COURT WELFAR.

COURT WELFARE IN ACTION
Practice and theory

**Adrian L. James
and
Will Hay**

HARVESTER
WHEATSHEAF

New York   London   Toronto   Sydney   Tokyo   Singapore

First published 1993 by
Harvester Wheatsheaf
Campus 400, Maylands Avenue
Hemel Hempstead
Hertfordshire, HP2 7EZ
A division of
Simon & Schuster International Group

© Adrian L. James & Will Hay

All rights reserved. No part of this publication may be reproduced, stored in a retrieval system, or transmitted, in any form, or by any means, electronic, mechanical, photocopying, recording or otherwise, without prior permission, in writing, from the publisher.

Typeset in 10/12 pt Erhardt
by Pentacor PLC, High Wycombe

Printed and bound in Great Britain by
Biddles Ltd, Guildford and King's Lynn

British Library Cataloguing in Publication Data

A catalogue record for this book is available from the British Library

ISBN 0 7450 13732 (pbk)

1 2 3 4 5   97 96 95 94 93

To our wives and our families

Contents

Acknowledgements		ix
Introduction		1
PART I *The context and theory of court welfare*		11
Chapter 1	The Path to the Present	13
Chapter 2	Policy and Praxis	35
Chapter 3	Polarisation and Polemic	58
PART II *The world of practice*		79
Chapter 4	Working with Families and Children	81
Chapter 5	Constructing Welfare Reports	103
Chapter 6	Organisational Issues	125
PART III *Social theory and court welfare work*		147
Chapter 7	From Practice to Theory: some emerging issues and problems	149
Chapter 8	Understanding Practice	168
Chapter 9	Synthesis and Synergy	189
References		209
Index		219

Acknowledgements

As always, there are so many who contribute, both directly and indirectly, to the process of researching, writing and publishing a book that it is difficult to know where to begin. However, in this instance we were both in no doubt that our major debt is to all of those in the probation service without whose willingness and co-operation the research, and the subsequent writing of this book, would not have been possible.

This is a large and far-reaching debt of gratitude and it is always invidious under such circumstances to name particular individuals. Suffice it to say therefore that we owe a great debt to all concerned: from the early stages in the research, to the Civil Work Committee of the Association of Chief Officers of Probation, when preliminary discussions were held about the proposal and whose support was vital to facilitating access to probation areas; to those Chief Probation Officers who had the courage to agree to let us loose in their professional backyards to rummage around, as is the wont of researchers; to those managers and other staff, such as research and information officers, who agreed to be interviewed and to provide us with various pieces of information on top of the everyday demands of servicing a probation area; and most of all, to those court welfare officers whom we interviewed and who gave so unstintingly of their time in terms of completing various statistical returns.

We must also acknowledge with gratitude the support of the Lord Chancellor's Department, both nationally and regionally. In particular, we would also like to thank the President of the Family Division, Sir Stephen Brown, whose support to the research was vital in helping us to resolve delicate issues of access to crucial materials, as well as enabling us to interview judges, whose perspectives are such a key component in understanding court welfare practice.

The research around which this book has been written was funded by the ESRC (Grant Number R 000 23 1589), without which it would never have been done and the book would not have been written. Such financial support was crucial after a sustained search for funding from other sources, including government departments and charitable organisations, had been unsuccessful. It provides, in our view, clear evidence of the vital role played by organisations such as the ESRC in facilitating research which may be of both inherent interest and practical relevance, but which may still not attract funds for various reasons quite unconnected with the quality of the research proposal.

Similarly, we wish to acknowledge our debt to the publishers for enabling us to develop our ideas in this form. In particular we should like to thank their Senior Commissioning Editor, Clare Grist, for her support and assistance in resolving some of the many problems that can occur in the production of a book such as this, and their anonymous external assessors for their helpful comments at various stages in the project.

In the course of a project which spans several years, we are conscious that many colleagues have contributed in various ways and to various degrees to the thinking involved in making sense of the complex social phenomena which are the focus of research such as this. Our thanks to all of these. In particular, however, we should like to express our gratitude to Robert Chester, for his many critical insights, good humour and for his encouragement and exhortations to 'repine not' in the face of yet another rejection for funding, and for his helpful comments on early stages of the draft manuscript; to Robert Dingwall, particularly for his important contribution to the early stages in the development of this research, his more general support, and for being a seemingly inexhaustible supply of stimulating insights into the world into which we were enquiring; to Ronald Drinkwater for making available some of the historical material used in Chapter 1; to Robert Harris, both for his general support for the research and for his helpful comments on a later stage of the draft manuscript; and in particular to David Greatbatch and Christopher Walker for their painstaking and vital contribution to the analysis of our sample of welfare reports. Needless to say, however, responsibility for the final version rests solely with the authors.

It has become almost *de rigueur* to thank secretarial colleagues for their good humour and patience in producing endless versions of manuscripts, coping with illegible handwriting and so on. It is a sign of the times that we have less need to do this on this occasion and that if we acknowledge anyone for this thankless aspect of production, it should be ourselves and the well-known manufacturers of 'fruity' desk-top computers whose products are so easy to use that even we can manage to do it! Nevertheless, as mere novices in such skills, we should like to express our gratitude to Sharon Saunby, who provided us with invaluable, willing and always cheerful secretarial support throughout the project, to Claire Hairsine for her additional help and support and to Joan Wilson for her indispensable 'consultancy'.

We must also acknowledge our debt, in so many ways, to our wives and families. Without their support, encouragement and forbearance when faced with partners who spend days and weeks away from home doing fieldwork and then spend hours and days tapping away, often irascibly, in front of computer screens, such ventures would be impossible.

Adrian L. James and Will Hay
February 1993

Introduction

The work of court welfare officers has undergone unprecedented change in the decade since Mervyn Murch published his seminal study, *Justice and Welfare in Divorce*, in 1980. This change has followed the increased demand for welfare reports, a fact which has been thrown into sharp relief by the increasing emphasis within the probation service on its work with offenders and the relegation of civil work to the lowest priority.

Of perhaps greater significance, however, has been the impact of conciliation, both as a concept and as a movement, on both the legal and social work discourses. It has contributed to a proliferation of new approaches to court welfare work which have sought to minimise the acrimony surrounding divorce which was, according to the proponents of such developments, a product of a system constructed around an adversarial model of justice. However, conciliation has also contributed to the development of a very different conception of divorce, as both a social and a legal process, which has had profound implications not only for those working within the legal system but also for parents and children, whose involvement is only transitory but whose needs the process purports to meet.

These changes have precipitated a high-profile inter-disciplinary debate about the principles and practices involved in these new approaches, some of which have been seen as antithetical to established approaches and some of which have also attracted very public criticism from the judiciary. However, some exploratory research (Dingwall and James 1988; James and Dingwall 1989) suggested that in spite of the apparent polarisation of positions reflected in the rhetoric of this debate, differences in practice were not always so great as might have been expected. In addition, it also revealed that in spite of the extent of these changes, a wide range of issues (including resourcing, training and the development of performance indicators) was being dealt with apparently in the absence of any recognition of the nature and extent of the sea-change which had occurred in court welfare practice.

It is against this backcloth that the Economic and Social Research Council funded a two and a half year project to study the civil work of the probation service. This research, completed in 1992, was the first large-scale, detailed and systematic study of court welfare practice undertaken in this country. It had three main aims, the first of which was simply to collect new information. Because of the growth in the number of divorces, the many substantive and procedural changes in the law relating to divorce and the debate amongst both policy-makers and practitioners generated by this, major questions about the development of policy, practice and the management of court welfare work were raised in the 1980s. Such questions were timely and appropriate but the answers which were being generated, in the absence of any substantial and recent body of empirical evidence, took no account of the many recent changes.

The external symptoms of such changes were to be found in court delays; delays in the preparation of welfare reports; consequent delays in the making of crucial decisions concerning children; increased pressures on court welfare offices in an intrinsically demanding area of practice; and increasing difficulties for managers in a context of growing expectations of efficiency from central government and of making economical, efficient and effective use of resources. It was therefore important to generate new, up-to-date and detailed information about court welfare practice.

The second aim was to contribute to an understanding of the principles and practices of court welfare work. Policy on the civil work of the probation service had been almost complete neglected during the 1980s, substantially because of the increasing emphasis upon the work of the probation service within the criminal justice system. Therefore, many developments reflected initiatives by enthusiastic practitioners in different parts of the country rather than a process of planned and managed development. In consequence, many changes in practice were little understood, not only outside but also within the probation service.

This difficulty was compounded by the fact, revealed by the exploratory research, that the rhetoric used to construct the discourse about these changes did not necessarily reflect the realities of practice, which were influenced by a range of situational and other factors intrinsic to welfare encounters. The research was therefore intended to shed new light on the principles and contingencies which shape practice and to increase understanding of what are, of necessity, highly encapsulated and privatised encounters between welfare officers and families.

The third aim of the research was, through achieving the first two aims, to contribute both directly and indirectly to the development of policies, practice and management for civil work, given the pressing need to confront and deal with some of the major issues facing the development of welfare services within the context of divorce and the civil justice system. The aim was quite specifically to focus on perspectives on court welfare practice from within the probation service and therefore no effort was made to involve parents directly in the research, either as subjects or as sources of information.

The research was undertaken in six probation areas, selected in consultation with the Civil Work Committee of the Association of Chief Officers of Probation (ACOP) to represent a cross-section of areas in terms of size (of service, of area, of population), geographical location and approaches to practice. Thus although the study areas do not constitute a random or stratified sample in any statistical sense, they represent a broad spectrum of probation areas and approaches to practice.

In order to achieve the aims outlined above, we employed three main approaches:

- The collection of data on referrals over a twelve-month period by means of forms especially adapted to meet the needs of each area, and on a more detailed basis for referrals during the first three months of this period, together with the collection of data by means of a daily diary exercise conducted during our first month in each area.
- The collection of a sample of welfare reports from each area for detailed analysis (originally, we had planned to tape-record welfare officers' interviews but we abandoned this following resistance in our first study area, which effectively invalidated this approach in the remaining areas).

- The use of semi-structured interviews with court welfare officers, middle and senior managers, judges and other key legal personnel, as well as direct observation of court welfare officers at work.

The purpose of this strategy was to triangulate (see Hammersley and Atkinson 1983) three different data sets which, by combining both quantitative and qualitative data, would not only provide checks to corroborate the accuracy of findings and conclusions drawn, but would also afford a rounded and detailed account of court welfare practice.

The study areas

Throughout the book, we have not identified areas or court welfare teams other than by letter and number, in order to protect the anonymity of the study areas. Whilst this approach may seem somewhat prosaic, we wished to avoid the chore, not to say the ritual, of the social-scientific convention of concocting implausible and confusing (for readers as well as writers!) pseudonyms. However, in order to understand some of the practical and organisational issues which will be alluded to in the following chapters, it might be helpful for readers to have some brief information concerning the nature of our study areas:

Area A is a rural county, welfare officers operating from three offices, although one of these housed only a single officer, and the other two part-time officers. Staff in this area have adopted a system whereby all disputes are referred for out-of-court conciliation. If the matter is not resolved, then the court will be informed and a decision made regarding a welfare report which, if requested, is prepared by a different officer.

Area B has a single team operating from a central office covering all of the county. All reports for magistrates' courts were (at the time of the fieldwork) prepared by mainstream probation officers in field teams working with offenders.

Area C is a large urban and industrial county with four teams located in its main population centres.

Area D is a county characterised by town and country, with officers being based at three area offices.

Area E is also a large urban county containing five offices, although for reasons of practicality, data were not obtained from all of these teams.

Area F is a very large rural county with very few staff, operating from three offices with no specialist court welfare team.

In addition, although when quoting our respondents directly we have generally indicated from which area they came, where this might lead to their being identified (as in the case of Chief Probation Officers, for example), we have not done this.

The data-base

The research has generated large amounts of data. In terms of quantitative data, returns using the progress record sheets were received from 93 court welfare officers. Given that there were 526.5 specialist main grade and senior court welfare officers in post in England and Wales in 1990 (Home Office 1992a), in addition to a number of non-specialists, this represents a sample of over 15 per cent of all welfare officers from a sample of 11 per cent of all probation areas. In all, information was returned to us involving 2,159 cases, representing some 8 per cent of the reports prepared nationally in 1990. The number of returns from officers varied from only 1 to as many as 82. In general therefore, the data-base on which the research has been able to draw, which will be discussed in more detail in Part II but which is described in detail elsewhere (James and Hay 1992), is sufficiently large and representative to constitute a fair cross-section of the work of court welfare officers in England and Wales in 1990/1.

The qualitative data collected during the course of research by the authors consists of over 70 semi-structured interviews with court welfare officers, each lasting between 60 and 90 minutes. In addition, a number of interviews between welfare officers and clients were observed in each of the study areas. Interviews were also conducted with the Chief Probation Officers and other senior managers in each area, and with team managers and Research and Information Officers relating to various aspects of the management of family court welfare work. In total, 93 interviews were conducted with probation staff, all of which were transcribed. In addition, judges were interviewed in each study area, the total number of such interviews being nine.

A further and very important qualitative element in the research, based upon a detailed analysis of welfare officers' reports, was undertaken substantially by Dr David Greatbatch, then of the Centre for Socio-Legal Studies, Oxford. Delicate negotiations with the Lord Chancellor's Department (LCD), the President of the Family Division of the High Court and the Association of Chief Officers of Probation were necessary in order to overcome the problem posed by the confidentiality of these reports.

A sample of 230 reports was collected from our study areas which were subjected to detailed analysis of content followed by computer analysis. The sample was not randomised in any statistical sense. However, it was collected to represent the range of the work undertaken by all of the officers in the study areas and reflect the balance between types of referral and distribution between courts. In the larger areas, the number of reports we asked for from each officer was reduced in order to keep the sample to a manageable size, but the overall stratification of the sample was none the less applied. The sample consisted of reports from which identifying information had been removed and which had been filed at least six months before (in order to conform to the agreement made with the LCD and the President of the Family Division).

These reports were analysed by David Greatbatch, who had not previously seen a welfare report, using an entirely data-driven approach. The reports were studied in detail, gradually building up a picture of the issues and their presentation in each report, which provided a framework for the analysis of the sample as a whole. This aspect of the analysis was conducted, after discussion of the results of a pilot coding exercise by just one researcher, of the research team, in order to avoid any problems in terms of inter-coder reliability. The data were subsequently analysed by computer, with the invaluable assistance of Christopher Walker, using SPSSx. It was encouraging to note, however, that this approach produced almost precisely the kinds of categories which we might have sought to use. The significance of this approach is that it minimises the influence of any preconceptions held by the researchers and represents more objectively the data being studied – in this case, court welfare reports. The data are not 'squeezed' into pre-determined categories, but are allowed to 'speak for themselves'.

The aims and structure of the book

Our aims in writing this book are fourfold: firstly, to provide an overview of the family court welfare work of the probation service which is as up-to-date as possible (acknowledging that practice is, of course, continuously evolving), by examining key aspects of the policy context, the organisation and the practice of court welfare officers; secondly, to identify some of the key issues and themes which emerge from this analysis; thirdly, to explore some of the dilemmas and challenges facing court welfare officers and the origins of these; and fourthly, to identify some of the key elements in a theoretical framework for understanding and conceptualising court welfare work and similar forms of social work. In this, we seek to bridge some of the conceptual gaps left by many current theoretical frameworks by exploring the links between issues of inter-personal transactions and structural issues of inter-organisational relationships, and the significance of the shifting and differential possession and use of power by key actors in the context of the divorce process.

Part I will consider the context in which the family court welfare work of the probation service has evolved and exists, drawing attention to the complex web of inter-related issues – including social trends, policy initiatives and legislative changes, organisational dynamics and professional practice – which have helped to shape it. Chapter 1 provides an introduction to the recent history of divorce reform and a brief discussion of recent developments, such as the impact of the 'conciliation movement', the Children Act 1989 and the Law Commission's proposals for divorce law reform, in order to delineate key elements of the context in which the current debate is occurring. Chapter 2 provides an analysis of the background to developments in policy relating to court welfare work, in order to show how the cumulative effect of the policy environment has been to sow the seeds for many of the current issues in court welfare work, such as the power of practitioners and the problems of management, outlining recent policy and management initiatives. Building on the first two chapters, Chapter 3 offers a more detailed analysis of the emergence of current approaches to court welfare practice. Rather than discussing the substantive issues raised by a comparison of different methods of and approaches to practice, however, the focus is upon the related discourse which has been typified by being practitioner-dominated, high profile and highly polemical.

Part II builds upon these foundations by exploring key themes and issues in the world of practice and illustrating these by the selective use of the main findings of the research. By drawing on both quantitative and qualitative data, the richness and diversity of practice is revealed as the product of the highly complex, ambiguous and at times conflicting demands made on court welfare officers. Such issues lie at the heart of understanding the nature of their practice which is typified not only by substantial variations but also, paradoxically, by substantial consensus.

In Chapter 4, evidence relating to the nature of welfare officers' work with families will be considered. Since the polarisation in the discourse discussed in Chapter 3 revolves around certain key practices in relation to such issues as home visiting, contact with children, use of family meetings and use of co-workers, this chapter looks both at welfare officers' stated positions and at what actually happens in practice. Chapter 5 explores the welfare report as the main visible output of the court welfare officer, considering different aspects of the construction of welfare reports. These will illustrate some of the themes and issues to emerge from the study and begin to consolidate the foundations for the subsequent theoretical part of our analysis. Chapter 6, using evidence from the research relating to practice and drawing upon a range of other data relating to organisational considerations (including the views of judges, senior probation managers as well as practitioners), will explore such issues as economy, efficiency and effectiveness in relation to the organisation and management of court welfare work.

Part III of the book builds upon the preceding parts by considering further the organisational complexity and ambiguity of the court welfare task, both in principle and in practice. In doing so, it draws selectively on certain aspects of social theory that complement the empirical material which was the focus of Part II, in order not only to illustrate the inter-dependence of the worlds of theoretical and empirical enquiry, but also to outline an approach which takes account not only of 'structural' features of the system but also how people interact in specific contexts. In the process, some of the key issues which must be taken into account in the future development of family court welfare work are identified.

Chapter 7 outlines the main issues and problems that have emerged from the foregoing chapters and discusses some of the important implications which stem from a consideration of selected aspects of social theory and the contextualisation of practice: that it takes place within a complex set of inter-related social processes; that these are constrained in various ways by 'structural' factors and frameworks; and that within this, individual actors make sense of the rules and resources which are carried by structure and which are routinised, reproduced and stabilised over time. Chapter 8 considers how these theoretical perspectives might be used to understand court welfare *practice*. In particular, we discuss models of practice which have emerged and the theoretical foundations for these, using these as the basis for a discussion of different elements of court welfare practice. We also consider the extent to which court welfare officers respond to other important frames of reference and the extent to which different approaches to practice are beginning to merge and become more homogeneous, in spite of their different theoretical roots, as a result of contextual pressures.

The concluding chapter identifies the main issues arising from the research and focuses upon outstanding issues and dilemmas. These will be addressed in the context of the latest developments outlined at the start of the book in terms of the Children Act 1989 and the proposed reform of the law relating to divorce, both of which have major implications for current and future arrangements for the practise and organisation of court welfare work.

PART I

The context and theory of court welfare

Guessing the future is fun. Describing the present is harder work. Precision is difficult, certainty more difficult still, and there is an ever-present danger of being either misled by false pictures of the past or distracted by interesting visions of the future. The kindest thing we can do to the future, therefore, is to be as careful and accurate as we can about the present.

(Ferdinand Mount 1982: 348)

1

The path to the present

Divorce as we know it today is a recent phenomenon. Prior to the Matrimonial Causes Act of 1857, there was no judicial divorce in England and Wales. For the rich, full divorce with the right to remarry was available but only by a private Act of Parliament, only 317 of such Acts being passed between 1697 and 1855 (Home Office 1979). This facility did not disappear until the law was amended by the Matrimonial Causes Act of 1923. For the vast majority of the population, marital breakdown and separation were either a matter of social fact, dealt with by a variety of informal means, or they were dealt with under a system of canon law administered by ecclesiastical courts and based on the principle of the indissolubility of marriage. This was the result of the gradual assumption of control over marriage and sexual morality by the Church, a process virtually completed by the end of the thirteenth century which dominated the regulation of marriage until the nineteenth century.

The control over divorce by the Church and subsequently by the state is a major factor in understanding the history of marriage and the family. It makes difficult any interpretation of the relationship between the realities of marital life, the quality of this and its propensity for failure and breakdown, since the only readily available indicator of marital breakdown is the relatively crude one of divorce, recourse to which has been tightly restricted until comparatively recently. The extent to which the dramatic increase in divorce, particularly since the Second World War, is primarily a product of improved access to divorce or of changes in attitudes towards marriage and divorce is therefore problematic. However, most commentators believe that, quite apart from improved access to divorce and legal aid as a result of progressive changes in the law, there has been an increasing incidence of marital breakdown and an increasing readiness to choose divorce as the solution (see, for example, Burgoyne *et al.* 1988; Chester 1971; Dominian 1982; Goldthorpe 1987; Philips 1988; Stone 1990).

Nor is this phenomenon exclusive to Britain. Certainly, Britain has one of the highest divorce rates in Europe, which in 1988 was exceeded only by that in Denmark, and certainly divorce in Britain has grown faster in the last thirty years than in either France or Germany (Family Policy Studies Centre 1991). However, divorce across Europe tripled between the early 1960s and the present, with about one-third of divorces in many European nations occurring within five years of marriage (Dormor 1992). Nor are high rates of marital breakdown and divorce restricted to the most socially progressive, liberal or affluent nations as is commonly supposed. As Dormor shows, the highest levels of divorce in Europe are found in the former Soviet Union where rates are now approaching those of the United States of America, with nearly two out of every three contemporary marriages being expected to end in divorce.

The explanation of such changes constitutes a major exercise in its own right and one which is well beyond the scope of an introductory chapter, but the debate and the issues are well documented (see, for example, Burgoyne *et al.* 1988; Chester 1971; Dominian 1982; Dormor 1992; Gathorne-Hardy 1981; Goldthorpe 1987; James and Wilson 1986; Mount 1982; Philips 1988; Rimmer 1981). Stone (1990: 410–16) summarises the principal issues which are of importance in understanding the rise in divorce and about which there is broad agreement. Of the various statistical trends which have made a contribution to the increasing divorce rates in Britain, the following are of particular significance:

- Divorces are taking place earlier in marriage.
- An increasing proportion of marriages are remarriages of the divorced, which are more likely to end in divorce.
- The overall decline in age at first marriage, which is of importance since young, especially teenage marriages, are more likely to end in divorce.
- The impact of large numbers of the unskilled lower social classes on the divorce market.

Of a wide range of political factors, perhaps the most significant are the following:

- The impact of two world wars, both of which led to a major increase in marital breakdown.
- The progressive easing of divorce laws (in particular, the use of unreasonable-behaviour grounds by women).
- The increased availability and granting of legal aid to the poor in 1914, 1920, 1949 and 1960, which is arguably more important overall than the other two factors.

Stone also argues, in common with other commentators that 'the expectation of sexual and emotional fulfilment from marriage has recently risen to quite unrealistic levels. . . . As a result, many marriages which would have been regarded as tolerable in the past are today seen as unendurable' (1990: 414). He also cites as important factors a decline in influence of parents and kin; the egalitarian ideology of feminism; the removal of moral stigma from marital breakdown and divorce; and economic changes and patterns of employment, particularly of women.

This is not intended to constitute an exhaustive list, let alone discussion, of the many and complex issues which must be borne in mind when considering the causes of marital breakdown and divorce in England and Wales today. It is merely to identify some of the many important processes – personal, social, political and economic – the subtle interplay of which goes to produce the sociological phenomenon of the divorce rate. It is also to hint at the interaction between *public* and *structural* factors – and within this particularly the role of the state and the legal system – and *private* and *individual* factors which contribute to people's solutions to the problem of marital breakdown, which constitute the human experience of divorce.

The principal conduit for this interaction is the law, through the machinery and influence of the courts. The functioning of the law therefore occupies a major place in our understanding of marital breakdown and divorce, not only because of what it *allows* but also because of what it *prevents* and, in consequence, precipitates and encourages in terms of extra-legal solutions. As Stone argues, from the Reformation to the present day, husbands and wives, together with their lawyers (and, as we shall argue, more recent players such as court welfare officers) have contrived to use, to adapt, to circumvent and to deceive the law in order to deal with the facts and consequences of marital breakdown. Thus, in eighteenth-century upper-class circles,

Close kin and often neighbours were . . . nearly always deeply involved in a failing marriage at all the critical stages of its disintegration, beginning with attempts to shore it up and ending in mediation to see fair play at separation and to keep the scandal of the break-up out of the courts. (1990: 3)

In addition, Stone points to the evidence that: 'private separations always involved delicate prior negotiations between spouses about custody and visiting rights', the reality of such negotiations being 'very different from the patriarchal absolutism exhibited when cases came before the common law courts' (1990: 174). The 'shadow of the law' (Mnookin and Kornhauser 1979) has thus been a long-standing influence on the behaviour of those involved, either professionally or personally, in the divorce process. Before considering some of these issues in more detail, it is also important to locate some of the most significant of these changes in a temporal as well as a conceptual framework.

Divorce reform and the growth of marriage-saving

Although the Matrimonial Causes Act of 1857 made divorce available through the secular courts for the first time, divorce was not to be the main solution to marital breakdown for the majority for some time, largely because of the prohibitive costs incurred in the process. It is therefore to the work of the magistrates' courts that attention needs to be paid. The Matrimonial Causes Act of 1878 first gave wives the right to seek relief in the summary courts on the grounds of assault by their husbands. The powers of the magistrates' courts to grant separation, maintenance and custody orders were progressively extended, and by the 1930s, they provided the main legal remedies for marital breakdown for those unable to afford the costs of a divorce action in the High Court, making three times as many orders in domestic proceedings as the High Court made in divorce cases (McGregor *et al.* 1970).

Concern about the growing number of such cases was reflected in the Summary Jurisdiction (Domestic Procedure) Bill. Introduced in 1934, this included, *inter alia*, proposals for the establishment of special domestic courts and for a 'special conciliation' summons to enable courts to require either spouse on the request of the other to appear before the court, which would then try to help them to resolve their marital problems. In the event, this provision was shelved in favour of a Departmental Committee which was 'to enquire into the social services connected with the administration of justice in courts of summary jurisdiction, including . . . the application of conciliation methods to matrimonial disputes' (*Report of the Departmental Committee on the Social Services in the Courts of Summary Jurisdiction* 1936: vi). The Committee's report (1936: 6–9) showed that although there were local variations in the practice of courts, informal attempts at conciliation, mostly by probation officers, were widespread. However, such activities, whilst appreciated, were not acknowledged without some reservations. For example, the Committee stated:

> We cannot help feeling that under the present system there is a real risk that conciliation may be carried too far. The practice adopted in so many Courts of allowing the probation officer to see all persons who come to them in matrimonial difficulties may well tend to lead to some denial of justice. . . . There is a strong temptation to the zealous officer to settle as many cases as he can out of Court, and he may even be actuated by personal convictions as to the sanctity of the marriage tie. (1936: 12)

In commenting on the report and the subsequent Summary Procedure (Domestic Proceedings) Act 1937, the Metropolitan Magistrate, Mr Claud Mullins, also expressed some dissatisfaction that probation officers were still interposing their authority between applicants seeking summonses and the courts: 'It is most important that probation officers and all who are doing the work of matrimonial conciliation should curb their religious enthusiasm and be quite certain that they are not denying legal rights to anyone' (Mullins 1938: 6). However, he also stressed 'the importance of this work in connection with juvenile crime as all agree that there is no greater cause of crime amongst children than an unhappy or divided home' (1938: 7). This perceived link provided a significant part of the rationale which underpinned the development of the civil work of the probation service in tandem with its work with offenders, resulting in a spread of responsibilities which was to prove significant in terms of subsequent developments (see Chapter 2). The seeds of another part of the subsequent debate were also evident in comments made by the Medical Director of the Tavistock Clinic:

We have realised recently how important the broken home and the unhappy home are in the production of delinquency and neurosis. . . . I am not at all sure myself of the value of the 'patched up home'. I find myself sometimes differing from Probation Officers who, perhaps from wishful thinking, have the idea that all will sort itself out once they can get people to live together again. . . . I personally feel that sometimes it is wiser and better that they should be put asunder. (Rees 1939: 81–2)

The Summary Procedure (Domestic Proceedings) Act 1937 resulted in such work becoming part of the statutory duties of the probation service. This was partly to legitimate the work already being undertaken. However, it was also clearly intended to reassert a degree of judicial control over an informal system that had emerged as a result of grass-roots initiatives and which, it was recognised, was open to the vagaries of idiosyncratic practice and personal beliefs. Thus, in addition to the availability of legal remedies for those who could not afford divorce proceedings in the High Court, social-work help was also made available following the Act, with the intention of reducing marital breakdown (and thereby subsequent delinquency in children) through conciliation.

It should be noted, of course, that in this context, conciliation refers to what is now termed *reconciliation*, although the two concepts were not as far apart as might be thought. In a report prepared after the war for the Probation Training Board at the Home Office, the work of probation officers was classified

> under three leading activities which indicate the main functions, as well as the essential nature, of that work. They are: Supervision, Conciliation and Investigation. . . . Conciliation . . . refers almost entirely to matrimonial conciliation work, with or without court intervention . . . many put it ahead of supervision [of offenders] in order of difficulty. . . . At the same time, there is a certain similarity . . . viz. that each person concerned should feel that he is participating . . . in conciliation, each party in the resumption of married life. This cannot be emphasised too much, since the more strongly each feels that the conciliation is not being imposed by an external authority, the more lasting the conciliation is likely to be. It is not enough to invite and obtain the *co-operation* of the parties. That is important but, by itself, remains largely a half measure. It should lead to the generation of a genuine feeling of participation. (Frisby and Wilson 1946; emphasis in original)

Apart from the emphasis on the *resumption* of married life, much of this holds true in the work of court welfare officers today. It is interesting to note that this report, too, makes clear links between the civil work of probation officers and their work with offenders.

Such themes and concerns continue to be evident during this crucial period in the evolution of divorce. In the same year as the Summary Procedure (Domestic Proceedings) Act, the Matrimonial Causes Act was also passed, bringing about the first major extension of the grounds for divorce to include, in addition to adultery, cruelty, desertion and insanity of the other spouse. The result was an immediate increase of almost 50 per cent in the number of divorces granted annually. It may thus have been more than mere coincidence that a year later, in 1938, the Marriage Guidance Council was formed.

It is perhaps not surprising therefore that, even during the years of the war, the Metropolitan Magistrate, Mr Claud Mullins, expressed his concerns about the rise in domestic proceedings and the increasing availability of divorce:

> Before the war I often used to find that about a third of the cases in my list had been reconciled. Now reconciliations are few. . . . Matrimonial morale, as I see it, has slumped badly. . . . Today . . . all women who come to our domestic courts alleging desertion, persistent cruelty or adultery against their husbands can legally apply to the High Court for divorce; and most of them can get free legal aid to do so. In 1938, 4,301 more matrimonial petitions were filed than in 1937. What would have happened if the war had not come? I dread to think. (Mullins 1943: 58–9)

He went on to argue that all divorce cases should receive some form of 'social help':

> for divorce in such cases [where the parties have children under 17 and preferably under 21] is vastly more than a matter for lawyers. The object of conciliation . . . would not be directly to prevent divorce, but to see that those seeking it understand the practical consequences of divorce . . . Thus through conciliation people can make a wise choice for themselves and their children. . . . Compulsory conciliation procedure exists in some countries. Why not make a beginning here with cases involving children? (1943: 59)

This reflects the widespread anxiety during the 'thirties about the condition of the British family. As Eekelaar and Dingwall comment: 'it is probably more appropriate to analyse both the extension of court-based social work and the establishment of marriage guidance as part of that general concern than to relate them to specifically legal developments' (1988: 4).

These concerns were reflected in the work of the Denning Committee, established in 1946 in response to the strain placed on the legal system by the sudden increase in the number of divorces. The Committee's report (1947) considered *inter alia* ways of expediting divorce cases and reducing costs, paying considerable attention to the question of reconciliation:

> Its main strategy was to build upon the experience of the probation service in the magistrates' courts since 1937 . . . [recommending] that this role should be extended to divorce cases in the High Court, envisaging that a welfare officer would review every petition in cases involving children, with the power to investigate the position of the children and to attempt to reconcile their parents. (Eekelaar and Dingwall 1988: 6)

Concern about the *costs* to the legal system of divorce was an issue which was to become another significant theme in successive reviews of both substantive and procedural issues relating to divorce law reform.

The following year, in response to the recommendations of the Denning Committee, a further committee was established 'to consider how marriage guidance could best be developed with the assistance of Exchequer grants' (Bochel 1976: 196), as part of which consideration was given to the possible contribution of the probation service. That Committee specifically rejected the possibility of expanding the probation service in order to make such provisions, partly because of the stigma associated with the criminal work of probation officers, but also because of concerns about the resource implications of any such expansion and, implicitly, the effect this might have in detracting from the work of the service with offenders (*Report of the Departmental Committee on Grants for the Development of Marriage Guidance* 1948).

However, as a result of these two reports, the direction for the development of the probation service in divorce was clearly set. There was to be no *general* extension of the service's responsibility for marriage guidance, Exchequer grants going instead to the National

Marriage Guidance Council, the Catholic Marriage Advisory Council and the Family Welfare Association. The then Secretary of the Marriage Guidance Council envisaged a partnership with the probation service in this enterprise, commenting that they had always 'welcomed the service of probation officers, as committee members, as lecturers, and as counsellors serving our Marriage Guidance Councils' (Mace 1947: 104). However, there was to be a social-work service to the High Courts, developed from the work of the service in the magistrates' courts, through the appointment of court welfare officers with powers to advise and guide, as well as to investigate, parents on the care and welfare of their children, both before and after divorce.

Although the primary emphasis was still on reconciliation, there was increasing concern about provisions to ensure the welfare of children. This, linked with pressure for reform of the divorce law and in particular the abolition of the matrimonial offence as the ground for divorce, led to the establishment in 1951 of a Royal Commission on Marriage and Divorce (known as the Morton Commission), which reported in 1956. The majority of the Commission rejected any move towards no-fault divorce and emphasised the importance of further developing services for marriage guidance and reconciliation. However, as Eekelaar and Dingwall have pointed out, since collusion or condonation of any matrimonial offence constituted a bar to divorce, 'Any attempt at reconciliation was likely to be inhibited by the possibility that apparent condonation could compromise the chance of a divorce if the attempt failed' (1988: 7), a disincentive against reconciliation which was not dealt with until the Matrimonial Causes Act 1963. However, in spite of this, there had been considerable scope for agreement on the whole range of ancillary matters in divorce, including the custody of children, which was endorsed by the courts from as early as 1945.

The Royal Commission also considered the possibility of seeking welfare reports in every divorce application involving children, much as had been suggested thirteen years earlier by Claud Mullins, but this was rejected as being both impractical and undesirable. Parents, it was thought, should have impressed upon them their continuing responsibility for taking decisions concerning the future welfare of their own children, rather than leaving this to the court (Bochel 1976: 199). Nevertheless, the Commission recommended the extension of the scheme for appointing court welfare officers, which had been initiated in the High Court in London, to all areas in the country where divorce cases were heard. They rejected, on balance, the possibility of giving this work to the recently formed Children's Departments because of the greater experience of the probation service, both in dealing with matrimonial work and in working with the courts. The Probation Rules were subsequently amended in 1959 to make such work a statutory responsibility for probation officers (Bochel 1976: 200).

When divorce was extended to county courts in undefended cases by virtue of the Matrimonial Causes Act 1967 (a process subsequently taken even further by the Matrimonial and Family Proceedings Act 1984, largely in response to the growing number of matrimonial causes and especially divorce petitions), welfare officer appointments were also required. Thus, in spite of the desire of the Royal Commission to restrict the use of welfare reports, with the greater availability of personnel *and* the increase in divorce, the number of reports prepared for the divorce and magistrates' courts increased dramatically from 3,370 in 1961 to 12,916 in 1971 (James 1988). Therefore, the development of court welfare work during this period

> amounted to the provision of facilities for the making of social enquiries connected with children at the request of the judges. They fell short of the conciliation service envisaged by the 1947 Denning Committee, where the responsibility of the officers would have included the provision to appellants on request of advice and of casework help if necessary. (Bochel 1976: 200)

This particular feature of the growth of the court welfare function was to have significant implications for subsequent developments.

This trend was given a further boost by the Divorce Reform Act 1969, which was passed in no small part due to growing criticism (see, for example, SPCK 1966) of the offence-based divorce law. It reflected the recommendations of the Law Commission (1966) for the introduction of a 'dual system', based upon 'irretrievable breakdown' as the sole ground for divorce, a ground which was, however, to be proved by evidence of one or more of five facts – adultery, cruelty, desertion, two years' separation with the respondent's consent and five years' separation – thereby *effectively* retaining the matrimonial offence. However, as Dewar has argued, there was evidence that court hearings in such cases were perfunctory, serving no obvious function and therefore 'Partly in recognition of this, but also (and more importantly) out of a desire to reduce the growing burden on the civil legal aid budget of matrimonial costs' (1989: 170), the streamlined 'special procedure' was introduced by the Matrimonial Causes Act of 1973 and eventually extended to all undefended petitions, with legal aid being restricted to disputes over ancillary matters – changes which 'probably did more to alter the nature of the divorce process than any substantive change introduced by the 1969 Act: divorce, it has been said, has become an administrative process' (Dewar 1989: 171).

Such changes were clearly evident in the divorce statistics. In the two years between 1970 and 1972 alone, the number of divorce decrees made absolute increased from 58,239 to 119,025 (OPCS 1980). The general upward trend was therefore set to continue dramatically and inexorably until the mid-1980s – a more than sixfold increase from 1960 to 1985 – when it levelled out (Table 1.1). This increase brought with it an even greater increase in the demand for welfare reports – nearly eightfold from 3,370 in 1961 to 26,410 in 1990 (Home Office 1992b: Table 9.2). It is important to note in passing that the early 1970s also witnessed the start of a revolution which had profound effects on the work of the service with offenders. They saw not only 'the collapse of the rehabilitative ideal' (Bottoms 1977) but the growing disillusionment with positivist and deterministic explanations of offending, calling into question the assumed links

Table 1.1 Decrees absolute granted, England and Wales (000s) 1960–90

1960	1965	1970	1975	1980	1985	1990
24	38	58	120	148	160	153

Source: Stone 1990, Table 13.1 and Family Policy Studies Centre, 1991

between marital breakdown and delinquency which had been a major philosophical justification for the matrimonial work of the probation service. They saw the birth of a new era of penal policy, dominated by a neo-classical view of crime and punishment, stressing the significance of choice in offending behaviour and 'just deserts' in sentencing, and the search for alternatives to custody in the face of an ever-increasing prison population. They also saw, in the face of the growing crisis in the economy of welfare, increasing demands for cheaper and more cost-effective methods for dealing with offenders. Thus the resources of the probation service came under increasing pressure from the criminal justice system, with demands for the development of ever more community-based measures for offenders and for rapidly increasing numbers of social inquiry reports (James 1988).

An important effect of this was to initiate a debate about the fundamental role of the probation service – was it to offer a broadly based social-work service to the courts, including the civil courts, or should it focus more clearly on its developing role in the criminal courts? The House of Commons Expenditure Committee (1972: ix) certainly regarded matrimonial work as a 'natural candidate for removal' in the face of the increasing demands from the criminal justice system; the Home Office regarded the provision of alternatives to custody as 'a strategy for the service . . . for the next twenty years or so' (Haxby 1978: 23–4); and the Finer Committee (1974), which was indirectly to have a profound influence on court welfare work, regarded the association with offenders as disqualifying the probation service from work in the family court (James 1988). The impact of this debate on court welfare work will be considered in more detail in Chapter 2.

Thus, not only was divorce becoming predominantly an administrative process, but the work of probation officers in matrimonial proceedings had largely become one of investigating and reporting on issues relating to the welfare of children, with referrals to probation officers for matrimonial reconciliation plummeting from 46,728 in 1961 (Home Office 1966) to 11,523 in 1973 (Home Office 1976). The report of the Home Office working party (*Marriage Matters* 1979), set up to consider the provision of marriage guidance, represented a final attempt to revitalise interest in and commitment to marriage-saving, but as Eekelaar and Dingwall argue: 'Reconciliation had played its part in making divorce law reform palatable: it was now to be discarded' (1988: 11).

The restructuring of reconciliation and divorce

The report of the Finer Committee (1974) represented a watershed, heralding a new era and redefining the discourse about marital breakdown and divorce. This was not so much because it produced *new* ideas – in many ways it reflected current ideas, such as the Practice Direction on Matrimonial Conciliation, issued in 1971 by the President of the Family Division, allowing adjournment of cases for conciliation to resolve disputes by agreement (Parkinson 1986: 63–4). However, it brought them into clear public focus, linking a number of important social policy issues with a new vision of family law.

Consequently, it was 'to serve as an important symbolic legitimation for many proposed initiatives in family policy' (Eekelaar and Dingwall 1988: 12) of which the conciliation movement, which developed from 1975 onwards (see Fisher 1990; Parkinson 1986), was arguably *the* major example, representing in effect a modernisation of the concept of reconciliation.

Simultaneously with the growth of independent out-of-court conciliation services, the probation service progressively adopted the *new* model of conciliation offered by the Finer Committee, adapting working practices accordingly (see Chapter 3). The aim was to reduce the conflict so often surrounding marital breakdown and increasingly being acknowledged as harmful to the long-term welfare of children (see, for example, James and Wilson 1984b; Richards and Dyson 1982; Rutter 1975; Walczak with Burns 1984; Wallerstein and Kelly 1980).

Although this has been described as reflecting a shift from marriage-saving to child-saving (Murch 1980: 189), this simple dichotomy fails to reflect the extent to which *re*conciliation had been concerned with child-saving and child-protection in terms of the perceived likelihood of future delinquency. Thus, in 1962 the Departmental Committee on the Probation Service (known as the Morison Committee) took the view that matrimonial conciliation work was very relevant to the preventive work of the service

> on the grounds that work resulting in the preservation of, or help to, families 'reduces the risk of delinquency and other maladjustment'. Matrimonial work might well come into supervision work, and the problems and techniques of matrimonial conciliation were 'not of a different order from those associated with probation work'. (Bochel 1976: 210)

Indeed, it is arguable that the child-saving component of conciliation has been used by the probation service in a way which is directly comparable to the child-saving philosophy of *re*conciliation before it. Thus, for example, in a recent policy statement on civil work, the Central Council of Probation Committees (CCPC 1991) commented of conciliation that: 'the implications for the prevention of crime and delinquency should not be underestimated', whilst a joint statement by the three main probation organisations commenting, *inter alia*, on civil work, drew attention to the contribution of family breakdown to a wide range of social problems, stating that 'Both directly and indirectly it contributes to the incidence of crime' (ACOP, CCPC and NAPO 1987: 6).

The supposed links between marital conflict and future delinquency have therefore provided a legitimising rationale for the continued involvement of the probation service in this area of work, by bringing it much closer to the concerns of policy makers and the increasingly central role of the probation service in the criminal justice system. Like reconciliation, conciliation also represented an attempt to soften the instrumental concerns of the legal process with issues such as cost and efficiency, by acknowledging the *human* costs of marital breakdown.

Murch's dichotomy also gives insufficient recognition to a number of significant contemporaneous changes in the social, economic and political climate (James 1990a) and the extent to which conciliation represented an attempt to 'reframe' the negative consequences of divorce *for parents*, by identifying positive *means* of achieving positive *outcomes* from the generally negative experiences of marital breakdown. In addition, conciliation came to occupy a similar cost-saving and procedural-expedition role in the surrounding policy debate. Thus, in the 1970s and 1980s, much as in earlier periods, 'the dominant influence is neither marriage-saving nor child-saving but cost-saving. Again and again one is confronted by the struggle of civil servants, judges, and court administrators to cope with the pressure of a continuing rise in the demand for divorce' (Eekelaar and Dingwall 1988: 17).

The development of in-court conciliation by the probation service was, in particular, both a product and a victim of this pressure: a product in that many courts endorsed and encouraged such schemes because of the prospect of saving both time and money, even though it was not a statutory duty of the probation service and there were no specific statutory provisions to enable courts to authorise such methods; a victim because it led to forms of practice which led Davis (1983) to question whether it could be called conciliation at all. However, in-court conciliation schemes developed rapidly in the 1980s 'as a consequence of the growing alarm over the escalation of costs in matrimonial litigation' (Eekelaar 1991: 155), and by the time the Booth Committee reported in 1985, the cost-saving agenda remained as clear as ever, although the solution was seen to lie in conciliation rather than *re*conciliation.

This view is endorsed by Davis, who also argues that 'The rationing motif dominates our civil justice system' (1988a: 109), a view implicitly supported by statistics relating to in-court conciliation. Since such data began to be collected by the Home Office, the indications are that this has been an area of substantial growth in general (see Table 1.2). In particular, however, the largest proportional growth has been in the magistrates' courts *without* the use of adjournments (showing a 40 per cent increase between 1989 and 1990), the category which also shows an increase for all courts, compared with adjourned conciliations which have decreased across the board. Although such data need to be treated with caution, a point to emerge strongly in the recent Thematic Review of such work by the Home Office Inspectorate (Home Office 1991b), the evidence of such growth is persuasive.

Table 1.2 Conciliation cases on which the probation service began work by type of court and type of case

		1986	1987	1988	1989	1990
Magistrates' courts:	in court	780	810	1071	1120	1560
	adjourned	970	860	780	860	800
	total	1760	1660	1850	1980	2360
High and county court:	in court	5400	5790	6140	6390	6940
	adjourned	2780	2260	2160	2120	2060
	total	8190	8050	8290	8510	9010
All courts:	in court	6180	6600	7200	7510	8500
	adjourned	3760	3120	2940	2980	2860
	total	9940	9720	10140	10480	11370

Source: Home Office (1992b: Table 9.3)

The continuing concern with costs more generally is equally clear, as evidenced by the following:

- The terms of reference of the Inter-departmental Committee on Conciliation, established in 1982 'to report on the nature, scope and effects (*including financial and manpower consequences*) of existing facilities and services' and to consider the possibilities for development '*within existing resource planning*' (para. 1.1, Robinson Committee Report 1983; italics added).
- The terms of reference of the Matrimonial Causes Procedure Committee (the Booth Committee 1985), which was to consider possible reforms to the Matrimonial Causes Act 1973 'having regard to the desirability of achieving greater simplification *and the saving of costs*' (para. 1.1; italics added), and which concluded

by stating their belief that the implementation of their recommendations 'would achieve not only greater simplification and the saving of costs, but would also provide further for the welfare of the children and for the parties themselves' (para. 5.14). (It is interesting to note in passing the priorities implied by this, the concluding sentence of the report!)

- The terms of reference of the Inter-departmental Review of Family and Domestic Jurisdiction, which was 'To examine the feasibility of the establishment of a unified [family] court . . . to identify the main options for such a court and *to assess the resource implications* of each of these options' (para. 1.1; italics added).

- The terms of reference for the Conciliation Project Unit (1989), established in response to substantial criticism of the Robinson Committee's report, which was to compare different forms of conciliation to assess and compare, *inter alia*, 'the costs of different types of conciliation schemes, having regard to the cost of operating schemes, the effect on legal aid costs and lawyers' fees, and the cost of processing divorce cases through the courts' (para. 1.4).

Such approaches all reflect the concern of the legal system to *manage the legal processes* consequent upon marital breakdown more effectively, rather than the concerns of practitioners (both court welfare officers and independent service conciliators) to *manage the family processes* more effectively.

Recent developments

Thus, the issue of child-saving has, until recently, only been addressed *indirectly* and to the extent that it has reflected adult-orientated agendas, such as marriage-saving or conciliation, and can be cost-effective. Although the welfare of the child was elevated to the first and paramount principle as long ago as 1925 by the Guardianship of Infants Act, then hailed as a landmark in the legal protection of children, this did not reflect a child-protection philosophy so much as part of the fight of women for joint guardianship over their children during marriage (Maidment 1984). Indeed, divorce has, until very recently, always been an adult-centred process – it is only since the early 1970s, with the provisions of s.1 of the Guardianship of Minors

Act 1971 and of s.41 of the Matrimonial Causes Act 1971, that children have moved centre-stage in divorce proceedings. The Children Act 1989 is the latest and clearest expression of this trend, s.1(1) making the welfare of the child the paramount consideration. As Eekelaar has argued: 'The significance of these provisions in promoting a reformulation of the problems seen to be central in divorce from being adult-centred to child-centred cannot be overstated. But the shift was incomplete and threw up a whole set of new questions' (1991: 123). Questions such as what constitutes the welfare of the child? What constitutes the preferred 'family setting' in which children should be brought up? What weight should be attached to their wishes and feelings? Are the claims and abilities of mothers and fathers as parents regarded as equal? Questions on which the statutory provisions gave no guidance.

In principle the Children Act gives the power and the responsibility for making many of these important decisions to the parents. However, courts have amply demonstrated that they have clear views on such issues and may yet use their wide discretion, to which they have been long accustomed, to intervene in parental decisions whilst parents may yet seek to involve the courts in the decision-making process (James 1992a). The extent to which the check-list of factors to be borne in mind when considering a child's welfare (s.1(3)) will aid the interpretation of the welfare test also remains to be seen (Eekelaar 1991: 127–8).

The stress which the Act places upon parental responsibility as opposed to rights is also of substantial significance, reflecting the emerging ideology that not only do parents have obligations towards their children but that decisions about children should always, where possible, be made by the parents, and not by the state or, indeed, the courts. However:

> The ambiguity in the word 'responsibility' permitted an unperceived shift from the idea that the law should insist that parents should perform their parental duties towards their children . . . to the opposite idea that child care was best performed by parents with minimal state intrusion. (Eekelaar 1991: 128)

As we shall show in later chapters, such ambiguities are reflected in the emerging ideology of court welfare, which reflects the latter meaning of 'responsibility' through, paradoxically, the use of various forms of pressure on parents to accept the 'responsibility' of parenthood by making the decisions concerning their children's future, rather than the courts.

Such issues are also clearly reflected in the most recent proposals for the reform of the law relating to divorce (Law Commission 1990). These aim to encourage parental responsibility and agreement and to minimise possible harm to children, in the context of a simplified system of divorce based unequivocally on the principle of irretrievable breakdown, to be proved 'by the expiry of a minimum period of one year for consideration of the practical consequences which would result from a divorce and reflection on whether the breakdown in the marital relationship is irreparable' (para. 7.2). The availability of counselling, conciliation and mediation services during this 'cooling off' period is regarded as an integral part of these proposals. This signifies the continuing concern about the prevalence of divorce and the need to make provision for marriage-saving activities in the context of proposals which opponents are likely to view as another step towards a totally administrative system of divorce.

The Children Act 1989 and the proposals of the Law Commission outline and reflect an ideological position concerning the relationship between the family and the state. However, they also serve to highlight areas of continuing tension and ambiguity – for example, the proposed 'cooling off' period might conflict with the principle of minimising delay in the child's interests, embodied in the Children Act, and might consequently encourage parents and lawyers to seek orders under the Act, contrary to the principle of minimal intervention. Moreover, although the language is that of empowerment, Eekelaar (1991) argues that these proposals reflect a concern not only to *regularise* divorce procedures and to ensure that cases are processed efficiently and without doing any further harm, but also to *regulate* divorce through the imposition of a waiting period, designed to prove that the breakdown is, indeed, irreparable; to provide the opportunity to reflect on the consequences of divorce (and the possibilities of reconciliation); and to provide an additional delay before remarriage becomes possible.

Themes and issues

A number of themes and issues emerge from this brief and necessarily selective review of the recent history of divorce. In particular, it is evident that a highly significant *leitmotif* throughout these developments has been the search for more economical and efficient methods for dealing with the ever-increasing strain on the legal system posed by matrimonial issues. Thus, although there has been a major shift from reconciliation to conciliation which has had a profound effect on court welfare practice and parents' experience of the divorce process, the issue of cost-saving has informed the political and the legal response to both approaches. A further issue of particular significance for the involvement of the probation service in matrimonial work, is the postulated link between marital breakdown and delinquency. Whilst there may be less credence given to this link in the prevailing climate of criminal justice policy than previously, it continues to be significant as part of the discourse about the role of the probation service and the place of civil work within this. These provide some of the threads of continuity in this history.

In addition however, there are some important threads of structural and conceptual continuity. Firstly, there is clearly a growing perception that the ability of the legal process to deal with such issues is inherently limited. In spite of the principles which inform legislation and which underpin the practice of the courts, parents continue to conduct their lives in a *socially* rather than a *legally* defined and managed context. In the main, the courts and the law impinge only briefly upon their lives at the point of divorce and are used, both then and subsequently, primarily as a means of pursuing inter-personal agendas which can be constructed and prosecuted as disputes through the legal system. Such legal disputes are therefore *symbols* of essentially human conflicts.

The most recent developments represent another step towards a predominantly administrative divorce system which would maximise self-determination, minimise state intervention and be the most effective way to reduce costs. And yet it can be argued that there are fundamentally important reasons for continuing to locate such disputes within the legal framework: 'the supervisory elements of family law have a significance beyond the facts of any individual case in their statement of the desirability of child protection and of substantive equity' (Dingwall and Eekelaar 1988: 177). Moreover, as long as the law requires that children's interests are paramount, the state will have a duty in individual cases to ensure that parents take account of their needs and, if necessary, to prevent parents from reaching settlements which may be convenient for them but detrimental to the children. Although they acknowledge that welfare can be a more insidious form of social control than law (see, for example, Davis and Bader 1985; Dingwall 1988; Piper 1988), they argue that parents are not

> invariably the best judges of their children's interests, although their unique access to information about their own children's needs must mean that their views should carry considerable weight ... the principle that children should not be avoidably prejudiced in their life-chances by the behaviour of their parents compels us towards endorsing some measure of supervision. (Dingwall and Eekelaar 1988: 179)

In addition, it is clear that a wholly administrative process may selectively disadvantage certain groups who are less competent or effective bargainers and there is no reason to believe that such a system will necessarily be any more effective in eliminating conflict.

Secondly, it is evident from this that particular attention must be given to the difference between the *ostensible* and the *latent* functions of the law, a difference largely created by the success of the clients in manipulating the court system for their own purposes, reflecting the very real extent of their power in such situations. Thus, although the ostensible function of the law is to reflect the legitimate interests of the state by regulating the behaviour of individuals in relation to marriage and divorce and, latterly, by protecting the interests of children, Stone has argued that an important latent function of the law is to provide 'an institutional structure based on concepts of justice, but moulded and twisted by changes in secular morality and conflicts of legal structures, as well as by the selfish interests of both clients and lawyers' (Stone 1990: 300), through which to give legitimate expression to changing social, professional and personal values.

Thirdly, evident throughout this history is 'the principle of unexpected consequences, the wide gap between intentions and results ... [which] reigns supreme over all the laws of marriage and divorce in England during the last five hundred years' (Stone 1990: 26). This is intimately linked with the *process* by which change has occurred, which Stone argues has consistently taken place in three stages (Stone 1990: 18–20): firstly, impetus for change came from clients themselves as they pressed for the law to meet their needs and began to find ways around the constraints imposed by the letter of the law; secondly, lawyers and judges attempted to bridge the widening gap between the theory of the law and its practice by modifying it through judicial reinterpretation; and finally, when the hypocrisy and manipulation became so extreme, the law was changed to bring it more into line with current social practice and moral attitudes.

This process is evident most recently in the context of the Divorce Reform Act 1969, which arose from a growing demand for divorce, increasing attempts to manipulate the law in order to achieve this, leading to 'a perception that the legal requirements imposed by a fault-based divorce system had driven a gulf between reality and the version of a divorcing couple's matrimonial life presented to the courts' (Eekelaar 1991: 24).

It is also evident in the current Law Commission proposals, which reflect concern about 'the degree to which the allegations of "fact" which may be made . . . might, be totally unrelated to the real reason for the marital breakdown' (Eekelaar 1991: 139), a direct and unintended consequence of the retention of the notion of 'fault' when the law was reformed in 1969:

> It had been the Law Commission's hope that most divorcing people would opt for the 'two years' separation and consent' condition, and that the 'adultery' and 'behaviour' conditions would be used only in emergency cases where a rapid remedy was necessary. Experience has belied these hopes. In 1988, only 18.8% of divorces were based on the consent condition; 29.7% on adultery and 43.6% on 'behaviour'. . . . People wishing to divorce are unwilling to wait longer than necessary. (Eekelaar 1991: 37).

Since maintenance and property issues cannot be settled until a decree has been granted, and since such settlements are particularly urgent when children are involved, it is not surprising that the 'adultery' and 'behaviour' conditions are used far more in such cases.

A further unintended consequence for which there is evidence (Davis and Murch 1988; Eekelaar and Clive 1977) is that this use of the 'behaviour' condition, which encourages the petitioner to embellish complaints about the conduct and personality of the other partner, can *increase* hostility during the divorce process. This has undoubtedly contributed to the growth of conciliation as a means of finding extra-legal solutions to the problems consequent upon the breakdown of marriage.

Fourthly, there are major issues raised concerning the nature of gender relationships after divorce. For example, perceived discrimination against fathers in custody decisions led to a growing demand for joint legal custody of children from the mid-1970s, which facilitated the articulation of the principle of joint parental responsibility embodied in the Children Act 1989. However, concern has been expressed that this may damage the position of care-giving mothers (Brophy 1989; Smart 1991) by giving fathers an equal status in the eyes of the law as 'responsible' parents and that such equality should only be conferred on fathers when they also take an equal share in the burdens of caring *for* as well as caring *about* their children.

However, it has long been a major argument of the feminist movement that women and men should be equal in the eyes of the law and to argue that because women do more in terms of caring *for* their children, they have a stronger and therefore *un*equal claim to custody arguably legitimises a division of labour and responsibility in marriage which weakens claims for equality (if not equity) in other aspects of the marital relationship. In addition, to assert a stronger claim in these terms is also to re-inforce socially ascribed gender-based roles of women as care-givers, which have been attacked as reflecting the patriarchal assumptions upon which the law and society are based (issues which are discussed in more detail in Chapter 8).

Of much greater significance is that this debate signifies the fact that divorce is adult-centred, dominated by the needs, wishes and views of adults. Despite the apparent shift from adult-centred to child-centred divorce and the introduction of the welfare check-list as the symbol of this, conflict between adults concerning the rights of men and women, of mothers and fathers, has not been and is unlikely to be defused, since even child-welfare-orientated decisions are based upon assumptions which are often gender-based or are capable of being defined as such. Thus, even child-welfare-orientated decisions based upon the primary care-giver criterion 'can be represented as prejudicial to men' (Eekelaar 1990: 136) *precisely because* parental relationships are, of necessity in the large majority of cases, unequal, at least to the extent that they are based upon a complementarity of marital roles and a division of labour, and because both men and women as mothers and fathers have interests in their children which are not amenable to equal division when parental relationships break down.

These themes and issues will be very much in evidence throughout the remaining chapters of this book.

2

Policy and praxis

In order better to understand the recent development of the court welfare work of the probation service and the milieu in which the themes and issues identified in Chapter 1 are played out, it is essential to consider the policy, practice and management contexts which serve to 'structure' court welfare officers and the way in which they work.

This is not to suggest, as constructivist legal theorists such as Teubner (1989) do, that the people the law deals with, such as court welfare officers, are merely constructs or products of the closed, self-referential system of law (see also King 1991; King and Piper 1990), or that they are solely determined by the constraints of policy and organisational boundaries. Such a view is consistent with neither our data nor our theoretical perspective, which acknowledges the actors as fully self-conscious players. It is to suggest, however, that the boundaries of the stage on which they play are defined substantially by how they choose and are enabled to play their parts and by contextual determinants. Even when 'off-stage', to pursue the theatrical analogy a little further, welfare officers' actions both shape and are shaped by these same considerations. This perspective also explains our use of the term 'praxis' which, although perhaps more common in Marxist discourse, serves to emphasise not only accepted practice and custom, but also the creative and transformative aspects of action (Craib 1992: 34) which have been so much a feature of the history of court welfare work.

In seeking to clarify the contextual boundaries provided by policy, practice and management, it is necessary to identify different levels of analysis which, for our purposes, are reflected in the national, regional and local dimensions. These provide the horizontal bands for a matrix (Figure 2.1) which can be divided vertically by identifying key organisations or 'groupings', such as the Home Office, the courts, the Association of Chief Officers of Probation, probation officers (and within this, court welfare officers) and probation committees.

Figure 2.1 The policy context of civil work

	Home Office	Courts	ACOP	Probation officers	Probation committees
National					
Regional					
Local					

This list is not exhaustive, excluding as it does, for example, the Department of Health, which has assumed a significant role in the wake of the Children Act 1989, and independent mediation services, with which many probation services have developed close and mutually supportive links. However, it does provide an analytical template which can be used to analyse both the development of policy and the management of practice.

Within this structure, there are clearly some organisations in which there has been and still is no *formal* policy. We must therefore consider *de facto* policy, in so far as this can be inferred from what happens and from the disparate nature of the organisations involved. Furthermore, the concept of policy and the processes of policy-making clearly differ between these organisational groupings and do not necessarily operate at each of these levels. There may also be problems distinguishing between regions and local areas, particularly where the latter are large. Therefore, whilst not precise, the template does draw attention to conceptual and practical distinctions which are important in understanding the complexity of the policy and practice contexts of family court welfare work.

It is informative to consider, in passing and by way of comparison, policy developments in the criminal work of the probation service using the same template. This suggests comparatively clear objectives, improving co-ordination and purposeful management, contrasting with a picture of relative uncertainty, confusion and management inaction which has largely typified the development of the civil work of the service.

The context of policy

The Home Office
Nationally, there has been no formal Home Office policy on the civil work of the probation service, although clearly the process of formulating one has begun (Home Office 1993). Given the far-reaching changes in the work of the service with offenders, the sustained pressure to bring this centre-stage in terms of the criminal justice system during the 1980s (see Bottomley *et al.* 1992; Mair 1989) and the political significance of such policies, it is perhaps understandable that work in the civil courts should take second place and that there might be doubts about such work remaining the responsibility of an agency the orientation of which is changing so dramatically. It is difficult, therefore, to avoid concluding that the changes which are under way are driven largely by *necessity*, brought about by the continuing responsibility of the Home Office for this area of work. In addition, the recent review of family court welfare work by the Inspectorate (Home Office 1991b) made it clear that there were major issues concerning the funding, organisation and management of court welfare work which could no longer be dealt with by a *de facto* policy of benign neglect.

Home Office policy has also been bounded more recently by a further policy dimension – that of containment. The Statement of National Objectives and Priorities for the Probation Service in England and Wales (SNOP), issued by the Home Office in 1984, made it clear that civil work was the lowest priority for the probation service and that 'The proportion of resources allocated to civil work should be contained at a level consistent with local circumstances and the foregoing priorities' (SNOP, priority (e)), the level becoming accepted by most services being approximately 10 per cent of the budget (Home Office 1991b: para. 5.1), with any local expansion being at the discretion of Chief Probation Officers out of existing resources. In practice, this figure was calculated according to a variety of different formulae and, in so far as can be determined with any accuracy, some areas have been allocating less than 7 per cent of their resources to civil work (Home Office 1991b).

It is also noteworthy that an earlier draft of SNOP recommended that 'The growth of civil work should be *contained* by concentrating it, so far as possible, in specialised units' (Lloyd 1986: 49) and although this did not appear in the final version, having been resisted by ACOP, the growth of civil work as a specialism since that time is a matter of record. As Lloyd has also pointed out, since it referred only to statutory work, taken literally SNOP therefore excluded any type of conciliation, even in-court conciliation involving a specific request by a judge, since there was no provision for such work under the Probation Rules, 1984, only for *re*conciliation (Home Office 1984, r.35(e)).

This undoubtedly had the effect, intended or otherwise, of marginalising or making ambiguous the status of conciliation within civil work, creating a situation whereby any such developments might be construed as a form of organisational 'deviance' if presented too overtly. This ambiguity was heightened by the paradox that conciliation was increasingly being seen as a means of *reducing* the costs of civil work since, it was argued, successful conciliation removed the need for a welfare report and 'the general threat to civil work resources ... led areas to seek to portray all facets of their civil work as being carried out as efficiently and effectively as possible' (Lloyd 1986: 51). It also encouraged, in conjunction with the requirement to provide a civil work service 'consistent with local circumstances', the negotiation with local courts of idiosyncratic arrangements which attempted to accommodate these conflicting imperatives.

The Home Office cannot be said to have regional or local policies as distinct from the national, although the Inspectorate represent one of the means by which the Home Office seeks to 'manage' probation services within the regions. However, the extent to which the Inspectorate can be described as 'managing' practice, particularly in the absence of any clear national policy, is debatable and it is not always easy to discern links between thematic reviews and other forms of inspection and the practice of probation officers at team level. Thus the *de facto* policy of the Home Office has been largely neutral or negative, except for the imposition of financial limitations, allowing conflicting pressures and ambiguities to develop.

The courts

Courts cannot be described in conventional organisational terms, particularly since the creation of a unified family jurisdiction by virtue of the Children Act 1989, which necessitates the inclusion not only of the professional judicial services provided by High Court, the Principal Registry and the county courts, but also the lay element provided by magistrates' courts. We must also include the Lord Chancellor's Department (LCD), particularly since it now has overall responsibility for all courts in England and Wales having taken over magistrates' courts in 1992. This relationship is difficult to define in conventional terms of policy-making and practice because of the constitutional independence of the courts, and yet to separate the two would not make analytical sense.

Similarly, it is difficult to describe the courts as having policies collectively, whether nationally or locally. However, we should consider the following: the role of the President of the Family Division, the High Court and the Principle Registry, whence come various Practice Directions; the role of the LCD in framing and giving voice to policies which affect the civil work of the service; the role of the judiciary in influencing practice through case law; and the role of the courts in dispensing justice locally.

In general, the judicial structure tends to be reactive in terms of framing statements about policy and practice. As long as there are no specific problems or major developments in legislation, such as the Children Act 1989, policies about practice tend not to emerge. However, where problems do arise in specific cases, judges have been critical of court welfare practice – e.g. in *Scott* v. *Scott* ([1986] 2 FLR 320 and in *Re H* [1986] 1 FLR 476). Such judgments have clear implications for policy, management and practice in their own right. However, where issues relating to the principles underpinning court welfare practice have arisen therefrom (such as the need to distinguish between conciliation and welfare reporting and the injunction that an officer involved in a failed attempt at conciliation should not be involved subsequently in preparing the welfare report), these may be reiterated by the President of the Family Division (see, for example, [1986] Fam Law 197 and [1987] Fam Law 181) and underlined by Practice Directions from the Principle Registry (see *Registrar's Practice Direction*, 28 July 1986) which *should* shape the practice of both subordinate courts and court welfare officers.

The LCD, not having direct responsibility for the civil work of the probation service and not wishing to impose administrative constraints on the judiciary has also had a *de facto* policy of benign neglect. This also reflects the fact that, like the Home Office, court welfare work is not a high priority on a crowded policy agenda and a general view that if reforms of the substantive law are right, procedural issues will fall more naturally into place. Thus, although there have been and are still important inter-departmental working groups (such as the Family Law Administration Working Party) involving the Home Office and the LCD, as well as other departments, discussions concerning court welfare work have been circumspect, reflecting sensitivity to the respective responsibilities of and proper boundaries between departments.

Consequently, court welfare work falls into the interstices between departments – it is provided for the civil courts (for which the LCD is responsible), by the probation service (for the provision, cost and servicing of which the Home Office is responsible), which has a key role in the private law provisions of the Children Act 1989 (for which the Department of Health has major responsibilities). In addition, the LCD has also been slow to determine key issues for which they *do* have responsibility, such as the future of conciliation which has profound implications for court welfare work. Failure to resolve this has, arguably, contributed to the state of confusion and uncertainty which has dominated the development and management of court welfare work.

It is even more difficult to describe the courts as having a regional structure. Circuits are primarily administrative rather than policy-making structures and they do not include magistrates' courts, bearing little relationship to other administrative boundaries. However, locally, it is clear that many courts do have policies, sometimes reflecting the interests of circuit judges, the practices of court welfare officers, or arrangements negotiated with probation services. This results in considerable variations in service to people using the courts, in spite of the relative uniformity which should, in principle, result from the judicial procedures described above. As Lloyd commented: 'in this field of probation work, as in many other areas of work with the courts, local services' objectives will reflect the idiosyncrasies of their particular relationships with local courts' (Lloyd 1986: 51; see also Dingwall and James 1988; Silbey 1981).

In the course of our research we interviewed judges in five study areas, a significant majority of whom, including both circuit and High Court judges, admitted either ignorance or lack of detailed knowledge of the judgment of Mr Justice Ewbank in *Re H* referred to above. The following comments by judges indicate some of the tensions which exist within the judicial system and reflect the more pragmatic views which hold sway in many county courts:

> Once a court welfare officer embarks on a report, then they should stick to reporting. But that doesn't mean that if they feel there is a chance to get the parties to talk together that they should ignore it. It is always desirable that the parties should be brought together if there is scope for it. [. . .]* It is all very well for judges in London and big centres to lay down these rules. I don't dissent from them in principle, at all. I can see the reasoning behind it, but when you are in a small county with a small probation service [. . .] I think that it puts a great strain on the service to divide up the work in that way. It is hard to comply with.
>
> If in the process of preparing the report, the welfare officer senses that they are not very far apart and that there could be agreement between them, then I don't see why he or she shouldn't try to bring that about, but they mustn't lose sight of the fact that they are preparing a report for the court.
>
> I see no reason why, because a welfare officer is trying to get the parties together to resolve the conflict that he or she shouldn't, at the end of the day, prepare a report for the court.
>
> In the long run, the object is to look after the interest of the child, and the interests of the child must be by conciliation of some sort. [. . .] You try to get people together to behave reasonably and if you can achieve that, then it is much better than giving information and having a fight, isn't it? If Mr Justice Ewbank doesn't agree, then I disagree with him.

Thus, conciliation or settlement seeking activities and welfare reporting are *still* combined in many areas as a result of local policies and practices in spite of the fact that such views, no matter how much they seem to reflect common sense, apparently conflict with the separation of tasks required as a result of the judgments and Practice Direction referred to above. One High Court judge commented:

> Obviously, the county court judge has to decide cases in accordance with the law; both the statutory law and the precedent law derived from

---

* We have adopted the convention of using '[. . .]' to indicate where speech has been omitted, to distinguish it from ' . . . ' indicating a pause by the speaker.

reported cases. If an individual county court judge were to ignore or reject precedent law derived from reported cases, he would be vulnerable to appeal and correction.

However, our research suggests that the legal system is not well equipped to oversee judicial practice in relation to such issues and although magistrates' courts did not figure largely in our research, it is not surprising that other research has revealed similar variations and accommodations in these courts (see, for example, Guymer and Bywaters 1984). Although the new organisational arrangements created by the Children Act 1989 – including the designation of particular circuit judges to be care judges, the formation of care centres to which courts are assigned, and the introduction of innovations such as regional Family Courts Services and Business Committees – may lead to the framing of local and regional policies and greater consistency between courts, the extent to which this happens, either by design or otherwise, remains to be seen.

Therefore, in terms of the organs of central government, there has been and still is a substantial policy vacuum which has had profound implications for the development and practise of court welfare work.

The Association of Chief Officers of Probation

In contrast, ACOP has a national policy-making process which has generated a civil work policy, largely through the sustained efforts of their Civil Work Committee. This has consulted with the President of the Family Division and others on a number of important issues (see, for example, ACOP 1989a) and formulated clear policies addressing practice issues (see, for example, ACOP 1987). A major problem which it faces, however, is lack of authority, since no Chief Probation Officer or court welfare officer is bound to comply with ACOP guidance. It must therefore operate through consensus which is hard to find, not least in the area of civil work. Given the variations between probation areas' responses to Home Office initiatives (see, for example, Lloyd 1986; Bottomley *et al.* 1992), it would be more than a little surprising if ACOP's policy on civil work was *not* responded to selectively.

ACOP also has a regional structure which enables local factors to be taken into account in relation to national policies. Thus, regional training for court welfare officers may be provided because of the need to pool training resources, which may lead to the gradual emergence of a regional approach to court welfare work, although none exists at present. Locally, however, ACOP does not have a policy-making structure or a management function and its polices may, as argued above, influence local policies and practices selectively and differentially. Local service provision is determined by a range of contingencies, of which ACOP polices are a relatively small part.

Probation officers
The policies of probation staff organisations such as the National Association of Probation Officers (NAPO) have until recently, as with other organisations, reflected civil work's perceived unimportance in terms of the political agenda and its contribution to the overall workload of the service. As the debate within the service about practice has become more heated and a split has developed between what we shall call, as a form of shorthand, the 'traditional' and 'conflict resolution' approaches (see Chapter 3), so have probation staff begun to develop policies.

However, because of the lack of consensus amongst probation staff, these have tried to cover all options (see, for example, NAPO 1984) and in consequence were contradictory (NAPO 1988). Moreover, as with ACOP, NAPO are not able to 'manage' the implementation of their policies, partly because of a lack of authority in organisational terms but also because of a perceived lack of representativeness and consensus. Smaller and more specialised staff groupings, such as the National Association of Court Welfare Officers, have only recently been formed and have yet to make a major impact on the debate.

Historically, regional groupings of court welfare officers have produced important policy/practice documents (e.g. NW Regional Divorce Court Welfare Officers 1976) which have been very influential. However, during the recent period of rapid change, their role has virtually disappeared and currently, probation staff have no real regional policy-making forum or capacity. However, there is a regional focus for their activities, particularly through training and practice development events aimed at the pooling of resources and experiences. This, together with the movement of staff between probation areas, means that services are by no means hermetically sealed against cross-fertilisation of ideas and practices. There is therefore the possibility of increasing regional conformity emerging, the significance of which lies at least in part in the fact that it represents change by 'organisational osmosis', rather than a policy-driven process of managed change.

Overall, however, there is little local consensus amongst probation staff. There are allegations of elitism from those working with offenders; there are sometimes resentments about the 'closed shop' view of some court welfare officers who resist returning to work with offenders, thereby blocking staff movement and preventing others from gaining experience of civil work; there are ambivalent or even antagonistic attitudes towards senior and sometimes middle managers, often reflecting a view that management 'don't understand court welfare work'; and there are very real disagreements about the benefits of change versus continuity in staffing court welfare teams, related to issues such as staff mobility policies.

Even within civil work teams with an apparent consensus about policies and practice, our research revealed that welfare officers often 'accommodate' their preferred practices within shared team philosophies in such a way as to preserve their own autonomy without compromising team solidarity. Such accommodations are possible, particularly in the absence of co-working with colleagues, because of welfare officers' control over access to what are highly 'encapsulated' encounters with clients. This allows them and indeed, as we shall argue later, *requires* them to operate with a degree of flexibility and to respond to the exigencies of work with individual families and parents.

Probation committees

The Central Council of Probation Committees, representing those who actually employ probation officers, has not had policies in relation to civil work in the past any more than any of the other organisations considered and it was only in October 1981 that it decided to establish a Civil Work Sub-Committee. Like the judiciary, it is a relatively loosely knit organisation, with the additional problem that it consists of lay members of lay committees. However, CCPC has clearly become much more active and influential since establishing its specialist sub-committee, responding to key government initiatives such as the Robinson Committee (1983), the Booth Committee (1985) and the consultation paper circulated by the LCD arising out of the Cleveland child-abuse inquiry.

In the process, it has also recognised that civil work presents the service with a number of issues which will not go away. It is also an area in which, as an organisation consisting of magistrates many of whom sit in domestic courts, it has strong practical interests. Many of these coincide with those of ACOP and NAPO, as evidenced by the 'Next Five Years' document (ACOP, CCPC and NAPO 1987), reflecting a consensual commitment to the retention and future development of civil work by the probation service. However, until its most recent policy statement (CCPC 1991), it has failed to formulate a clear policy statement, partly reflecting the ambiguity which has hitherto surrounded the policy-making and management roles of probation committees which have only recently been addressed by the Home Office Blue Paper (Home Office 1991a).

Probation committees do not have a significant regional identity, their main scope for policy-making being local, but they have a problem of 'getting in on the act'. They are often effectively excluded from the policy-making process, being unable to get close enough to the issues to do much more than simply concur with the recommendations of the Chief Probation Officer, who remains the professional adviser to a lay committee. This relationship, which currently dominates the perceptions and work of probation committees (Holdaway and Mantle 1991, 1992), draws attention to a key feature of area probation services as organisations – they are 'loosely coupled' in the sense that the organisational links between the different elements of the organisational hierarchy are loose and attenuated, rather than closely integrated. Consequently, the probation committee is loosely coupled to the managerial world of chief officers, which itself is loosely coupled to the world of practitioners.

Another potentially significant issue identified by Holdaway and Mantle is that the primary reference point for magistrates as probation committee members is the work of the probation service in the magistrates' courts, leading to a lack of appreciation of the overall needs of a probation area and, by implication, the needs of other courts requiring a court welfare service. Recent proposals (Home Office 1991a) certainly have the potential to enable committees to become much more active in their role as policy makers and managers, but such changes will require a substantial shift in the culture of probation committees as depicted by Holdaway and Mantle (1991, 1992), the possibility of which must be questionable.

The context of practice

Ultimately, it is locally that policies must seek to influence practice and where it is hardest for them to do so, not least because of the enormous diversity of practice, reflecting the emergence over the past decade of a grass-roots revolution in court welfare practice, few areas having remained totally untouched by the search for alternative approaches to dealing with family breakdown and divorce. However, this has largely been practitioner-led and a major problem to emerge subsequently has been for management also to try to 'get in on the act'.

There are several reasons for this. Probation officers in most spheres of probation work are not easy to manage because they are low-visibility, front-line workers whose practice with their clients is, with few exceptions, encapsulated within a confidential professional relationship. To this must be added the high level of commitment to and sense of ownership of locally developed approaches to court welfare work, creating resistance to management actions which might represent intrusion or the threat of change. In a number of areas, this difficulty has been compounded because welfare officers have formed strong alliances with the judiciary, who may either share a similar view of court welfare work, or simply appreciate the fact that fewer contested cases are appearing before them. There is also, as argued above, often a resistance to management based on the view that management do not understand civil work:

> I don't think they understand the complexity that there can be in a welfare report. [. . .] The other side of the coin is that we do something very special which nobody can understand and we don't really want them to understand. Management feel kept at a distance. (Area B)
>
> We're generally being managed by people who are not managers [. . .] who have lost touch with their roots and don't know what is going on. (Area C)
>
> I don't think there's very much dialogue between management and practitioners [. . .] civil work is very much different in that for several years the practice of civil work was managed by practitioners. Current policy, by and large, reflects what civil workers have been attempting to achieve over the last few years. (Area D)
>
> Most management simply don't know enough about us and are at a loss and have tried and have other things on their mind. Belatedly they have tried to pick the issue up. [. . .] They are threatened in the realisation

that we know much more about it than they do, and they are threatened by the specialism which has grown up. (Area E)

Although not all court welfare officers are critical of management, these comments reflect the views of a significant number. They hint at ambivalence about the perceived failure of management to understand court welfare work and the simultaneous importance of sustaining this ignorance, in order to protect cherished practices from scrutiny and possible change.

It seems evident, however, that until there are clear policies about the aims, objectives and priorities of court welfare work, practice cannot even begin to be managed effectively, and until there is a degree of consensus about these aims, objectives and priorities, policies cannot begin to be framed. Thus the policy context is an integral and inseparable part of the context of practice. Given the complexity of the situation, any such consensus is going to be difficult to achieve and local solutions to particular problems will always tend to emerge and be perpetuated by local arrangements and relationships.

However, the context of both policy and practice are also shaped significantly by the statutory framework within which court welfare officers work. In particular therefore, practice must now take account of the fundamental changes introduced by the Children Act 1989 and, more speculatively, the Law Commission's proposals for the reform of the law relating to divorce. Embedded in these changes are a number of important principles which clearly should be reflected in policy and practice. Although much discussed and written about, it may be helpful briefly to restate these because of their significance in relation to the framing of practice and our discussion of this in subsequent chapters. They are as follows:

- *The welfare principle:* that courts must treat the child's welfare as the paramount consideration in all questions about his or her upbringing.
- *The principle of parental responsibility:* that in the interests of the child, parents retain responsibility for their children, even after separation.
- *The principle of parental involvement:* that in exercising their responsibilities, parents should be as fully involved as possible in making decisions relating to the upbringing of their children.
- *The principle of positive intervention:* courts shall not make orders unless satisfied that it will be a positive contribution to the interests of the child.

- *The principle of minimal delay:* delay in court proceedings is generally harmful to a child and must be kept to a minimum.

However, it is also important to acknowledge that these important principles contain certain contradictions or ambiguities which contribute significantly to the context of practice (see also Chapter 1). Since, in many respects, these provide some of the key themes for the rest of the book, we will do no more here than to list them. Thus, for example:

- There are few absolutes about what constitutes the best interests of the child and how best to achieve this, and key actors may have divergent opinions.
- The responsibility of parents for their children must be balanced with the responsibility of the state to ensure that parents exercise their responsibility in a way that does reflect the best interests of the child.
- Parental involvement of any substance must require welfare professionals to relinquish some of their power.
- Parental views of what constitutes positive intervention may differ from the courts, and more orders may be sought than is currently anticipated.
- Minimising delay where welfare professionals are involved may have implications for resourcing, organisation and practice, leading to conflict between courts and welfare officers. It may also conflict with other objectives such as the Law Commission's proposals for a 'cooling off' period in divorce proceedings.

In particular, the principles of parental responsibility and involvement, in the wider context of consumer power, citizens' rights, and organisational accountability which is evident in so many aspects of social policy and service delivery, have potentially major implications for the provision of welfare services in divorce and for the context of practice.

To summarise, therefore, the main elements which comprise the context of policy and the practice of court welfare work are as follows:

- A policy vacuum at central government level, reflected in benign neglect, containment and negative resource management.
- Consequent organisational uncertainty/ambivalence over the place of court welfare work.

- A policy credibility and implementation problem on the part of relevant professional associations at national level.
- A loosely coupled organisational structure, with lay employers' committees loosely coupled to the managerial world of chief officers, which is loosely coupled to the world of practitioners.
- Diversity of practice and lack of consensus amongst probation staff.
- Probation officer control over highly encapsulated, low-visibility encounters with clients.
- Variable but sometimes very close working relationships with the local judiciary, who often actively support divergent practices in different areas or even within the same area.
- A generally sceptical attitude towards management by probation officers, which can be particularly marked in civil work.
- Continuing ambiguities and tensions stemming from both the statutory framework provided by the Children Act 1989 and the principles underpinning this.

The context of management

Much of the context of the management of court welfare work is framed by the not unproblematic context of policy and practice we have just outlined. It is also shaped by trends in the operational environment of the probation service, particularly the current emphasis on inter-agency and inter-professional co-operation, reflecting developments in criminal justice and child-protection; by the nature of the probation service, which is framed not only by its responsibilities but its location within the ethos and infrastructure of social work in terms of its training, values, functions and history; and by its nature as an organisation, straddling the worlds of central and local government, which is increasingly constrained to provide locally relevant services meeting minimum national standards within cash limits defined by the centre. One could scarcely *design* a more complex context for management!

What, therefore, are the main issues confronting probation management arising from this analysis? There are at least five *main* areas of concern which, for analytical purposes, can be laid out in another matrix (Figure 2.2). This suggests that whatever the starting point, because of their inter-dependence no one area can be considered in

Figure 2.2 Main issues in the context of management

	Organisation and resources	Management	Inter-agency initiatives	Practice	Training
Organisation and resources	■				
Management		■			
Inter-agency initiatives			■		
Practice				■	
Training					■

isolation from the others. These five main areas should also be considered in terms of the different *levels* of analysis suggested in Figure 2.1, since there are national, regional and local issues raised by each area of policy concern which need to be identified and addressed.

Organisation and resources
As we have argued, the organisation and resourcing of civil work are typified currently by the following: the absence of direction from the Home Office, the LCD and, in some cases, from local management; a policy of benign neglect; and the low priority which it is accorded, reflected both in status and resources. The latter is clearly illustrated by current approaches to funding whereby, in the absence of any logically necessary connection between the two, expenditure on civil work is linked to expenditure on criminal work, rather than being separately and specifically calculated (Home Office 1991b: para. 3.31). The impact of such issues is attested to with silent eloquence by the exclusion of court welfare work from the proposed formula for the introduction of cash-limited probation funding by the Home Office (1991c: paras 36–9).

These issues are mirrored in divisions amongst probation staff over whether court welfare work is still an appropriate task for the probation service, or whether it might not be time to relocate this function, which rests with the service by virtue of history rather than by the expectations of the probation service today and which, arguably, might be located elsewhere if designing a court welfare service *ab initio*.

A major problem in the context of management must therefore be the absence of government policy concerning the aims, objectives and provision of court welfare services. Not until such issues are clarified will managers be able to plan ahead and overcome the planning blight resulting from uncertainty about the organisation and funding of court welfare services.

Management

The Home Office review of family court welfare work (1991b) offers a thorough analysis of many of the issues confronting managers, confirming that probation committees have rarely been given the opportunity to consider civil work issues. Consequently, in the light of the proposals for restructuring committees, revising their policy-making and management roles, and emphasising their role in the provision and management of services for which they will be accountable to government, probation managers will need to ensure that committees are more closely involved in future (Home Office 1991b; paras 7.77–8).

The emphasis on value for money in the public sector has also been a major factor shaping recent management practice in the probation service (see Audit Commission 1989, 1991), reflected in the drive by the Home Office to devise a financial and resource management strategy (Humphrey 1991) with appropriate indicators for monitoring performance. Consistent with its low priority, such developments have scarcely touched civil work (Home Office 1991b: para. 7.84). However, with arguments for the specific funding of civil work inevitably comes the need to monitor performance. This too, however, is inseparable from the issue of policy, aims and objectives. As the review noted:

> Where a service had identified specific objectives for civil work, senior management was in a position to formulate a view of the effectiveness of the use of resources made available. . . . In most areas, not only was there an [sic] lack of clear objectives for civil work but monitoring systems were notable only for their absence. (Home Office 1991b: para. 7.85)

Therefore, a further and increasingly pressing component of the context of management, having major implications, is the need 'to establish an accurate statistical data base for civil work, which will address local and national requirements' (Home Office 1991b: para. 3.30) and to develop appropriate performance indicators for monitoring court welfare work.

In addition, however, there are related issues concerning the *management of practice*, many of which will be explored in detail in the following chapters; the *management of practitioners* in the context, for example, of the increasing development of mobility policies requiring staff to move from specialist posts after a pre-determined length of time; and the *management of relationships with the courts*, which have hitherto been conducted predominantly on a highly individualised basis between court welfare officers and 'their' judges (or *vice versa*, from the judges' perspective!) or individual magistrates' courts.

Inter-agency initiatives

The growth of the conciliation movement in England and Wales (for a detailed discussion of which see, for example, Fisher 1990; Forster 1982; James 1990a; Parkinson 1986) has been a significant factor in the background of many of the developments described in this chapter and, in particular, in the changes in court welfare practice which will be discussed in more detail in Chapter 3. Indeed, it is arguable that many of the emerging issues in the contexts of policy, practice and management are a direct consequence of the impact of both the concept and the practice of conciliation. In this sense, the development of independent conciliation services, although important in both practical and symbolic terms, has been only one expression of the much wider impact of the conciliation movement.

However, it is important to note that the development of independent services (of which in 1992 there were some 55 in operation using the services of some 300 conciliators) has taken place in spite of the lack of financial support from central government. In many instances, their development has been actively supported – both directly, in terms of staff (professional and clerical) and premises, and indirectly, in terms of training, consultancy and membership of management committees – by local probation services (Home Office 1991b; James 1992b; Parkinson 1986; Wells 1990), not least because of the view that the availability of such services, apart from being desirable in their own right, would reduce the demand for welfare reports (Lloyd 1986). Indeed, many independent services might not have survived without such support. Probation services and court welfare practitioners have therefore had a substantial but largely unacknowledged influence on the development of such services and practice within them.

The probation service is committed to continuing to support such services and to close liaison with them both locally and nationally (ACOP 1987). Indirect support through various means is therefore likely to continue but, in addition, probation committees now have the power by virtue of s.97 of the Criminal Justice Act 1991 to fund them directly. Various local contractual arrangements are therefore likely to emerge, although the cash-limiting of probation services may have implications not only for the funding of civil work activities but also for the willingness of probation committees to give such direct financial support.

The Law Commission proposals are also of particular relevance because they focus upon the availability of marital and divorce counselling, conciliation or mediation, and other such services which they see as 'an important element in developing a new and more constructive approach to the problems of divorce and marital breakdown in the interests, not only of the adults and children directly involved, but also of society as a whole' (1990: para. 5.31). This clearly locates such facilities in the context of the tradition of providing social-work services in matrimonial proceedings, of which the probation service has been and still is an integral part (see Chapter 1), whilst also highlighting the need and potential for the development of locally based inter-agency strategies to ensure the provision of a range of services, making this another important element in the context of management. As Wells has argued, reflecting the position of ACOP (1989b): 'In the years ahead, the civil work of the service will increasingly be committed to the concept of partnership . . . to be part of a co-ordinated approach to the problems arising as a result of separation and family breakup' (1990: 46).

Practice
It is clear from our discussion of the context of practice that there are many practice issues which form an important part of the context of management. The detail of many of these will become clear in the chapters which follow, but two issues in particular are worth stressing at this point.

The first, which is an issue of process, is the question of how management can 'get in on the act' concerning court welfare work which it has either ignored or has been prevented from getting close to. If managers are to engage effectively with the issues outlined above, they must have and be seen to have relevant knowledge about practice. More importantly, and perhaps more problematically, the management of court welfare practice must be accorded legitimacy by practitioners. Resistance from some welfare officers seems likely because if management is successful in achieving this aim, practice may in future be located more firmly in the context of the legal system from which, for a variety of reasons, we shall argue it has become separated or distanced. Practice may also have to change in line with management strategies, involving loss of grass-roots control in an area regarded by many court welfare officers as the last bastion of relatively autonomous 'social work' practice in the probation service. These concerns about process raise questions about both management skills and methods, consideration of the adequacy of which must also form part of the context of management.

The second is an issue of substance concerning the changes brought about by the Children Act 1989. It remains to be seen what impact the Act will have on the report-writing, mediation and supervisory functions of court welfare officers, but it is clear that they will be exercised in a very different statutory context and that achieving the changes required by the Act will require management. It is also clear that the related procedural mechanisms and administrative structures will require not only a more co-ordinated approach between the different parts of the system, but also greater probation service accountability for the adequacy of the service provided to the civil courts. In one vital respect, these changes also offer an opportunity for management to become involved, since this necessity for change means that the *status quo* has been altered and the system will consequently be more open to entry and to further change.

Training

The final major component of the context of management is training. Like practice, training is dynamic. Not only is it constantly changing and evolving in response to a variety of internal and external pressures, but the very ideas about what constitutes practice and training are subject to the same pressures and processes of change. Thus, the main constituents of practice – the roles, tasks, knowledge, skills and competencies – which come together to make court welfare practice are not static, any more than are the ideas about how to incorporate these into training. Thus, the management of training must encompass not only these constituents and the organisational and practice contexts of court welfare work, but also the changing statutory context of practice; the changing structures of social work training (e.g. the demise of Regional Staff Development Units, the creation of their successors and the developing role of the Central Council for Education and Training in Social Work both at pre-qualifying and post-qualifying levels); the development of regional training strategies and programmes; and, of course, the resourcing of training.

In addition, it is crucial, particularly with the growth of mobility policies, that the processes of staff management and development, which form an integral part of training, are also effectively managed. Few welfare officers interviewed in the course of our research recalled satisfactory management of the process of transfer, training and induction into civil work. When asked about what training they had received, replies included:

> I didn't have an induction period. I was just left to get on with it. I feel that I've wasted about six months of this year just floundering around. (Area A)
>
> I just picked it up. [...] I haven't been to a specific course. (Area B)
>
> I spent some time with another officer and went to court as an observer and that was it, straight in. I've learned by doing. (Area C)
>
> It's up to management [...] to train me accordingly. They don't train us and I think that the probation service is woefully inadequate in what they claim they train. (Area D)
>
> It's difficult joining a new team. [...] I'm still finding it difficult. [...] I don't think the induction worked particularly well for me. I was able to observe and read, but I would have preferred more practical training. (Area E)

Recent developments

Partly as a result of the review of family court welfare work (Home Office 1991b), and the occasional *cause célèbre* such as the judgment of Mr Justice Ewbank in *Re H*, probation managers have begun to engage with the problems of managing family court welfare work. They have not been helped, however, by the nature of the policy, practice and management contexts outlined above. In contrast, the criminal work of the service has been the subject of policy-making at all levels, a growing consensus about objectives and priorities at all levels and often across organisational boundaries, and a veritable flood of consultation documents, papers of varied hues and requests for action plans, which have produced a very clear if somewhat crowded management agenda. The two 'arms' of the service could hardly be more different.

However, there are clear signs of change. ACOP and NAPO have recently produced a joint policy statement on civil work (ACOP/NAPO 1991), whilst CCPC has also produced a statement (CCPC 1991) concerning aims and objectives, reiterating their commitment to developing the civil work of the probation service. Perhaps more significantly the Home Office (1993), in the wake of the Thematic Review and after consultation with ACOP and CCPC, have produced a draft document for publication in 1993 outlining a national strategy for the development of family court welfare work. This proposes dropping the term 'civil work' in favour of 'family court welfare work', a term thought to describe the work more accurately and to be more in line with the spirit of the Children Act 1989, although significantly the use of the term 'family court welfare service' is not favoured since this implies 'an undesirable degree of separation from the remainder of the work of the probation service' (Home Office 1993: para. 2) which there is now clearly a wish to avoid.

The strategy document indicates that probation areas are required to produce local family court welfare work policy statements. These will in turn be informed by the functions, goals and values for the probation service identified in the recently published Three Year Plan (Home Office 1992c) and will provide the framework for the efficient and effective management of family court welfare work, in the light of the provisions of the Children Act 1989. It also comments *inter alia* on the recent change, effected by the Probation (Amendment) (No. 2) Rules 1992, making dispute resolution at the request of the court, directed towards achieving agreement out of court, a statutory duty. This reflects the Home Office view that '*appropriately directed*, this is a sensible use of resources . . . which can be an important factor in enabling couples to reach agreement over the future of their children' (1993: para. 6; emphasis added) and signals the introduction by 1994 of a framework of 'best practice' to be defined in national standards. In addition, there are also indications of movement within the LCD, not least in terms of a new or renewed interest in the development of alternative dispute resolution as part of the legal system more generally (Roberts 1992) and of family mediation within this (James 1992b).

What is clear above all else is that court welfare practice has developed dramatically during the last decade, in spite of these problems, because of the imagination, commitment and enthusiasm of court welfare officers. They have acted and, paradoxically, been enabled to act within the legal system in response to a growing tide of dissatisfaction with the shortcomings of the present legal system and the effects of these on parents and children. Praxis, in terms of the creative and transformative aspects of action, is indeed central to these developments. The nature of these such changes, the impact of conciliation and the discourse surrounding these are the subject of the next chapter.

3
Polarisation and polemic

In considering the emergence of current approaches to court welfare work and, in particular, the impact of conciliation, we shall be only indirectly concerned with the substantive issues concerning different approaches to court welfare practice. Thus, we shall not enter into the debate about the advantages and disadvantages of, for example, different models of family therapy compared with conciliation or what might be described as 'traditional' investigative approaches, since this is covered more than adequately in the material on which we have drawn in this chapter and throughout this book. Moreover, many of these issues will also become apparent in subsequent chapters from the views of court welfare officers themselves. Rather, our intention in this chapter is to take a meta-view of the discourse which has developed in order to understand the underlying issues. This discourse, in all its forms and aspects, has been conducted in a wide range of forums, with varying degrees of publicity.

At its broadest level, the discourse has been evident in the growth of the alternative dispute resolution (ADR) movement representing 'a serious new effort to design workable and fair alternatives to our traditional judicial system' (Edwards 1986: 668). It has been dominated largely by lawyers and has centred on the growth of informal justice (Matthews 1988) in the face of increased questioning of the appropriateness of adversary justice, drawing upon cross-cultural literature about disputes and negotiations (e.g. Griffiths 1988; Gulliver 1979; Minamikata 1988). The latest developments in this wider debate in the United Kingdom have been the investigation by the LCD of the potential of ADR in the civil justice system (Roberts

1992) and the report of the Beldam Committee (1991) to the General Council of the Bar, recommending the development of a court-based, mediation-focused scheme for ADR, using experienced litigators as mediators. Such developments have generated concerns (e.g. Davis 1985; Greatbatch and Dingwall 1989; Piper 1988; Roberts 1983, 1992) that, even where the impetus for reform comes from grass-roots sentiment, as with family conciliation (James 1990a), rather than from the policies of central government, 'developments will be co-opted by the powerful, so that "bad" form takes over from "good" substance ... [leading to] rampant interventionism, a system of indirect controls and pervasive reliance on professional expertise' (Freeman 1982: 19). In essence, these are 'discourses about the form of law' (Freeman 1982: 8) which reflect fundamental issues about the relationship between adjudication and ADR, between the state and the individual (Roberts 1983, 1992). However, they are also discourses about process which reflect inter- and intra-professional power struggles about who should provide and therefore control the definition, practice and development of ADR.

Within this general context, there has been a discrete discourse about family conciliation and divorce which has been informed by this wider debate (Roberts 1983). This has been reflected in and developed by various official reports (most notably that of the Finer Committee and the Booth Committee), by research (e.g. Conciliation Project Unit 1989; Davis and Bader 1985; Dingwall 1988; Greatbatch and Dingwall 1989; James and Dingwall 1989; Kingsley 1990; Piper 1988; Simpson *et al.* 1990) and by contributions from pioneers and practitioners (e.g. Davis and Roberts 1988; Parkinson 1986). It has also involved a more diverse range of participants including lawyers, academics and practitioners, reflecting a diversity of perspectives and claims about the nature of conciliation and its role in divorce.

Settlement-seeking and court welfare work

The most intense and specific part of this debate has been within the probation context. This sub-discourse has arguably been the most important for formative purposes and is the most significant in terms of understanding the issues involved for welfare officers, providing the frameworks for and shaping court welfare practice. The most overt representation of this sub-discourse has been the published output of a relatively small group of academics and practitioners, particularly in the form of articles and correspondence in both legal journals (in particular *Family Law*, one of the most widely read journals amongst court welfare officers) and social-work journals. This symbolises some of the ambiguities and tensions which exist for welfare officers, as social workers practising in a setting in which they have a long history and much experience but which is dominated by the legal profession, legal values, legal perspectives and procedures. This has led commentators such as King (1991) to argue that law dominates this discourse and has 'enslaved' the welfare discourse, although this conclusion is debatable (James 1992c).

In particular, the journal of the National Association of Probation Officers provides a unique insight into the development of the discourse. In 1972, an article written by A Group of Devon Probation Officers appeared, arguing that in divorce, parents can lose a sense of proportion and that 'fights for custody are not always undertaken out of a genuine desire to care for their off-spring but often to deprive and hurt the other partner' (1972: 41). The argument was essentially about the use of resources and the need for specialisation in order to make the best use of these, in order to meet the needs of children in the context of the increasing demand for welfare reports.

Nothing further appeared until an article by Scarr in 1978, referring to the work of court welfare officers in Minnesota whose role had changed from

> investigator to mediator . . . taking the problem out of the adversary system and bringing both parents together with their new partners and children where appropriate. The emphasis is on the best interests of the children. The focus is on parenting qualities not the causes of marital breakdown and discord . . . hostility and bitterness could be avoided if we were introduced at the beginning of the process as mediators rather than as laborious report writers when much more damage has been done. (1978: 26)

Scarr argued that the probation service should re-evaluate its approach in view of the increasing volume of divorce court inquiries referred by the courts, suggesting impartial 'counselling' in a neutral environment as a step towards achieving satisfactory compromises.

The following year, three articles appeared (Bretherton 1979; Chapman 1979; Straker 1979), raising various issues about court welfare work. In the first, Chapman referred to NAPO's evidence to the Marriage Matters working party. This concluded that, in spite of the decline in matrimonial work, the service had an indispensable role in this field, exhorting the service to respond to the consultation document sent out in the wake of the report: 'The real question is whether we can meet this challenge and prove that probation officers are in favour of continued involvement in matrimonial work' (1979: 59).

In the second, Bretherton enlarged the debate, discussing the place of court welfare work in the divorce process, the tasks and objectives of welfare officers and the theoretical principles governing the work. She argued that the welfare officer was concerned primarily with the welfare of the children, to help the court reach a decision on this and to offer appropriate help to the parents and children from a position of neutrality. In a situation where a speedy divorce depended often upon proving unreasonable behaviour and magnifying faults, 'The court welfare officer can talk about the areas where the parties agree and can allow them to acknowledge the good as well as the bad in the relationship' (1979: 75).

The tasks she described as threefold: seeking information for the preparation of the report; conciliating; and acting as a counsellor for either or both parties or the children: 'The process of conciliation will usually involve *counselling* but the object of counselling . . . is to help [parents] disentangle their own needs and feelings from those of their children' (1979: 76; italics original). She argued that the adversarial system was inappropriate for settling family disputes and that the welfare officer, a neutral 'spokesman for the child', should help the court 'by providing factual information about the child and his family and the theoretical basis upon which the court may take its decision' (1979: 80), referring to the maintenance of the *status quo* espoused by Goldstein *et al.* (1973), whose work was particularly influential at that time (see Murch 1980; Wilkinson 1981).

In the third article to be published that year, Straker described the development of divorce experience courses in Leicestershire, which were 'an expression of a fresh approach . . . a major response to the problem of those who are affected by family splitting' and a reaction against 'the anachronism of over-using an adversarial system in an area which calls for information, negotiation and mediation' (1979: 81). He argued that such developments were essential because court welfare work had been reduced to a massive reporting operation with limited resources, focusing conflict on the children, the resolution of which was put into the hands of people outside the family.

These articles reveal some important issues. Firstly, they clearly acknowledge the change in the nature and scale of the problem of divorce, the need to respond to the challenges which these presented to court welfare officers, the perceived inadequacy of traditional approaches and the growing desire to develop new responses to familiar but increasingly unmanageable problems. This is linked with growing concerns about the resourcing and organisation of court welfare work and, in the light of the declining traditional role of the service in relation to *re*conciliation, questions about the appropriateness of probation service involvement in family court welfare work (see Chapter 1).

Secondly, this transition highlighted the need for a new language as new concepts began to emerge from the old. The traditional language of counselling merges with new ideas stressing the importance of neutrality, of reframing negative experiences, of reducing conflict and encouraging parents to focus upon and agree about children's needs. This is linked with a transition from prevailing theoretical perspectives, such as those of Goldstein *et al.*, to new perspectives such as those of Wallerstein and Kelly (1980), already influential in the United States and which were filtering through to the United Kingdom.

Many of these issues are reflected in the first book to be devoted exclusively to the subject, by a court welfare officer, Martin Wilkinson. In this, he acknowledged the slow progress in the move towards the family court advocated by the Finer Committee (1974), arguing that

> Those concerned for the welfare aspects of family courts cannot therefore afford simply to wait upon events. The Probation and After-Care Service ... should even now be considering how best to give some immediate and tangible demonstration both of its commitment and of its potential performance. (1981: 188)

Part of this demonstration 'has been its response in social work terms to the new demands made of it. . . . Central to this part of its work is the concept of conciliation, which seeks as far as may be possible to heal the emotional wounds of the marital breakdown' (1981: 5–6). He argued that court welfare officers had a dual role of reporter and conciliator and that 'counselling' may modify attitudes towards a former partner, influencing the final balance of the completed report:

'The two processes of investigation and conciliation are thus inextricably interwoven and very largely interdependent' (1981: 8).

In an interesting footnote, Wilkinson commented on the clear separation of these functions in some American courts. He argued that although there may be difficulties in combining the two, such as if a client wished to keep information provided for the conciliation confidential for the purposes of the report, the distinction was unnecessarily artificial and that there was added depth and quality to the report, 'which gets much closer to essential attitudes and feelings when it actually embraces the conciliation aspect' (1981: Chapter 2, n. 1). This prescient comment is interesting, not only because it identified what was to become a crucial issue in refining the definition of court welfare work, but because it was consigned to a brief footnote! In addition, during the same period, further articles reflecting the growing impact of conciliation on court welfare work were published elsewhere in the social-work press (e.g. Burrett and Gibbons 1981; Fraser 1980)

Disagreement about agreements

A year later, two further articles appeared in the *Probation Journal* (Davis 1982; Howard and Shepherd 1982), signifying the first signs of tension between some court welfare practitioners and outside commentators and the first salvo in what was to become an increasingly acrimonious exchange. Davis's critical appraisal of the growing use of conciliation in court welfare work identified conciliation in the process of preparing welfare reports as the most problematical form of conciliation being practised. He acknowledged that facilitating agreement in the course of preparing a report was not new and that not only could welfare reports act as a vehicle for achieving settlement but that 'the conciliatory and even-handed approach of the welfare officer may enable a genuine accommodation to be reached' (1982: 125). Such an approach, welcomed by many parents, had led to the development of 'new style' welfare reports focusing on the outcome of negotiations.

He argued, however, that conciliation and welfare investigation had different objectives and were based on different principles:

> The focus of conciliation is conflict resolution, whereas the Divorce Court Welfare Service has a predominantly child welfare orientation . . .

the risk is that a preoccupation with the welfare of the child may undermine parents' authority. . . . If conciliation were viewed purely in terms of the children's interests, it could take on an authoritarian guise, with value judgements (as in many welfare reports) being freely imported.' (1982: 125–6; see also Chapter 5)

This echoes the concerns that led to the Summary Procedure (Domestic Proceedings) Act of 1937, about probation officers exceeding their legitimate authority by defining their role and constructing their encounters with clients in a different way from that intended by the law (see Chapter 1). Davis also cautioned that conciliation may not be the best method for most people, even though most family conflict is settled informally, and that the probation service needed to be flexible and establish clear boundaries between different areas of its civil work.

In contrast, Howard and Shepherd asked why the court welfare system had changed so little, describing the development by their specialist court welfare team of a family-focused approach to the preparation of custody and access reports which involved active parental participation, which fostered conciliation and which provided colleague support, whilst guarding against assuming the responsibilities of the parents, through conjoint working. They espoused a simple philosophy: 'the basis of a child's best interest lies in an agreement between the parents regarding the arrangements for their child' (1982: 87). This entailed fundamental shifts in practice involving increased contact between parents by 'a process of conciliation', a shift from judgements by welfare officers to problem-solving and parental agreement, and a move from assessment of individuals to assessments of families as groups of individuals.

However, they argued that such shifts in methods had implications for both the general 'frame work' of reports and the specific techniques of interviewing, going on to describe how they framed the purpose of the welfare enquiry in introductory letters to parents in terms of exploring: 'the possibilities of reaching an agreement about the children's best interests that will be acceptable to the court', and their decision to prepare welfare reports using interviewing techniques derived from various models of family therapy

> by a process of conjoint interviewing, which can be termed as conciliation. The point is that we do not see conciliation as something

apart from preparing welfare reports but that the two are intrinsically combined . . . there is a shift for the worker from an investigator to a conciliator. (1982: 92)

They argued that reports are requested because of parental disagreements and if these could be resolved, the report should simply outline the terms of the agreement, there being little justification for further investigation at that stage. This approach they contrasted with 'traditional welfare reporting', in which the worker investigated separately the parents' views of the situation, arguing that although the new approach demanded greater professionalism and was more demanding, it was more satisfying than 'traditional' court welfare work.

Thus, as the discourse developed, there appeared to be a growing consensus, articulated by those practitioners advocating a change of direction for court welfare, about both the arguments for and the implications of such changes. They identified dissatisfaction with the traditional court welfare role and an increasing wish to frame welfare interventions in a more positive way, by enthusiastically embracing conciliation. In order to do this conciliation was defined or, as commentators such as Davis argued, *re*defined as being not just about conflict resolution but as being the best means of ensuring the child's best interests, thus legitimating court welfare involvement in such activity. It is interesting to note in passing that at this stage in the debate, the approach of Howard and Shepherd not only stresses parental agreement as the best means of ensuring the child's best interests, implying choice, but also the acceptability of agreements to the court. This, of course, implies constraint but also legitimation of this approach.

It is also significant that the need for the report is located in the disagreement of the parents rather than the court's need for information. It can be argued that the framing of the report in this way, from which the type of report produced flowed quite logically, made a significant contribution to the development of practices which subsequently led to serious judicial criticism of some welfare officers' lack of attention to the information needs of the court. Locating the need for reports in the disagreement of parents also legitimated the use of techniques derived from family therapy as a means of resolving those disagreements, a practice regarded by critics as inappropriate in the context of welfare investigations. It is also interesting to note the juxtaposition of greater job satisfaction with the advantages to parents and children of the new style of welfare reporting compared with the traditional approach. Davis's challenge to these developments and the thinking behind them signified the start of a major power struggle over the control and definition of the language of conciliation, and its practice.

A year later, further research (James and Wilson 1983; see also 1984a and 1984b) shed more light on court welfare practice and raised further questions. It revealed that a substantial minority of officers regarded conciliation as an integral part of their work, with many references being made to family therapy (implying therapeutic intervention as well as investigation) and concluded that probation officers 'already have a substantial but covert involvement in conciliation during the process of report preparation and that increasingly areas are becoming both directly and indirectly involved in setting up and running conciliation schemes' (1983: 54). Questions were also raised about the adequacy of training for court welfare work, about investigation practices in terms of people interviewed and agencies contacted during the course of enquiries, and about contacts with children during the course of enquiries.

The consolidation of therapy

At the same time, based on experience in a specialist team, Guise expressed concern about conciliation in independent schemes which failed to include children routinely in conciliation interviews with parents. The team's approach to conciliation was based on a view that

> For quite a number of these families there is a specific social work task; to help them deal with and resolve the emotional trauma of their failure to make their relationship work, before they are free to make lasting and effective decisions about their children's future. . . . Some families come to us particularly entrenched and even here we have been able to achieve some movement by working at greater lengths with them on a therapeutic basis by using the family therapy approach. (1983: 59)

This clearly identified a therapeutic *process* using therapeutic *methods* which was required before agreements could be reached.

Guise advocated framing enquiries by making clear an expectation that both parents and children should attend a joint interview with two officers, this being the team's normal method of working, arguing that this approach produced more consent orders, shorter reports, fewer supervision orders, better family adjustment to the post-divorce situation, more job satisfaction and that welfare officers had the necessary skills for such work:

> Enabling and facilitating separating couples to find a new role as parents is a social work skill ... the Probation Service has the social work skills to staff conciliation services effectively and ... should now actively seek to be the main provider for future conciliation services. (1983: 60)

This clearly represented a bid for 'ownership' of the definition and provision of conciliation, defining it as a social-work process requiring social-work skills, working towards what are essentially social-work goals concerned with adjustment and change in individuals and families, rather than reaching agreements. It also reflected the growing desire to move beyond the perceived sterility of simply investigating and reporting on families, to a form of social-work intervention which not only provided increased job satisfaction but also met some of the requirements of the legal system. The inclusion of the latter suggests a growing awareness of the need to acknowledge the welfare officer's role in meeting the needs of the legal process, as well as those of parents, children and court welfare officers, reflecting some of the concerns felt in the legal system about the need to manage the increasing workload. This, in turn, explains in part how welfare officers were enabled to promulgate such developments.

The following year saw two further articles which took the discourse a stage further. Shepherd et al. (1984), reacting against the argument for the separation of conciliation and report writing, argued that conciliation was not something to be tried but for which a traditional welfare report could be substituted in the event of 'failure', but was 'at the very heart of the welfare principle'. In addition, they maintained that conciliation was not just about agreement but was

> a *process* of encouraging the parties to a divorce to take up their responsibilities as parents. . . . An over-emphasis on 'getting agreements' runs the risk of losing sight of this process. . . . This may serve the interests of the courts, but not necessarily those of the children. (1984: 21)

They also emphasised the problems created for the legal system by parents who had difficulty in separating from each other and who therefore disputed issues of custody and access, to which conciliation provided the only answer.

Moreover they argued that, in principle and in effect, conciliation and investigation were contradictory – that conciliation rested upon the assumption of parental competence, whereas investigation by its very nature questioned parental competence. Whilst acknowledging that sometimes courts had to adjudicate, they argued that in doing so they should not rely upon

> a pseudo-professional judgement by the welfare officer about which is the more reasonable or suitable parent... any *opinion* offered should be confined to an assessment of the emotional environment and dynamics of the family, as a way of accounting for the persistence of the problem. (1984: 23; italics original)

This demonstrated a wish to control the information which the court received by framing the task solely in their terms, rather than responding even in part to the courts' view of the welfare officer's task (although, as we argued in Chapter 2, some courts undoubtedly condoned this approach, sometimes for reasons of processual expediency, sometimes because of sharing the same view, and sometimes for both these and other reasons). They concluded by pointing out a judicial paradox: 'the law requires that the interests of children be safeguarded, yet to do so it must employ a system which in its application actually works against their interests' (1984: 24).

The deepening divide

Pugsley and Wilkinson (1984) reacted to Shepherd *et al.* by asserting that court welfare officers 'must ultimately retain their statutory responsibilities for child welfare and protection, and be prepared to make recommendations in contested cases'. They went on to criticise their theoretical framework of family therapy, arguing that although it was an elegant model, often satisfying in its application, 'it appears somewhat free-floating and ill related to the base of our work in the Courts' (1984: 89).

In addition, they questioned both the elevation of the assumption of parental competence to a 'fundamental principle', because this ignored both the impact of the emotional upheaval of divorce and the issue of child abuse, and the implied fundamental rejection of the legal system, pointing to the danger of

> seeming to want to deny people recourse to the courts, of undervaluing what can sometimes be achieved in court or at the door of the court. There is a rose-tinted look to the assertion that if conciliation is perceived to have failed, it is because the conciliators have not been skilful enough and because the system allows all concerned too readily to resort to the adversarial process. (1984: 90)

Pugsley and Wilkinson also challenged the accusation of making 'pseudo-professional judgements', arguing that the proposed alternative involved making highly subjective judgements about parents when attempting to describe the dynamics of a family and that:

> there are some cases (and we all know them) where one parent is better able to meet the needs of the children, and it behoves us to say so. This is not a pseudo-professional judgement; it is a judgement based on experience and informed inquiry which can and should be questioned in court. (1984: 91)

They saw *no* fundamental conflict between conciliation and reporting, drawing attention to cases which did not fit into the family therapy model. Whilst affirming their belief in the potentially important contribution of conciliation, they concluded that 'If we were to allow a blanket assumption of parental competence to supersede the long established values of child welfare, and where necessary child protection, we would at last find the baby had vanished with the bathwater' (1984: 92).

Pugsley and Wilkinson therefore identify a false dichotomy created by Shepherd *et al.* between the approaches. Part of the background knowledge about divorce which informs both conciliation and other approaches to court welfare work is that parental competence is often reduced, albeit temporarily, by the emotional and social upheaval of divorce. Thus, in so far as the view held by Shepherd *et al.* of conciliation is partly about *enhancing* parental competence, it also implicitly *questions* this by focusing on parents' failure to achieve separation, assuming that this is the *only* reason for failure to agree – i.e. that disagreement *necessarily* signifies some kind of dysfunction in the family and can have no rational or situational basis. Conversely, investigation can also be about facilitating agreement, reducing conflict and *assuming* a degree of parental competence, whilst also protecting child welfare concerns. This false dichotomy symbolises the battle for control over the definition of conciliation and the court welfare task. Essentially, as Pugsley and Wilkinson implicitly argue, Shepherd *et al.* are seeking to reframe the welfare task, the welfare officer, the parent and the court, asserting simultaneously the superiority of therapeutic over judicial process. It is this set of assumptions which gave rise to much of the criticism of this approach which was subsequently encountered.

The following year, Davis (1985), in a 'combative review of recent conciliation literature', argued that the concept of conciliation had been 'stolen' by court welfare officers to serve their professional biases. According to his analysis, conciliation had two key features, neither of which could be found in either adjudication or welfare investigation – party-control and dispute resolution – and that court welfare officers' preoccupations and concerns with child-saving and therapy were not part of conciliation. In his inimitable style, he stated:

> The pendulum swings from child-saving to therapy – and then back again. . . . They're all for 'conciliation', presumably because it's the flavour of the month, and yet they want to merge this with their habitual orientation, whether it be therapeutic or child-saving. . . . It appears that if POs can't be family therapists or child-savers, they can't function. (1985: 10)

He argued that conciliation was best left to people with no such pretensions.

In an acerbic and at times personal reply, Shepherd and Howard argued that Davis had framed conciliation in a particularly narrow way and that they were more concerned with the processes of practice they had developed than whether this was or was not conciliation as Davis, as an academic, would define it. They argued that as practitioners, they had to address

> the questions of what happens after his form of conciliation has left the conflict unresolved. How *should* welfare officers carry out their enquiries for a Welfare Report? How *do* you seek to promote the welfare of children in such circumstances? What is the best way for such conflicts to be resolved? (1985: 60)

In another response to Davis, Jones identified the problem for welfare officers of reconciling the principle of party control with their position within the legal structure, arguing that

> the powerful impetus to in-court conciliation provided by judicial and legal voices has had some unfortunate consequences. . . . The problem with a restrictive definition of conciliation as mediating towards agreement is that it ignores the context of our work, the emotional complexity of divorce as a family experience. (1986: 21)

He went on to 'take issue with Gwynn Davis that conciliation, directed as it is towards resolving disputes, in not a form of counselling or therapy . . . the welfare of children can[not] be separated from the welfare of parents, or the welfare of the family' (1986: 23).

A year later, in their book, Howard and Shepherd pointed to the remarkable variety of different threads running through the basic concept of conciliation and argued that its variety of ends and objectives helped to explain

> how readily conciliation as a concept can be taken along different paths in seeking to achieve a multitude of seemingly desirable objectives. It is, however, the . . . claims regarding legal savings and children's welfare which are the most contentious and potentially liable to move the concept in different directions. (1987: 9)

What Davis also overlooked in his critique was the extensive involvement of the probation service in independent services, and the child-saving and therapeutic pretensions of such services themselves, many of which operate on the assumptions that parental co-operation and agreement will benefit the children and that children should be able to grow up knowing both parents, reflecting the movement away from the theoretical perspectives offered by Goldstein *et al.* (1973). Thus, Forster commented in relation to the work of conciliation services: 'Wallerstein and Kelly may have done for children of divorced parents what Bowlby . . . did for children in care and in hospital some thirty years ago' (1982: 11). The NFCC's aims and objectives revolve around the resolution of disputes involving children the needs of children, parental relationships with children and agreeing plans for children's welfare (Fisher 1990), all to be achieved through *parental* agreement. Also, as Dingwall commented of Parkinson's (1983) listing of the positive features of conciliation: 'conciliation also confers third-party benefits. The principal recipients are identified as children. . . . Once again, the emphasis is on their psychological development and the mitigation of the stress and emotional trauma of divorce' (1986: 17). And as Parkinson herself observed: 'One of the main arguments used by supporters of conciliation services was that children would benefit from parental agreement and co-operation over custody and access arrangements' (1986: 69).

It is thus unclear whence might come the people without child-saving pretensions to whom conciliation should be left. Unless justified on the grounds that agreement *per se* is 'a good thing', or on grounds of cost and expediency, there must be a *purpose* for reaching agreements through conciliation, many proponents of conciliation seeing this as the reduction of harm and suffering caused to children. Therefore, conciliation became for many a means to that end and, both in principle and in practice, part of the child-saving philosophy.

This further exchange reflects the continuing struggle for 'ownership' of conciliation and the definition thereof; the struggle of practitioners to respond positively to the demands of practice as part of a legal process which was increasingly being widely criticised for failing to address certain issues; and the evolutionary and dialectical nature of the process of change in practice.

The judicial backlash

In responding to Davis's critique, Jones also commented:

> Over the course of our interviews with families, we may assist them to separate effectively and thereby reach a resolution of those differences concerning arrangements for their children. We then convey the terms of that agreement to the court in a succinct statement which is usually acceptable in lieu of the traditional report. (1986: 23)

This view of the acceptability of such reports proved to be a little complacent as a series of hard-hitting and highly critical court judgments made clear. In 1985, Lord Justice Dillon (in *Scott* v. *Scott* [1986] 2 FLR 320, [1986] Fam Law 301), whilst confirming that successful conciliation was desirable, commented on a 'completely unsatisfactory' report produced by a particular court welfare department [which] has misconceived its function. It regards its function as solely to endeavour to produce a conciliation between the parties and the settlement of disputes. . . . In this case, probably through a lack of competent leadership in the department, there has been a serious failure on the part of this welfare department and there has been no sufficient investigation of this case.

He was soon followed by Mr Justice Ewbank (in *Re H* (Conciliation: Welfare Reports) [1986] 1 FLR 476), who commented on a series of reports from one area in particular, which had been drawn to his attention, in which welfare officers had attempted conciliation, observing that

> none of them that I have so far seen have shown any real investigation at all. The reports . . . which I have been shown are useless and unacceptable. If it is the policy of this office to write reports of this nature, then the policy must be changed. This is not a matter which is open for discussion.

A year later, in December 1987, Lord Justice Purchas (in *Butler* v. *Butler*, CA, 11 December 1987, *Lexis*), commenting on another report from the service criticised in the case of *Scott* v. *Scott*, observed:

> there has been no change in policy or direction in this department. I can only say, speaking for myself, that I find that utterly deplorable. I propose . . . that a direction is sent in relation to the issues in this case to the court welfare service that they immediately investigate, as they must in the proper discharge of the court's order, the relationship and existing circumstances in each of the homes, established by the mother on the one hand and the father on the other with their new-found partners, with the children there in the home so that these specialists – because that is what they are – can give the court the benefit of their observation and expertise on the detailed relationships established within the ambience of each home. Without that, it is quite impossible for a responsible report to be made by a court welfare officer. Included in that must be such investigations as they think will be fruitful to determine where truly the inclination of the children involved lie. How that is to be done . . . is a matter for the expert attention of the ladies concerned, but it is a vital part of their duty to investigate that aspect and report upon it to the court.

We have commented upon these cases, the latter at some length, in order to illustrate both the strength and the nature of the criticism. Such swingeing criticism was clearly intended to bring dissident court welfare services to heel, symbolically confirming the enslavement of welfare-within-law (King 1991). However, it was also clear that, in addition to giving simultaneous but implicit support for conciliation, the courts were doing several other things in the process: there was no general criticism of welfare officers and reports, only of particular areas where local practices had diverged too far from what was acceptable to the courts and others involved in the process such as registrars; there was clear criticism of the failure of management to manage; there was a clear statement about the nature and purpose of welfare reports and the role of the welfare officer; and there was a clear distinction drawn between that upon which courts could properly rule – the *content* of investigation and reports – and that which lies within the expertise of the welfare officer – the *process* and *method* of investigation.

The emerging synthesis

A year later, in one of the last articles to be published on the subject in the *Probation Journal*, Hurst argued that changes in practice did not represent a move to conciliation, but a major re-orientation in method, stemming from a recognition that:

> in most cases the only risk to the children was the parental dispute itself . . . and in response to this recognition, we have seen not a move to conciliation but a quite radical change . . . using, but modifying, an approach derived from conciliation itself. Its purpose is not to help parents reach an agreement but to help them to identify and resolve those problems which are preventing agreement. (1986: 95)

Hurst went on to argue (drawing upon the definitions offered by the Booth Committee, 1985, paras 4.59–60) that whilst conciliation was voluntary and privileged, taking place in an unconstrained, neutral atmosphere, none of these conditions applied to court welfare work, and that this new approach had changed the nature and focus of the welfare report, from one which attempted to assess parental competence, to a document concerned to explain and interpret the context in which parental dispute takes place – and its effects upon children. . . . The purpose of reports is not to chose between parents . . . but to ensure that the information given to the court is sufficient for the court to make an informed decision about the children's future. The level of information provided will vary by the types of problem identified and the degree to which parents have been able to resolve these difficulties in the family meetings which have been held. . . . In most cases parents can be helped to manage their conflict. (1986: 95–8)

Thus, the child-saving focus remained clear, although now there was acknowledgement of the need to provide the courts with the information they required. However, it is also clear that this did not represent capitulation to the control of the courts or the enslavement of welfare, but a strategic minimalist accommodation of judicial expectations and a restatement of professional autonomy – welfare officers retain the power to control the definition of what constitutes sufficient information, which will depend upon their expert diagnosis of problem type. There also remains an expectation that family meetings will be therapeutic to the extent that problem resolution and change will be sought.

This position was further refined by Cantwell and Smith, who argued not only for the need to accommodate the courts' expectations of the welfare officer's function but the importance of *incorporating* these into the welfare officer's theoretical and practice 'frame work':

> to replace the word 'family' with the word 'system' and to assume that we work conjointly with a system that includes the family and the Court. . . . It is helpful to consider that during the period of separation, divorce or other conflict, the legal system itself becomes part of the family system. During this period, a judge or magistrate, like other adults in the family, can become too rigid or disengaged in his/her behaviour towards the rest of the family; he/she is also open to all the same risks of being 'sucked in', that are faced by family therapists. . . . The job of the systemic Divorce Court welfare officer is to attempt to retain a 'meta' position to the 'dance' that is occurring within the temporarily enlarged family . . . [which] can prevent over-identification with either the legal system or the family belief system. (1990: 128)

The implications of such a perspective are clear – it is not the welfare officer or the welfare discourse which are enslaved, but the courts and the judiciary which are enslaved by the conflict within the family system *and* by the welfare discourse, which is employed to restructure the legal discourse in order to retain professional autonomy and the power to define practice (James 1992c).

In an important article which addresses this issue, Fineman argued:

> The professional language of social workers and mediators has progressed to become . . . the dominant rhetoric. It now defines the terms of contemporary discussions about custody and effectively minimizes contrary ideologies and concepts . . . [culminating] in a substantial redistribution of decisionmaking authority from judges and lawyers to the helping professions. . . . [This] derives in part from their ability to present the debate over divorce and custody as one involving the treatment of an emotional crisis rather than a solution to a legal problem. (1988: 730–3)

Increasingly, therefore, in order to defend and sustain their professional autonomy and their chosen style of practice without falling foul of the higher courts and the defenders of conciliation, welfare officers have argued that, since welfare enquiries are neither privileged or voluntary, whatever they do in the context of report preparation cannot be conciliation, no matter how much it might resemble conciliation as a *process* or be concerned with conciliation as an *outcome* (see, for example, Jackson 1992). This might reflect significant changes in practice, some of which have indeed occurred. However, it is also a semantic device to 'reframe' and win control of the definition and practice of *welfare* which, interestingly, incorporates and relies upon the *legal* concept of privilege and the *judicial* authority inherent in the recommendations of the Booth Committee. Thus, this new approach to practice has effectively been separated from conciliation and the claim for control over the definition of conciliation has been relinquished. It is also interesting to note that Davis subsequently distanced himself from 'conciliation' because of the confusion surrounding the use of the term, preferring 'to use "mediation" to refer more precisely to the specific form of third-party intervention' (Davis and Roberts 1988: 7) used by the independent conciliation service he studied.

The discourse between the legal and social-work professions has been about more than the ownership of conciliation – it has been about which profession, which procedures and which value system should dominate the process of resolving family disputes. Attempts to bridge these gaps have been made in the context of the development of comprehensive mediation (Parkinson 1989), but this has yet to make a significant impact.

A major problem for the probation service throughout this period has been the lack of any statutory authority to provide conciliation and therefore the inability to resource its development directly. The dispute has not been about whether conciliation could or should be undertaken by court welfare officers – the Booth Committee clearly implied that it could (4.59–63). It has been about how to develop and resource it in the context of an apparent legal consensus that conciliation and investigation should be separate functions. In consequence, conciliation activities have been 'smuggled' (with varying degrees of concealment) into the legitimate and accountable activity of welfare reporting. Although this has clearly constrained welfare officers and shaped some of these developments and the associated discourse, it is also clear that the prevailing attitude of many local judges and judicial administrators, the lack of central Home Office guidance and, in many cases, the absence of effective local management has enabled such developments to occur.

Between 1986 and 1992, the *Probation Journal* published nothing on court welfare work, concentrating instead on developments in the criminal justice system, penal policy, the implications of these for the probation service and, in particular, on issues of race and gender and the struggle to ensure anti-discriminatory practice in probation. In one of the last of such articles to appear, Pugsley (1986) described some of the tensions, produced partly by this debate, generated between three teams in Birmingham and the difficulty they had in sharing a common identity. These involved a polarisation concerning certain key issues: between adherence to a particular theoretical perspective and taking an eclectic approach; between therapy (however defined) and investigation; between encouraging agreement and allowing couples their conflict; between avoiding and making judgements and recommendations; between detachment from and involvement with the court process; between being a 'free professional operator' and a 'servant of the court' and who should determine this; between whether welfare officers provide a service to families or to the courts; between children's views as opposed to parental decision or court decision; and between professional judgements about the best ways of working and the need to experiment with these, and the rights of 'consumers' to have their resistances and anxieties taken into account.

She concludes that these differences are not 'threatening as perhaps they once were; we perceive them more now as inevitable and necessary counter-balances' (1986: 64). This analysis reflects much of the current diversity of practice, the syntheses arrived at after a decade of intense debate and many of the continuing tensions and dilemmas which we found in our research. It therefore represents a good point to move on to Part II which will explore these issues in much more detail.

PART II

☐

The world of practice

> Occupying ground somewhere between parents, courts and conciliators are probation officers who work as divorce court welfare officers. . . . By statute their role is to investigate the circumstances of divorcing families and to report to the courts. By training they are social workers inclined towards helping those whose needs warrant attention. By aspiration many are conciliators working in and out of court.
>
> (Clulow and Vincent 1987: 206–7)

4

Working with families and children

As we pointed out in Chapter 1, complex problems arise when trying to understand the family in modern Britain because of such issues as the growth of single-parenthood, the impact of divorce, the increase in remarriage and the ferment that has occurred as a result of pressures to redefine the terms by which men and women organise their mode of work and child care according to gender divisions (see, for example, Elliott 1986; Finch 1989). The context of work with families is therefore one in which some basic assumptions about the family and family life are increasingly being questioned.

The *raison d'être* for the involvement of court welfare officers in the lives of divorcing families is located in their statutory duty to investigate and report on, at a court's request, any matter relating to the welfare of the children in any given dispute. Within this legal framework, court welfare officers are called upon to address the impact of a variety of welfare issues concerning the best interests of the child which are both complex and diffuse, reflecting some of the broader uncertainties raised by the discourse about the family. Perhaps unsurprisingly, therefore, court welfare officers frequently disagree amongst themselves on a number of interrelated issues including, *inter alia*, the value-base upon which court welfare work rests, the kind of information concerning families and children deemed to be appropriate for the court and the method and process by which that information is obtained.

In our research, these differences of opinion manifested themselves in a variety ways both within and between areas. In this chapter we shall consider the nature of these differences as they were reflected in practice in each of the areas studied, drawing principally upon data collected from eighty-five interviews with court welfare officers (including senior court welfare officers) and statistical data gathered from 681 referrals for welfare reports (for a more detailed account of which, see James and Hay 1992). This data is, in turn, informed by observations of court welfare interviews with parents and their children during various stages of the report-writing process.

It should perhaps be said at the outset that there was a heavy bias towards data from the larger areas and from Area C in particular. However, it has to be recognised that such areas, with large budgets and large establishments, contribute disproportionately to the overall number of reports prepared nationally. In this respect, Area C is one of the largest single producers of court welfare reports in the country, producing some 10 per cent of the annual total in 1990. We do not therefore see this bias as being too problematic. Indeed, we feel that the data-base upon which the research has been able to draw is sufficiently large and representative for us to believe that it represented a fair cross-section of the work of court welfare officers in England and Wales in 1990/1 (James and Hay 1992).

Contact with parents

Court welfare officers gather information in a variety of ways, including office visits with individual parents, home visits and joint or family meetings.

Office contact with individual parents

There are a number of reasons why interviews with parents may be conducted in an office setting. Some court welfare officers whom we interviewed preferred such an arrangement on the grounds that it provides a 'neutral' space within which to conduct the interview. Others claimed that it was important to be 'in control' of the interview and that this can be done most effectively in an office setting:

> I somehow feel that there is something to be said for meeting people on your own territory. You go to homes and sometimes they have several members of the family round. I find it difficult if I have to say that I prefer to discuss this privately, or ask them to turn the television off. (Area C)

Data relating to individual meetings in the office is important for two main reasons: firstly, it provides a useful starting point with which to compare different modes of working; secondly, as we shall demonstrate later in this chapter, a number of disputed issues centre around the use of joint meetings. Information about individual office contact with parents therefore leads us to ask some important questions about how many were the *negative* result of parents not wishing to meet with their former partner and how many were the result of *positive* decisions made by welfare officers that an office interview was appropriate. Therefore, practice in terms of the use of office interviews cannot be separated entirely from some of the deep-seated problems that underpin parental disputes, particularly in those situations when one or both of the parents proclaim that they cannot (or will not) meet with the other parent.

Our data reveal that practice differed between the areas in relation to office interviews with parents as individuals. Welfare officers in Area B, for example, saw at least one of the parents on an individual basis in the office in 67 per cent of cases (30 referrals) compared with 37 per cent of cases (454 referrals) and 30 per cent of cases (34 referrals) in Areas C and D respectively. Marked differences were also to be found in the numbers of interviews involving fathers and those involving mothers. Generally, with the notable exceptions of Areas E and F, fathers had more office contact than did mothers. This is in contrast to cases involving home visits (see below).

There are a number of reasons for these differences. For example, fathers may be allocated more appointments by officers (consciously or unconsciously) as a means of rectifying the imbalance that seems to exist in a legal and social work system which, arguably, so often appears to favour mothers and which may lead to a sense of frustration and anger. The extra involvement with fathers in terms of office contact may also therefore reflect time taken to placate unhappy or frustrated fathers.

In contrast, it is probable that the children are resident with their mother, hence mothers may feel that they have less to lose, and thus need less time to explain their position. It may also be a reflection of the fact that if fathers feel that they are having particular difficulties in seeing the child(ren), then they are more likely to attend a meeting with the court welfare officer at the office to discuss their position.

Such findings suggest a number of inter-related questions which might usefully be considered but to which our data do not provide the answers. Might it be possible and useful to draw up a typology of the kinds of problems that fathers bring to disputes and how these relate to different levels of intervention? To what extent are these differences, as we suspect, a reflection of fathers' marginalisation and consequent sense of frustration? Further questions might also be asked about the nature of the interaction between court welfare officers and fathers. Are the differences in timescales, in part, explicable in terms of them being attempts to placate fathers by seeking to convince them to be more reasonable, sensible, considerate or realistic? If so, to what degree would this support a marginalisation thesis? In raising these questions, we recognise that we touch upon and, indeed, may challenge some of the perspectives on such issues promulgated by writers in the volume edited by Smart and Sevenhuijsen (1989). We will thus return to the thorny issues relating to gender in Chapters 8 and 9.

It is instructive at this point to relate data on office visits to the general aims and objectives of each area. For example, welfare officers in Areas D and E predominantly sought to hold joint/family meetings with a view to seeing how conflicts might best be resolved (see Chapter 5). It is therefore interesting to note that in Area D welfare officers saw the mother alone in the office in 24 per cent of cases (34 referrals) and fathers in 30 per cent of cases. In Area E, welfare officers saw mothers alone in 41 per cent of cases (107 referrals) and fathers in 34 per cent of cases. Welfare officers in Area B, meanwhile, frequently sought both individual and joint and/or family meetings with parents and their child(ren) whereas, as we shall see, welfare officers' practice in Area C revolved around visiting parents and children in their own homes. We should not therefore be too surprised to note that in Area B, 67 per cent of a sample of 30 referrals involved at least one office interview when the parents were seen separately, this proportion being the same for both mothers and fathers, whereas in Area C (in a sample of 454 referrals) the comparative figures were 27 per cent for mothers and 37 per cent for fathers.

Some of these differences may be partly explained by geographical factors which may make it more or less difficult for parents to visit the office. However, given the nature of the areas, this cannot be the only explanation. Since such differences cannot easily be attributed to the varying demands of different cases, they seem much more likely to reflect different attitudes towards and approaches to this aspect of practice, reflecting differing views about the desirability and effectiveness of office visits. Most welfare officers in Areas D and E, for example, stressed that they saw parents on an individual basis only as a last resort. In this respect it is plausible to suggest that many of the occasions when either (or both parents) were seen alone were the result of welfare officers being unable to persuade the parents to meet jointly. It is also interesting to ponder whether welfare officers in Area E were better at encouraging parents to meet jointly than their colleagues in Area D or, indeed, whether they exerted more pressure for them to do so. Alternatively, it may simply be that welfare officers in Area D were more flexible in arranging both joint and individual meetings but not, of course, to the extent of welfare officers' practice in Area B.

Home visits
Whether court welfare officers should visit people in their own homes and, if so, under what circumstances, is a related question which divides officers quite markedly. Again, such divergence of opinion reflected the different approaches and philosophies adopted in setting about the task of preparing a welfare report. Some officers, notably many of those in Areas A and C, argued that visiting each of the parents in their homes was an essential part of the job for a variety of reasons. For example, a number of welfare officers in these two areas argued that home visits offered children and parents an opportunity to have their say in an environment to which they are accustomed. Many welfare officers also thought that the home provided a setting more conducive to the discussion of sensitive issues:

> People often feel more comfortable in their homes than in our office. We tend to take quite a long time when we see them in their homes. We want to see the children and speak to them. They seem happier in their own homes. You can go and talk to them in their bedroom or go and look at their pets. So you do all those sorts of things rather than sit down and ask what they think of this. You can get round to it in a situation where they feel more at ease. (Area F)

For some welfare officers, visiting people in their homes best embodied not only the kind of practice with which they felt comfortable but also their methodological predilections:

> I suppose I'm an intuitive type of personality and I get a lot more from feeling what it's like in the home. I suppose bits of things like family photographs and what the atmosphere in the house is like. How people are with each other in their home helps me a lot, and gives me clues about how to work with a family situation. (Area C)

Perhaps more importantly, welfare officers who regularly visited homes did so out of a belief that there is an imperative need to see for themselves (and in their role as the 'eyes and ears of the court') where the child will be residing and/or visiting. Moreover, contrary to folklore, the rationale for visiting homes was not necessarily restricted to assessing the material conditions of the home:

> I don't see that you can pick up on all the family dynamics when they are out of the family setting. I think it is important, too, to see the home [. . .] when there is going to be a choice of environment. It's actually important to look at the practical and physical aspects of what their home will be in case circumstances change from the *status quo*. So it's not just about family relationships, it's also about environment. (Area A)

Conversely, many welfare officers in Areas D and E and about half of those in Area F, argued that visiting homes was something that should not be done simply as a matter of course. They frequently refuted the argument that it is possible simply to observe a *natural* environment on the grounds that the welfare officer's presence in the home will inevitably affect people's behaviour. Many also argued that home visits were of little value in ascertaining the wishes and feelings of children mainly because, they asserted, the child is likely to be influenced by loyalty to the parent with whom they live.

In contrast, it was maintained, an office setting offers the child greater opportunity to be detached from parental opinions. Visiting someone in their home, they argued, was necessary only when the court requested it, or on child welfare grounds following an accusation from a parent that the home in which the child had to reside, or visit, was unsuitable. Notwithstanding this, welfare officers who adhered to this view frequently found themselves under some pressure to visit homes. In part, this was fuelled by knowledge of the importance that many judges and magistrates place on welfare officers seeing the home. Additionally, they were often acutely aware of the possibility of being cross-examined on their reports, an experience which, perhaps understandably, many found very threatening. Consequently, many felt that they had to cover a number of eventualities and to adopt what might be described as a 'defensive' approach to practice. In the words of this welfare officer:

> [I do a home visit] when the court requests it, or when of the parties raise some issue such as [saying that the home] is a pig sty, they haven't got any electricity or furniture, and that it is rat-infested. Some people have said that we're not interested in material stuff, only emotional stuff. Of course what happens when it gets to court is that material stuff becomes important because barristers make a great deal of the home conditions. [. . .] So you have to consider what the court might want. Whether you consider them necessary or not is another thing. Some people say that interviewing people in their own homes makes them more relaxed. My view is that having a social worker turn up with a briefcase under their arm adds a touch of stigma to the whole proceedings. (Area E)

It would be a mistake, however, to reduce this issue to a debate between two polarised factions. Indeed, many welfare officers committed to settlement-seeking said that they did not have a hard and fast rule about visiting homes:

> I don't often do home visits and I don't feel that I am being pushed into doing them. [But] I find it easier writing my report if I've done home visits because I'm more sure in my own mind of the different things if I've tested them out. (Area E)

A number of welfare officers whose practice was primarily office-based, geared around joint meetings and conflict resolution, argued that it was not always possible, for a number of reasons, to ascertain all the information they required for a welfare report within the time limits available in an office setting. In addition, they might require clarification of a particular issue which did not necessitate another joint meeting. Under such circumstances, they might visit the home. This is not to say, however, that welfare officers who were hesitant about home visits only did them as a matter of expediency, or that they were always seen in negative terms. As this welfare officer argued:

> Sometimes you learn something. I don't want to be dogmatic about this, because sometimes you can learn more. (Area E)

Meanwhile, officers in Area B adopted a midway position between these two modes of thought by combining home visits with individual office visits and joint/family meetings. Officers in this area tended to stress flexibility and the need to adopt particular approaches to suit each individual case and set of circumstances:

> There are cases when I don't visit the home, but in most cases I do. Not to inspect the premises but to see people and children in their own environment. I'm less keen on children in the office than some people are. It depends on the case. [. . .] My work is a combination. I don't work to just one or the other. (Area B)

> If it is a care and control case then [. . .] I see the parents jointly, and then [. . .] I see them once each with the children and then the children on their own. [. . .] At times we have a family interview here [. . .] but I visit the child at his or her home first so that I won't be a stranger to them. (Area B)

Our data relating to such issues suggest some wide variations in practice. Welfare officers in Areas A and C, for instance, routinely visited parents in their homes, whereas in Areas D and E the opposite was true. For example, the mother was visited in her home in 93 per cent and 87 per cent of cases in Areas A and C respectively, compared with 3 per cent and 16 per cent respectively in Areas D and E. When welfare officers in Areas D and E did make home visits, only 2 per cent of cases involved more than one visit. In contrast, it was not unknown for welfare officers in Areas A and C to have visited homes on up to five occasions.

It is perhaps important to note that in those areas where home visits were made regularly (all areas except D and E), mothers were visited at home more than were fathers: in Area A in 93 per cent of cases compared with 72 per cent for fathers; in Area B in 53 per cent of cases compared with 43 per cent for fathers; in Area C in 87 per cent of cases compared with 67 per cent for fathers; and in Area F in 64 per cent of cases compared with 42 per cent for fathers.

This raises some important issues about whether mothers and fathers are treated equitably. There may be a number of reasons why they may not be. Most obviously, mothers are more likely to have the child(ren) residing with them and this might well (and arguably should) mean that they will be visited more often than fathers. It might also be that court welfare officers visit mothers more often in order to try to facilitate improved contact arrangements with fathers. Other reasons might be a reticence (perhaps quite rightly) for women court welfare officers to visit fathers' homes on health and safety grounds, or the existence of evidence or allegations of child abuse (with the consequence that the child will not, under any circumstances, be visiting the homes of perpetrators) thereby arguably obviating the need for a home visit. Explicable though such differences may therefore be, there are nevertheless questions that can, and perhaps should, be posed about whether fathers are marginalised by such differences in practice and about how far they might feel a sense of injustice.

One long-standing and largely unresolved question relating to the investigative aspect of preparing a welfare report is whether it is desirable and/or appropriate to interview people other than the parents who play a key role in a child's life. What we do know is that parents frequently ask court welfare officers to canvass the views of, for example, a relative, child-minder or friend, on the grounds that this person knows the child(ren) well and will provide the welfare officer with evidence in support of their case. In addition, we formed the impression that the judges we interviewed would welcome the broadening out of the investigation in such a way. However, only officers in Areas A, C and F visited other people's homes on a systematic basis, although officers in Area B visited a 'significant other's' home in 17 per cent of cases. Officers in Area D did not visit a 'significant other's' home at all, and officers in Area E only in 2 per cent of the cases in our sample.

Joint meetings

Clearly, the marked shift towards alternative models of dispute resolution within the court welfare domain has highlighted issues associated with the practice of holding joint/family meetings. It is equally clear that court welfare officers hold competing views, not only about the appropriateness of joint/family meetings but also about their importance and role in the process of preparing a court welfare report.

Some welfare officers (albeit a small but vociferous minority, mostly in Area C) held the view that arranging a joint/family meeting with the explicit aim of resolving the conflict contravened the judgment of Mr Justice Ewbank in *Re H* ([1986] 1 FLR 476) that welfare officers should not confuse the tasks inherent in preparing a welfare report (investigating and reporting) with that of conciliation (dispute resolution). Meanwhile, other officers, whilst recognising the centrality of joint/family meetings, frequently found themselves attempting to resolve a number of tensions and dilemmas. For instance, is it *always* appropriate to hold a joint/family meeting? If not, what criteria should be used to determine the answer to this question? In the face of parental reluctance, how far should one go in seeking to persuade parents (usually the mother) that joint meetings are in their and their child(ren)'s best interests? At what stage in the process should a joint/family meeting be arranged? Should the children be involved and, if so, at what stage and in what capacity?

Our data relating to joint and family meetings indicate that answers to such questions will very much depend upon who is asked. Welfare officers in Areas A and C, for example, held a joint or family meeting in 25 per cent of cases (43 referrals) and 26 per cent of cases (455 referrals) respectively. Meanwhile, court welfare officers in Area B, D, E and F held joint meetings in 60 per cent (30 referrals), 73 per cent (34 referrals), 67 per cent (107 referrals) and 66 per cent (12 referrals) respectively. Similarly, in terms of frequency, whereas officers in Areas A, B and C held two or more joint meetings in only 3 per cent or less of referrals, welfare officers in Areas D and F held two or more joint meetings in over 50 per cent of cases. Clearly these marked variations in practice reflect, at least implicitly, some of the recurring divergences of opinion that permeate court welfare work about the following:

- The aims and objectives of the task.
- The form of contact with parents felt to be most appropriate in achieving those aims and objectives.
- The stage in the proceedings when a joint meeting can or should be arranged.
- The number of joint interviews needed to complete the task.

How then might we begin to account for such variations in the use of joint meetings? In beginning to answer this question, it is important to remember the impact that the conciliation debate may have had on welfare officers' attitudes towards holding joint meetings (see Chapter 3). In all of the areas studied, although not necessarily in all of the teams within each area, conciliation (in the sense of conflict resolution and settlement-seeking) was an integral part of practice. However, the way it was organised differed both within and between teams and areas in some important respects, including the stage at which parents were seen and whether conciliation meetings were conducted in or out of court. It is our observation that welfare officers were more inclined in some areas (notably in Area A and to a lesser degree those in Area C) to adopt the traditional model of practice following the failure of conciliation. Thus, whereas welfare officers in these two areas extolled the virtue of conciliation, they were less sure about the merits of bringing the parents together as part of the process of preparing a welfare report. This, in part, helps to explain this welfare officer's view:

> I don't argue that joint meetings and even joint meetings with children are inappropriate. I'm just saying that they are not always appropriate. I understand that in some areas officers would say that home visits and separate interviews are always inappropriate. I disagree with that. [. . .] I would certainly not rule out seeing the parties together. We would also see the parties with the children. But I suppose more often than not, when I look at my practice, I would be seeing them separately with the children. (Area A)

This comment is also important for other reasons. It demonstrates that there may be a gap between what welfare officers *say* they do, or *want* to do, and what they *actually* do in practice (see also James and Dingwall 1989). Additionally, this welfare officer affirms the importance of a particular approach to practice whilst simultaneously conceding that other forms of practice are legitimate. Implicit in this view is that there is not a *correct* or *all-encompassing* way of setting about the court welfare task.

Clearly the above comment needs to be located in the general practice framework that Area A had adopted in response to the distinction made by Mr Justice Ewbank that conciliation and reporting on the welfare of children should be separate and distinct tasks. However, welfare officers in other areas did not feel themselves bound by this strict division and their practice often reflected different concerns. For example, whilst welfare officers in Areas D and E placed a great deal of emphasis on the importance of arranging joint meetings from the outset, many welfare officers in Area C who held joint meetings asserted that, for a range of different reasons, they tended initially to visit parents separately and only then to see if there was scope for a joint or family meeting:

> I've a tendency to go out and see people, partly because I don't trust the system to let them know what they're in for. [. . .] If I'm honest, it seems more comfortable going out and assessing a situation and then

seeking to persuade people to come in together knowing that there is no intrinsic reason why they shouldn't. It seems more comfortable to me. (Area C)

Again, there are a number of possible reasons for this. Court welfare officers, for instance, frequently stressed that arranging individual meetings was very time-consuming. In this regard, joint interviews were seen not only to have strategic operational value but they were also seen to be functional in a number of other ways. For example:

> If they agree to a joint meeting [. . .] it's better than seeing them separately. It is difficult. It can be painful. [. . .] It's often very difficult for the first meeting because they haven't seen each other possibly for months. [. . .] They probably left overnight and a great big bubble burst. They may therefore have a lot of angry things they want to say to one another. But in the end it's valuable for them to be able to do that and to work through it. (Area E)

However, there were also a number of other reasons for preferring joint meetings. One of these originates in the knowledge that ultimately the court is effectively powerless to enforce an order without the co-operation of the parents (an issue which we discuss more fully in Chapters 7 and 8) and joint meetings are seen as more likely to facilitate or to achieve this. Another reason is the belief that the best interests of the child are met best by the parents reaching agreement. Welfare officers stressed repeatedly that parental disputes *in themselves* further exacerbate situations which are already fraught. Resolving the dispute is therefore, by definition, in the best interests of the child. Thus, parental agreement was, for a number of welfare officers, synonymous with meeting the child's best interests:

> The best interests of children are served by getting the parents to agree. It is as simple as that. (Area D)

A major corollary of this is that welfare officers feel that parents should be encouraged to make decisions about their children's future and to play as full a role as possible in their children's lives, a view which is clearly endorsed by the Children Act 1989. This manifests itself in practice by welfare officers conveying the message that if parents do not do this, they will be abdicating their responsibilities in favour of the court. The burden of the welfare officers' message is thus that it is parents' duty to co-operate with one another to fulfil these responsibilities. Viewed in this light, joint meetings are seen to have instrumental, therapeutic and symbolic value:

> I will encourage joint meetings because there is more scope for the family to sort things out jointly than if they don't. I find it much easier and I get a clearer picture much quicker. I also feel I can offer more. (Area E)
>
> My own practice is to just invite the parents [for the first interview]. This symbolises that they are the adults [. . .] that they have marital business which may be pretty private and something the children shouldn't hear about. Secondly, you are testing out how much they are able to make good decisions and take the heat off the children [. . .] to see how far you can push the parents into taking that responsibility. (Area E)

However, many welfare officers also argued that the benefit that can be derived from joint meetings do not end there. Joint meetings, they claimed, also provide the best forum for gaining the kind of factual information that the court needs to make a decision should the couple fail to agree. According to this line of argument, settlement-seeking and information-gathering are therefore neither mutually exclusive nor contradictory tasks. As the following observation illustrates, a welfare officer may have a number of aims and objectives which cannot be fully formulated until various unique features of the case begin to unfold:

> The aim is to get them in and see what it is about. I've got in mind the two rather different aims of conciliation and enquiry. When you get them together you get a feeling of which way you are going to go. Can you get them, with a little help and effort to agree? Or do you see, in fact, that they are not going to do that and there may be things to be concerned about? Therefore it is more of an enquiry mode. (Area E)

Welfare officers in Area F also did not have a consistent policy towards holding joint meetings. Whereas officers in some of the area offices held joint meetings as a matter of course, the reverse was true for probation officers in other offices. It must be borne in mind that, at the time of our fieldwork, staff within Area F were in the process of restructuring the way in which they conducted their court welfare work. In essence, the county wanted to make more explicit its commitment to a conflict-resolution approach. However, a number of disagreements were beginning to emerge in relation to this exercise, some of which concerned the issue of joint meetings. For some officers in Area F, joint meetings were a necessity and consequently they had changed their practice accordingly. For other officers, joint meetings were something that they could commit themselves to in principle but not in practice. It was difficult to pinpoint accurately the reasons for this difficulty, though we suspect that much of it lay in officers' reluctance to change traditional ways of working which, for them, were based on solid foundations.

Co-working

Issues revolving around co-working featured prominently in all of the areas studied. Almost all of those welfare officers in Areas D and E argued that co-working was an indispensable component of court welfare practice. They typically argued that 'two heads are better than one' and that practice was therefore, by implication, more effective; that the co-worker helped to keep the focus of the interview; that the co-worker assisted in the task of ensuring that each of the parties made equal contributions; and that it reduced the stress inherent in the job. Whilst senior managers conceded some of these points to varying degrees, the issue for them was much more about whether co-working could be justified on resource grounds. In this regard it might be noted, in passing, that some welfare officers (most notably those in areas D, E and F) also frequently co-worked when visiting parental homes.

Our data reveal that substantial differences in co-working patterns existed between areas. Welfare officers in Area A did not co-work in any of the cases (11 referrals). In contrast, welfare officers in Area B co-worked in 39 per cent of cases (18 referrals), Area C in 10 per cent of cases (115 referrals), Area D in 72 per cent of cases (25 referrals), Area E in 97 per cent of cases (72 referrals) and Area F in 60 per cent of cases (8 referrals).

The absence of co-working in Area A can perhaps best be explained by the fact that, following the failure of conciliation, welfare officers in this area adopted a traditional investigative orientation to the court welfare task. Meanwhile, court welfare officers in Area C informed us that they would have liked to have co-worked more often. However, a large majority of officers in this area also commented that they perceived the system as being geared up solely to the production of reports. This, in turn, was translated into the need to work on an individual basis primarily (though not exclusively) following the traditional model of practice. Consequently, co-working, which is more closely associated with a conflict-resolution approach, was viewed by welfare officers in Area C as a useful adjunct to good practice rather than a necessity, whereas for officers in Areas D, E and some officers in Area F, the reverse was true. Officers in Area B extolled the virtues of co-working, but did not argue (in contrast to officers in Areas D, E and F) that virtually all interviews involving seeing the parents jointly should be co-worked.

It must be borne in mind that important though these figures are, they do not, in themselves, reflect the broad range of models and disparate methods of co-working that we were able to witness. Some officers preferred their co-worker to engage with parents and children whenever their co-worker felt it to be appropriate. Others wanted their co-worker only to take notes of the interview on the grounds that co-workers frequently tended to digress or truncate fruitful lines of enquiry. Meanwhile, other welfare officers clearly expected their co-worker to ensure that they kept to the main task and that parents were given equal opportunities to speak.

Only welfare officers in Area E worked to a consistent pattern. In large part, this was due to the fact that their practice was informed by a systemic family therapy model, in which context they used a one-way screen behind which sat the co-worker who observed the interview and took notes. In keeping with this 'live supervision' model, the co-worker intervened at salient points during the interview by means of a telephone – for example, whenever she or he wanted a point of clarification, or felt that a particular question should be put to the parents or the child(ren). Additionally, the co-worker might want to suggest that the interviewer should pursue a different line of enquiry, adopt a different tone or allow greater time to one party or the other to express themselves, and so on. This approach, it was argued, enabled the co-worker to avoid being 'sucked in' to the dispute, whilst at the same time allowing the co-worker to observe both the verbal and non-verbal interactions between different members of the family and with the lead worker. Such differences reflect the varying but substantial influence that has been exerted by two schools of thought that permeate the family therapy discourse – those who advocate a psychodynamic approach and those who favour systemic family therapy (for a wider discussion of these approaches, see Preston-Shoot and Agass 1990).

In addition to asking about the value of co-working, we also invited welfare officers to comment on any problems of working in this way. A number of welfare officers, including some who worked in areas committed to a conflict resolution approach to working, drew our attention to two main difficulties. First, officers said that they found identifying times when they and a co-worker could meet a difficult and frustrating task. In practice this often meant delays which they said conflicted with their wish to deal with the matter as quickly as possible for the sake of all concerned. Given this, some officers preferred to set about the task by themselves. Second, a number of welfare officers said that they found co-working difficult because of inter-personal reasons such as not being able to relate to, or work with, some colleagues. Given the emphasis on parents working together to set aside their differences, it is perhaps interesting to note, in passing, that there is something of an irony here.

Family meetings

Ascertaining the wishes and feelings of the child(ren) is a thorny and delicate issue and one that generates frequent disagreement amongst welfare officers both within and between areas. Some welfare officers maintained, for a variety of reasons, that such wishes and feelings can best be determined by seeing the child(ren) in the presence of both of the parents.

> It is beneficial [to have the children present] when we need to look at the communication between the children and their parents. It is significant for older children because there is a bit of mystique built up around divorce, and it is important that children understand the situation and what is going to happen. I feel that it is therapeutic for them to know what is going to happen and what the plans are concerning them. (Area B)

> I like having children in joint meetings. I find them very useful in keeping parents civilised and giving lie to the more extreme statements, particularly things like 'she's terrified of him' when she is sitting on his knee pulling his hair. (Area C)

> Let's get the family together. [. . .] Working with individuals is limited in how productive it can be. My own view is that a problem is part of a family thing and [. . .] you should work with a group to enable people to identify the problem. (Area D)
>
> We normally invite the children in for the first interview unless there are good reasons why we shouldn't. We feel it helps keep the focus of the interview. And to some extent it can prevent the parents from lashing out at each other. (Area F)

Clearly, then, a number of welfare officers see value in seeing the children in the presence of their parents, although once again practice is as discrepant in this respect as it is in others. Court welfare officers in Area A, for example, saw the children with their parents in 30 per cent of cases (9 referrals) and welfare officers in Area B held whole-family meetings in 28 per cent of cases (18 referrals); however, in Area C this happened in 40 per cent of cases (113 referrals), whilst in Area D it occurred in 68 per cent of cases (25 referrals), Area E in 78 per cent of cases (68 referrals) and Area F in all eight referrals.

How can such differences be accounted for? Perhaps the most obvious starting point is that family meetings engender a number of risks and moral dilemmas. One particular difficulty arises over whether it is right to allow children to witness the kind of acrimonious disputes that frequently characterise joint interviews. This welfare officer spoke for many in relation to this issue:

> I don't think that being in a joint interview with two workers and their parents is any more damaging [to the children] than their experience of their parents separating has been already. I would say that one of the damaging things in marital breakdown is a sense of not knowing what is happening and why it is happening; of not knowing what is going to happen next. I think that any arena where the children can be given access to what is going on in order to clarify issues, especially in a safe and controlled environment has got to be in their best interests. (Area D)

Similarly:

> The reason I like the children there is to see how they relate to the parents. It is important, if at all possible, for the child to be part of the arrangements. Even for very young children, I think it is important for

the child to see that these adults are sitting round to do what is best for them. And I think it helps because children often feel guilty about the break-up of their parents' marriage. So it helps if we can let them know that it is not the child's fault. (Area F)

This is not to say that welfare officers lessened the severity or glossed over the difficulties of involving children in family meetings. On the contrary, as this welfare officer pointed out:

> You may put children under pressure. [. . .] We have to be aware that we may be increasing the stress by talking about things that hurt. Sometimes by inviting them to family meetings there may be some discomfort. But we would say not more than they have already seen and that it is necessary that we observe how it is so that in the long-term we can help to create something better. (Area E)

However, many welfare officers found such justifications insufficient and felt that this was at best an unsatisfactory way of gathering information and/or forming an impression of the family and at worst a quite unacceptable position. Some felt that, since it is the responsibility of parents to make appropriate decisions regarding their child(ren), it was neither necessary nor desirable for the children to be present, especially when young children are involved:

> I prefer children not to be present during interviews. [. . .] I think it's dangerous. A lot of stuff that comes out is not appropriate for children to hear. I prefer to bring them in when parents have redefined some of the issues and I like them to hear some of the positive bits. The idea is to bypass them. (Area C)

In addition, there may be adverse unintended consequences:

> I haven't found [seeing the children with both parents] too productive because the children have loyalties generally to the person who has custody, and it does tend to affect their ability to relate to the other parent. (Area C)

Other welfare officers were clearly ambivalent about the merits (or otherwise) of having children present. Some of this reticence lay in the difficulties of ascertaining the child(ren)'s wishes within the framework of a family meeting:

It is difficult for children to say what they want to say at a meeting in our office. They sometimes say it non-verbally and that can be important. [. . .] So whilst it is useful in some respects, I feel a bit uncertain about it. I haven't worked it out yet. [. . .] I don't know. It is probably just me really. (Area F)

Another facet of this dilemma is that welfare officers frequently argued that they found it difficult to predict whether having the child(ren) present would be advantageous or not. Thus:

It can be very damaging to children if they heard all that was going on. But there are times when it can be a good thing to invite children in. (Area C)

Such misgivings can also be combined with others, such as the question of the weight that should be attached to notions of empowerment:

I've got mixed feelings about it. I know that some people take the view that you shouldn't expose children to arguments that their parents have. My own view is that kids have seen it all before anyway. So I don't think that necessarily holds much weight. And sometimes parents behave much more sensibly when they are on someone else's territory. I'll be guided by parents on that. If you actually say the aim is to empower them, then you've got to respect their assessment of whether they think it is a good idea. And if they think 'no' – it's better if the decision comes from us – then you've got to give them the credit to do that for you. (Area C)

We also asked welfare officers for reasons why children did not attend joint meetings. Only officers in Area B indicated that it was the child(ren)'s wish not to attend joint meetings with their parents. In Areas A, B and C it was generally the officers' preference for the child(ren) not to be present when they saw both parents together, whereas the reverse was true for officers in Areas D and E. Within this general framework, the data nevertheless suggested some important differences of opinion between officers in Areas D and E – those in Area D preferred the child not to be present in nearly two-thirds of the cases, compared with officers in Area E, who did not want the child present in only a third of cases.

Clearly these data can tell us little about the reason why officers might not have wanted the child(ren) to be present during some or part of an interview with both of the parents. It might be, for example, that the child(ren) were very young and that officers therefore felt that there could be nothing gained from the child being present. On the other hand, some officers preferred to see the child regardless of age in order to observe individuals' behaviour and attitudes, or family interactions.

Contact with children

Issues relating to the involvement of children have always been to the forefront of court welfare work. Where, when and how should children be contacted and interviewed? How old should children be in order that their views be taken into consideration? These are familiar questions which are brought into sharp focus by the emphasis placed on establishing children's wishes and feelings by the Children Act 1989. However, it is clear that working with children is an area in which welfare officers have mixed views, abilities and levels of confidence:

> Since the Children Act we are focusing more on the children's views and looking at ways of improving our work with children. [. . .] People weren't confident about working with children, basically, and they made excuses why they didn't. Since they have, I've noticed that people are really struggling. But at least they are trying. (Area E)

> I don't feel any great strain in relating to children appropriately according to their age and cognitive development. I can judge how to pitch things. I know some colleagues do have problems in that area. If their experience is limited or non-existent, they can talk completely over the heads of young children. (Area F)

How then were these concerns translated into practice? The data we collected in relation to contact with children reflected some important differences of opinion between officers on a number of different dimensions.

Frequency of contact and setting
Welfare officers in Area A, for example, had contact with the children on two or more occasions in 51 per cent of their sample; Area B in 43 per cent; and Area C in 42 per cent. On the other hand, welfare

officers in Area E saw the children at least twice in only 18 per cent of cases, whereas welfare officers in Area D did not see the children more than once.

There were also divergent practices in relation to where children were seen. Thus, at one extreme, in Area C welfare officers saw the child only in the mother's home in 63 per cent of cases (337 referrals) whilst at the other, this was so in only 5 per cent of cases (20 referrals) in Area D. In contrast, welfare officers in Area B saw the child(ren) only in the father's home in 5 per cent of cases, whilst in Areas C, D and F, the comparative figure was only 1 per cent of cases. Figures for seeing the child(ren) in both homes range from 1 per cent of cases in Area E to 35 per cent of cases in Area A.

Our data concerning office contact with children reveal similar variations. Welfare officers in Area A saw children in the office only in 1 per cent of cases and in Area C in 4 per cent of cases, whereas welfare officers in Areas D and E saw children in the office in 90 per cent and 81 per cent of cases respectively.

Children seen alone

The issue of whether children ought to be seen alone proved to be a delicate issue. Some welfare officers indicated that they feared that children would be interrogated afterwards if they did not interview them in front of their parents. In addition, some court welfare officers said that children frequently told them things which they wished to remain secret, a wish with which welfare officers felt unable to comply. They therefore preferred to interview the children in front of their parents, although consequently this could often only be indirect.

Welfare officers' practice in Areas A and B in relation to this issue was broadly congruent: children were seen alone in 69 per cent of cases in Area A (35 referrals) and in 62 per cent of cases in Area B (21 referrals). Welfare officers in Areas C and F saw the child(ren) alone in 42 per cent of cases (366 referrals) and 45 per cent of cases (11 referrals) respectively. Perhaps surprisingly, welfare officers' practice in Areas D and E, which is geared primarily towards conflict resolution, differed in some important respects. Welfare officers in Area E saw children alone in only 4 per cent of cases compared with the figure of 32 per cent of cases in Area D.

In this chapter we have taken the first step in providing a descriptive overview of some of the key elements in the world of practice occupied by welfare officers. In the process, we have also described briefly some of the aims, objectives, methods and skills that they utilise in the process of preparing court welfare reports. In so doing, we have sought to detail some of the major variations in practice which exist, both within and between areas. In so doing, we have alluded to the sometimes conflicting rationales, values and assumptions which underpin the practices we have discussed, as well as some of the operational and situational factors which also affect practice. In the next chapter we shall elaborate on this description by reflecting upon the ways in which court welfare officers perceive their role as report writers, the factors which structure their perceptions and activities and how these perceptions give shape and meaning to particular practice orientations.

5

Constructing welfare reports

It is evident from Chapter 4 that the values, aims, objectives, and the skills and knowledge upon which welfare officers draw in their work with children and families, are all important elements in constituting their practice and locating this somewhere along the spectrum between conflict-resolution and investigation. However, these constituents and the practices produced by them do not exist in a vacuum, nor are they applied randomly. As Goffman (1974) argues, activities are perceived by participants in terms of the rules or premises of a primary framework, either natural or social. Such frameworks are not merely a matter of perception but correspond in some sense to the way in which that activity is organised. These organisational premises he terms 'the frame of activity'.

In this chapter, we shall look at welfare reports, the most obvious product of welfare officers' endeavours, with a view to discerning some of the 'frames of activity' through which they perceive their functions as report writers and which serve also to structure both their thinking and their practice. Shortage of space prohibits detailed discussion of the statistical material and the content analysis of the welfare report sample and readers are referred elsewhere for this (James and Hay 1992; James et al. 1992). Instead, we shall summarise our main findings and draw particularly on qualitative data to illustrate these issues.

Main research findings concerning welfare reports

There was a general consensus in our study areas that the optimum average output of reports is approximately sixty per annum and that the optimum number of reports current at any one time is approximately twelve. This is of particular interest given the considerable variations found to exist between areas, not only in terms of their geography and organisation of family court welfare work, but in terms of their varying approaches to practice, such as the balance between home visits and office interviews, which reflect fundamentally important issues about how welfare officers frame their activities. For example, many officers argued the importance of home visits, both for reasons of good practice and principle:

> I don't see that you can pick up all the family dynamics when they are out of the family setting, particularly children. I think it's important, too, to see the home environment [. . .] it's actually important to look at the practical and physical aspects of what their home will be, in case circumstances changes from the *status quo*. (Area A)

> I do most of my work through home visits with very little office-based interviews [. . .] even if I get a straight conciliation referral from the court, I do a home visit initially, rather than inviting people straight in, because I'm at pains to make sure that there's an informed consent to what's going on. [. . .] we've had conciliation referrals where the parties haven't even been in court when it's been heard, so they don't know what the hell's been going on. (Area C)

Others, however, tended to place much less importance on home visits and to use them strategically, depending upon the court for which the report is being prepared, the concerns raised by the other parent, their own assessment, or intuitive concerns about the home circumstances:

> Physical things like housing seem to me to be of little relevance because people do the best they can with their circumstances. [. . .] Normally I would do a home visit only if the court order it. [. . .] I still do an awful lot of it on gut feelings and no matter how objective you try to be, there is still the sense of the emotional atmosphere that each parent will provide for the children that is the most important factor for me. But then you try to justify it by information that you receive from interviews. (Area E)

Such comments show not only that officers placed different significance on factors such as home circumstances, but that the reasons for this reflect important differences in the way their approach to report writing was framed, which may then have determined what information was gathered. Thus although there were variations between areas and teams in terms of such issues, it should not be assumed that these were simple or consistent. It was apparent that even within teams, individuals had their own preferred approaches and responded differently to the exigencies of practice.

It was also evident that probation services in general had little knowledge concerning how long it took for requests for reports to reach them from the point at which cases were initiated, or of what happened to the large majority of reports once they had been filed. One officer, reflecting the experience of many welfare officers, commented:

> If I do a report for the county court, unless the judge drops a comment to the liaison officer who then relays it to me, you don't get feedback, unless you commit a gaffe [. . .] you work in a vacuum, and that's what I can't bear. (Area C)

Such a situation not only makes the monitoring of the report preparation process *overall* virtually impossible, it also separates welfare officers' work, both practically and symbolically, from other key elements in the divorce process. This, in turn, allows some officers to sustain the notion of the report as an end in itself, isolated in varying degrees from the legal process.

The research also revealed clear practice variations in the preparation of reports for different courts, with those for magistrates' courts apparently being 'investigated' (e.g. in terms of checks made, number of interviews, range and number of contacts with other agencies) to a lesser extent than those for the county and the High Courts. Such variations may have reflected the fact that reports for magistrates' courts are usually completed in a shorter timespan, or that such reports differ in important respects from those prepared for other courts – for example, they involve a higher proportion of access-only cases; they may involve younger parents, who have not been together long, with younger children; or they may involve more cases concerning young, unmarried mothers where the father had little or no chance of obtaining custody.

However, these differences may also have reflected different perceptions of magistrates' courts, which were generally regarded by welfare officers as being less 'professional' and having less 'expertise' and with whom welfare officers tended to have less personalised working relationships than the higher courts, leading to different practices.

> Magistrates' courts look to us to give them an answer, and to take them out of the realm of making a decision. County courts have a much more professional approach. Judges very clearly see us as being their eyes and ears in certain situations, and feeding back to them. (Area C)

> Sometimes it's quite difficult with magistrates' courts in only having six weeks to do the report, although they've been quite good about adjournments. Quite often, magistrates' courts will give you something quite specific to do and you have something very clear in mind to base your report on. [. . .] I sometimes feel that magistrates are really floundering, especially here because they may not have had much experience in dealing with these cases. (Area F)

Such variations and perceptions, whatever the reasons for them, raise important questions in the wake of the Children Act 1989 and the creation of a more coherent family jurisdiction.

There were also clear variations both between and within areas in terms of both *process* and *outcome* issues. Amongst process issues, we include the making of routine checks, the number and range of contacts with other agencies and the number of interviews with parents and children per report. Of particular importance in the light of the Children Act 1989 are the variations we found between courts and areas in the amount and adequacy of information in reports relating to children's welfare and, in particular, their wishes and feelings. Such information is central to the courts' deliberations concerning the best interests of the child(ren) and such variations raise important questions about practice, not only in terms of the nature and extent of direct contact with children, but also in terms of what information is gleaned from such contacts and how this is presented in reports.

There are also questions, again particularly in the post-Children Act 1989 era with its emphasis on joint parental responsibility and child protection, about the apparently differential treatment of non-custodial parents (usually fathers) and the comparative lack of enquiries relating to new partners which the research revealed. This must be of considerable concern in view of the importance of the latter as potential step-parents and of the growing body of research raising questions about the long-term welfare of children in stepfamilies.

Apart from general child care, they can have a pivotal role in the success or otherwise of access arrangements. The research also revealed substantial variations between courts and areas in terms of various *outcome* issues such as the time taken to produce reports, their length and the making of recommendations. The latter have assumed a particular symbolic significance in the court welfare discourse, areas often having fairly clear conventions or even formal policies concerning the making of recommendations. As one officer, from an area with a strong commitment to working with families and empowering parents argued:

> I don't really make recommendations. I make a recommendation in the sense that I would say something like 'this is an issue to do with the two parties arguing'. I might say 'one is more stuck than the other', or that 'one is doing this because it demonstrates to the other that . . . '. (Area D)

However, an officer from an area with a policy of *not* making recommendations argued:

> It seems to me that I'm not taking on the responsibility that I should be taking on if I don't make a recommendation. [. . .] I have to say my opinion. I don't get upset if the judge doesn't do what I want him to . . . that's his job. (Area F)

In contrast, two officers from Area E, which also has a strong commitment to worker neutrality and a family-orientated approach and has one of the lowest rates of recommendations, both adopted a more pragmatic view:

> We all make recommendations one way or another [. . .] I write my reports in such a way that at the end of the day, there is a message that the court will interpret as a recommendation. (Area E)

> I'm not sure how useful this word 'neutral' has come to be. It seems colourless. [. . .] It's hypocritical to write reports where conclusions are between the lines but we don't write them in terms of recommendations. (Area E)

Important outcome issues are also raised by the proportion of agreements reached, with no agreement being reached in well over half of the cases in our sample. It must, of course, be borne in mind that many of the cases reaching the welfare report stage will be more entrenched, with higher levels of conflict, and a number may be cases which have already 'failed' in conciliation. However, since many of the welfare officers we interviewed regarded this as the most significant performance indicator for evaluating the quality of their practice, such results may seem a little disappointing, particularly since they reflect the officers' own assessment of the level of agreement.

The existence of such variations between areas and teams in a number of aspects of practice raises difficult issues about standards, the nature of practice and its management which we have discussed in more detail elsewhere (James and Hay 1992). However, these variations obscure some important differences between officers within teams, in spite of some areas or teams having clear and apparently coherent practice ideologies, which raises interesting questions about how individual welfare officers frame their activities.

Contextual factors influencing the framing of reports

Our interviews with officers show that there are a number of issues concerning the context in which welfare reports are prepared which have a significant influence, although it is of interest and perhaps concern that one factor in particular which one might have expected to be of significance – welfare officers' statutory responsibilities – did not appear to be of great importance. In reply to the question, 'Do you know what your statutory duties are?', the following responses are typical of many welfare officers we interviewed:

> I don't know what they are. I think they're to provide reports for the court. I think that's it. To report non-accidental injuries if they're found. That must be it. (Area C)

> I'm not sure, but I'd imagine that it's the provision of reports and we are sometimes asked to do conciliations. The statutory responsibilities are just those two things. (Area C)

> I don't know what they are. (Area E)

> No, I don't actually, although I've got a list of them somewhere. (Area F)

Not only do such responses indicate vagueness or even a complete lack of knowledge, they also reveal inaccurate knowledge (e.g. conciliation was not then a statutory responsibility) and suggest a failure to recognise the relevance of these in terms of framing the welfare officer's functions and tasks.

Framework of divorce process
It is apparent, however, that there are a number of dynamic factors, both legal and inter-personal, that are inherent in the process of divorce which were highly influential in framing welfare officers' approaches to report preparation. Thus, processes of legal administration could be an important determinant:

> Because of their administration, the county and High Courts don't fix dates till they've received the welfare report. [. . .] the magistrates' courts are the only ones that fix dates. (Area C)

The statutory framework of divorce, particularly in the wake of the Children Act 1989, was also an important factor which was beginning to be of increasing concern at the time of our fieldwork. As one officer put it:

> Things are changing. With the Children Act, we're focusing more on the children's views and looking at ways of improving our work with children. [. . .] people weren't confident about working with children, basically, and they made excuses why they didn't. Since they have, I've noticed that some people are really struggling with the work, but at least they're trying. (Area E)

Also of importance were parents' reactions to the emotional impact of divorce and their involvement with the legal process, the way in which they presented issues, and the way in which welfare officers responded to these in preparing their reports:

> It depends on their own feelings about their ability to be effective parents. Some people are very hostile . . . they feel they're going into something that there's no way of them getting anything out of . . . they see it as interference. Some people just accept it as part of the process. (Area A)

> They might say the most awful things in affidavits, but usually one person who comes through that door doesn't want a divorce. (Area B)

It is also apparent that other key actors, such as solicitors, could be influential in shaping parents' expectations, sometimes causing problems for welfare officers wishing to frame their activities differently. Although solicitors were increasingly being regarded as sympathetic to what welfare officers were trying to achieve in developing new approaches to their work, this was not universally so and a frequent complaint was that some solicitors created expectations in their clients which welfare officers were unwilling to meet:

> I think a lot depends upon what they're told. . . . I mean very often the solicitor will say 'Somebody will come and talk to you, come and see you at home', and so they see you as somebody who has come to see *them*, to hear their story, so you have to get that bit over before you can do anything else. (Area C)

> Their solicitor had told them that I would see each of them individually, visit their homes, and that I would be writing a report on their homes; that I would be listening to what each of them had to say about the other partner and that I would be deciding who was right. We didn't do that and explained to them why we didn't. (Area D)

Whilst this might reflect attempts by solicitors to influence welfare officers' practice, it also implicitly indicates solicitors' perception of the potential influence of welfare reports:

> Solicitors will tell their clients that the judge is very unlikely to go against a welfare officer's recommendation and that a welfare officer has a lot of power in the court. (Area B)

> Even though I might say that it's the court who make the decision, they might say 'Oh, my solicitor says that you're really the one.' (Area E)

Thus, the distribution and use of power and the ambiguities created by this emerge as a key element in court welfare work which many officers implicitly acknowledged. Some explicitly recognised it as a central issue:

> Power is a big issue . . . my power, the court's power . . . who the hell are we to have all this power? . . . the power the parties have over the kids, the power of the parties against each other, power in the way you decide to send out your first appointment letter, power of parties over court

welfare officers, the power to make enquiries without letting anyone know you're doing them. (Area C)

In particular, what was often unacknowledged but was identified by this officer is the power of parents in this situation. In some important senses, parents *do* relinquish power when they enter the legal system, at least in terms of the formal aspects of the process and in so far as their participation in the system is only transitory. However, loss of power is not a *necessary* feature of the process, nor is it absolute or fixed – it varies between individuals and couples. As the following comments reveal, welfare officers are sometimes acutely aware that in the final analysis, power rests ultimately with parents rather than welfare officers or judges, who can be virtually powerless when confronted with determined parents:

> It was quite clear that the children loved their father and they wanted to see him. There was a sad ending because it didn't happen . . . it was one of those rare cases where the mother's will prevailed . . . she didn't assist the access and he didn't pursue it. (Area B)

> If the emotional issues that are separating the parents are getting in the way and if they aren't addressed, no matter what order the court makes, the parents will sabotage it. (Area C)

> Black people may feel that you are making judgements about whether their parents were married. [. . .] Asian people may fear that you are checking whether they are illegal immigrants or not. [. . .] They will give you the information they want you to know. (Area E)

Some officers also sought to play down any loss of power, emphasising the power that parents actually retained. This partly reflects the widely accepted principle of parental empowerment and the encouragement of parents to determine their children's welfare. Paradoxically, however, this also serves to empower welfare officers, the large majority of whom believe that facilitating parental agreement is the best way of providing for the child's welfare. By shifting parents' focus away from the external legal process of adjudication and the authority of the courts towards conflict resolution and the intra- and inter-personal processes of divorce, the focus is shifted towards divorce as a social rather than a legal problem and therefore towards the authority of the welfare officer. As one officer commented:

> I'm very careful to tell people that the courts are a rather toothless creature and although they can do certain things, it really is very dependent upon the parents doing things. [. . .] I try to remove it emotionally from the context of the court. (Area C)

Framework of the judicial process

In addition to those factors which are intrinsic to the divorce process, there are other important factors in framing welfare officers' activities which are a product of the judicial process itself and the welfare officer's place within this, which can *dis*empower parents. The courts themselves, in the way that they function as social and legal entities, and individual judges, can exercise a powerful influence:

> The judge has been known to say that 'I've read the report, I've read the affidavits and I think, Mr so and so, that you ought to go out of this court and get an agreement because I am minded to allow access to happen', or whatever. That's unfair really because it puts us in a very powerful position. I don't say that lightly or smugly, because it makes you aware that you've got to be pretty sound with your enquiries and to get it right. (Area B)

> The whole atmosphere is very pressured. People are told by their own solicitors that the main judge here is very pugnacious in the way he puts things over . . . you know, people must do this, that and the other . . . and being quite insistent without knowing the facts of the case at all. (Area B)

Within this context, the relationships which welfare officers develop with the courts, particularly locally, were an important factor in terms of their perceptions and responses. These provide an additional source of status and power for a number of officers, over and above that which inheres in the role, which contrasts with the relative lack of status experienced by many in criminal courts. Some derived considerable satisfaction from this, but also felt somewhat ambivalent:

> I suppose it can get a bit cosy but we've got a good relationship with the judiciary [. . .] officers could get a tough time in other areas but not in their own courts. (Area B)

> We can go into the civil courts with a recommendation based on what we consider to be the best interests of the child and it's like Moses

coming down from the mountain with tablets of stone. I feel that we have less basis for making some of these far more important recommendations than we do when we go into criminal courts. (Area C)

For others, however, instrumental advantages may also have accrued from this status by allowing them to frame their practice according to their own preferences. However, such advantages may not extend beyond the local courts, introducing an element of uncertainty into the preparation of reports for 'outside' courts:

> Our courts don't want reams of stuff. They trust us and if we say things are satisfactory, then unless there is some evidence to the contrary, I don't think they will say 'but you haven't told us about this, that or the other' [. . .] we may have less status in outside courts and that's an uneasy feeling sometimes. It's more theoretical stuff from London about what should be in reports, particularly from High Court judges, who perhaps have less close relationships with welfare officers. It's difficult, particularly because the pattern of civil work around the country is so diffuse and variable. (Area E)

It is also clear that welfare reports were often decisive in achieving settlements, even if parents could not be helped to agree in the course of welfare enquiries. This was also important for many officers in determining how they approached the construction of their reports:

> What actually happens of course is that very few matters actually go to trial because when they read the report at the solicitor's office [. . .] there is usually some kind of consent order. Sometimes it happens at the court portal [. . .] the detail in the conclusion is quite specific and I suspect that the barristers and solicitors say that 'This is what the welfare officer is saying and they've got no axe to grind, so look . . . '. (Area B)

> His solicitor rang me after reading my report to say that he'd capitulated. I suppose barristers go through the report and see if they've got a strong case or not. I suppose he could see the evidence was weighted against him. (Area B)

In addition, many welfare officers consciously made strategic use of this power and the devolved authority of the court as a means of exerting pressure on parents to accept the responsibility for deciding their children's future. Thus, one officer commented:

> What I say to parents right at the beginning is that the court has asked for a report. At the end of the day, if you fail to agree, or even if you agree, the court expects information about certain issues, about the children and so on. (Area F)

However, the same officer subsequently expressed a view suggesting a somewhat different agenda for making such statements to parents:

> Providing the court with information about the children merely clouds the issue and takes responsibility away from the parents.

Nevertheless, the fact of reports going before the court could exert a powerful influence on how they were framed. The judicial context which gives welfare officers so much power and status also presents them with very real imponderables, constraints and obstacles, which many welfare officers found threatening but to which they had to respond:

> If it's going before our local judge [. . .] she's going to understand what you're talking about, but it might go before someone else who doesn't have that understanding at all. If the judge is left unsatisfied or unhappy with the report, what happens? He might make a bad decision . . . he might adjourn it for more information . . . how does that help the children? (Area A)

> I'm much more conscious of the court being in the background than ever I was in criminal work . . . I suppose there's an element of self protection in that [. . .] all the time I'm thinking 'Oh, will the court say you should have done this, you should have done that.' . . . I'm slightly paranoid about it really. (Area C)

It is clear therefore that there was some sensitivity to the constraints of working in a court setting and that one of the strategies which welfare officers used in order to cope with some of the ambiguities which they face was 'defensive' report-writing. By this means, they anticipated possible criticisms and 'fireproofed' themselves against hostile cross-examination or embarrassing gaps in their knowledge which might be revealed in court.

However, welfare officers were not always successful in working as they deemed appropriate or achieving their preferred objectives:

> I've come across the practical difficulty of trying to persuade courts that it's actually going to be worse for the child to be put in this on-going conflict situation and where it might be better for the child not to see the other parent. But they won't grasp that because they see that as one partner winning and they absolutely won't have that because you can't flout the order of the court. (Area A)

> I know that there was criticism by courts of the kinds of reports that used to be submitted, because they didn't provide the kind of information the courts could use, so the information that is provided now in reports is much more court-orientated [. . .] one of the problems about our practice in the past was that we were perhaps too far removed from the court and the court smacked our hands, and we came back into order. (Area C)

Nevertheless, like parents, welfare officers are skilled at finding ways around judicial resistance and have the advantage of operating both within and without the court setting, giving them considerable scope for informal manœuvring. For example, one officer recalled a case in which:

> There were some quite articulate parents who wanted to agree joint care and control with the child living a month with one parent and a month with the other. The Recorder baulked at this and asked for a welfare report. [. . .] I might have been rather sneaky and said to them agree to joint custody and what you do between you after you leave the court is up to you. (Area B)

Framework of the organisational context

A further framework which serves to varying degrees to shape welfare officers' perceptions, expectations and practices is provided by the organisational context in which they work, including area policies or practices shaped by team ideologies. Such ideologies are frequently well formulated and clearly articulated, although previous research (James and Dingwall 1989) has shown they are not necessarily reflected in practice. However, they can result in shared approaches to the framing of welfare reports and the methods used. For example, many teams employed a standardised format for letters to parents which was important in laying the framework for subsequent encounters:

the way we word the letters to invite them to attend, it's a bit like they really have to have a good reason not to attend. (Area A)

What we do is send out a long letter explaining why we like people to come together . . . that we recognise that it's difficult for parents to meet together because of the conflicts that are around . . . point out that it's not that they get a bad mark if they don't come, but that we do think it is a worthwhile thing to pursue if at all possible . . . a good percentage of people respond to that and just come. (Area C)

In addition, teams were often seen to have a more general function in terms of providing a forum for the discussion of key issues and maintaining the cohesiveness of team practice:

The team is very forceful in looking after children's rights in making sure that they don't lose contact with one of their parents [. . .] we have a child-focused philosophy. (Area B)

At the moment, we have one member asking if co-working works, or can we go on co-working? But the rest of us are very firmly of the view that co-working is of the essence. (Area E)

However, it is also clear that some officers felt more 'loosely coupled' to their teams than others and would depart from apparently consensual approaches for a variety of reasons, framing their reports in ways which they found personally acceptable. So, for example, two officers in Area A had totally different views concerning home visits:

Some people investigate more. Some people pop in late at night and early in the morning. I disagree with that, because I don't see it as part of my job.

I pop in and do unannounced visits. [. . .] I believe that when I have to do a report, then an element of that is checking, being nosey. It's being a pain in the arse, and that's what's expected of me. [. . .] X doesn't do unannounced visits, where I do because I think I've got a responsibility to.

It is evident therefore that a number of officers preferred to preserve their autonomy and resisted pressures for conformity to a team approach:

> I know that, for instance, we have people in our midst who are more of a feminist view than I am and would be very aware of sex and gender and things. . . . I'm the wrong generation, you see . . . and I'm also confident enough in myself never to have to worry about it . . . nobody is going to stop me doing what I want to do. (Area C)

> I guess I'm different from other members of the team in some respects, as we all are. I go along with the general idea of the systemic family therapy approach but I haven't got the true faith about it. [. . .] my own personal style is that I go a lot on what I sense or feel. (Area E)

In addition, however, not infrequently there was disagreement between team members about whether a team approach existed in reality and, if so, what it was:

> We don't share a lot of things, actually. I don't know whether that's because we're so disparate in the sense that we're always out. There's not a lot of sharing. I think that's partly what having training days is about. [. . .] I have to be honest with you and say I have no clear idea what the philosophy of our area is [. . .] I think management is trying to change that. (Area F)

Alternatively:

> I think that we have a remarkably consistent viewpoint. [. . .] It seems fairly cohesive to me. There's not much general disagreement about the guidelines and how we want to operate. (Area F)

Such apparent disparities reflect partly the fact that many officers who seldom or only occasionally co-worked had little knowledge of how colleagues practised, and that, even in teams where co-working was the norm, there was often little knowledge of other teams' practice.

Although many officers continued to seek ways of reconciling their personal practice preferences with a variety of conflicting demands and imperatives, pressures for change could also reduce team cohesion:

> I don't know that there is anyone in the team who is desperate to co-work. The other thing is pressure of work. . . . I know there are arguments that by co-working you can actually get through the work quicker and in a more focused way, but in reality, if you're also doing

individual work, trying to tie in everything together can be quite difficult. (Area A)

We had a period where we used to see everybody together initially, but that was sat on. Sometimes we used to see them together all through... visit homes, write the report together, everything. [...] We haven't got the time now and the area is so vast, it's not possible. (Area C)

Management pressures were also evident in framing practice, although more so in some areas than others. In Area C, for example, in response to criticism from the courts, managers developed clear policies which produced mixed reactions amongst welfare officers:

> I'm actually quite happy with managers who say what their expectations are, because at least I know what is wanted of me. If I choose to shortcut that, that is my decision. Part of the problem is that management won't actually tell us what enquiries *not* to do, so the pressure is to do everything as quickly as possible. (Area C)

> I'm left with the feeling that management don't care how we work as long as they don't get complaints from the courts. (Area C)

> I'm sure that people would prefer to work in a different way, but we work in the way we've been told and within that we all aim to interview people together and possibly to get family meetings. [...] we've been told that to do a welfare report, we must do home visits... so okay, I do a home visit. (Area C)

However, such views were not restricted to this area alone – officers from other areas expressed similar concerns:

> One example which I find beyond belief is that we must check criminal records on the parties and the people they're living with if the custody is in dispute. For eight years we haven't been expected to do it... now, for political reasons, we're expected to do it. (Area D)

> We haven't made automatic checks with other agencies to date, but I think we're going to have to pretty soon. [...] I suppose it's a bit much really, but everybody is so anxious about child abuse these days, I think they're going to ask us to do it now. (Area F)

It is clear therefore that individuals within teams and areas were engaged in a process of balancing conflicting pressures and demands against their personal preferences or practice orientations and it is to identifying some of the determinants of these that we now turn our attention.

Paradigms of practice

In addition to the contextual frameworks which we have described, it is also clear that the use of the main elements of practice which shape the construction of welfare reports such as those described at the beginning of this chapter – the use of home visits and office interviews, the nature and extent of contacts with other agencies and with children, the making of recommendations – are also influenced by how officers frame their role as professional social workers. This determines some fundamentally important aspects of how they interpret and construct the task of the professional social worker in this particular setting.

There are as many approaches to court welfare work as there are court welfare officers. However, it is possible to discern broad orientations towards practice, defined substantially by different primary reference points. These reflect different perceptions about the sources and use of power and can be represented for analytical purposes as opposing paradigms on a continuum of practice. In describing these, we are seeking not to caricature but to delineate the complex groupings of attitudes and values which combine to form broadly comparable rationales which also frame the construction of welfare reports. Each of the paradigms described existed to varying degrees amongst welfare officers in each of our study areas.

The free-floating professional

The practice of the free-floating professional is determined primarily by professional judgements, derived from a theoretical orientation, about the most effective ways of working in order to achieve the objectives identified by the practitioner as relevant. The enquiries made, the methods used and the construction of the final report are determined in isolation from external points of reference such as those provided by the legal system, practice policies or families' perceptions of their needs. This orientation often reflects a justification of the means used in practice by the end of ensuring that the best interests of the child are being protected.

Although, in principle, this analysis could apply to any theoretical orientation, in terms of current court welfare practice, the most coherent theoretical orientation was provided by reference to the concept of families as dynamic social systems and to family therapy. Such an orientation tends to produce reports: based on more limited enquiries and fewer meetings; primarily using office interviews with few, if any, home visits; involving little, if any, contact with children on their own; and containing fewer recommendations. Thus, for example, these officers reflect the views of those whose primary point of reference was this particular professional orientation rather than their place in the legal system:

> I've evolved in the direction of therapy, some kind of therapeutic intervention as being the primary objective, so I've always identified the client, not the courts, as the client. [. . .] I wouldn't be working at this job if I couldn't work in a way that I wanted to and, in fact, I've come close to packing it in as there have been more restrictions. (Area C)

> The document which I produce is not part of the court process. [. . .] I've never done a home visit except once, when a judge ordered me to. [. . .] We are professionals in our own right. [. . .] I think that I am a professional person employed by the court and if I'm not professional enough to do it, then I shouldn't be doing it. [. . .] I'll carry on doing it my own way because I can survive and I believe sufficiently in my principles. (Area D)

Also typical of this orientation are officers who freely acknowledge their use of power in engaging people with their preferred approach to practice:

> We do, I think, put people under a lot of pressure . . . quite ruthlessly at times. It's a question of when you do that and why you do that down to being honourable. When you put people under pressure because it's more convenient, that's not on. But to place people under pressure to resolve their differences because we believe that to be in the best interests of the child is quite acceptable. (Area C)

> We're not about creating relaxation for people . . . these are strenuous occasions for everybody. [. . .] I think we have to work in the way we

think is most efficient and effective because we are the ones who define our task. (Area E)

> Normally, most people accept it . . . they're in a pretty powerless position, or they feel pretty powerless when they come here, so not many argue. [. . .] If I came here, I would be an awkward bastard. I wouldn't answer half the questions. I would want to see the person behind the screen. (Area E)

What is significant about this orientation is that, because the primary objective is to initiate or achieve some kind of change in the family system, the legal context of court welfare work, which is often otherwise an important element in framing practice, is marginalised. Moreover these officers are clearly aware of and justify the pressure which is put upon parents, acknowledging and even using their powerlessness in order to pursue the professionally defined agenda.

The officer of the court

The orientation of the officer of the court is determined primarily by reference to the requirements and expectations of the courts. The enquiries made, the methods used, and the construction of the final report are substantially determined by external points of reference such as those provided by the legal system, the role being symbolised by the expression, used by many judges and welfare officers, 'acting as the eyes and ears of the court'. Reports constructed from this practice orientation therefore tend to reflect officers' perceptions of the courts' needs and to be based on more extensive enquiries; a greater use of home visits; more effort to see children alone and in the homes of both parents; and display a greater readiness to make recommendations.

Many such officers (representing the majority of those whom we interviewed) also have their preferred theoretical orientations and frequently sought the opportunity, as we showed in Chapter 4, to help parents to find common ground and reach agreements. However, they were also quite clear about their primary reference point:

> I see myself as an officer of the court. I see myself as having a responsibility to the court to give an unbiased, unaligned view of the situation and I see myself as an expert witness in court. (Area A)

> The primary task is investigation because that's what the court expects me to do and orders me to do. To investigate and provide a report . . . they sometimes word it almost like that and that's what I'm about. If, in

the process of investigating [...] they agreed, I would not do all of the investigating bit, and maybe not as thoroughly as I would otherwise do them, but I would certainly see the child. [...] I would not simply take their word for it and simply send in an agreement, and indeed our judges here would simply not accept that. They've made it clear that they want a welfare report. (Area C)

Although many officers would not place quite so much weight on the court's needs, this orientation is, in key respects, not compatible with that of the free-floating professional because large areas of professional judgement (although not all) are suspended or made subservient to the needs of the court, which provide the principal frame of reference. Interestingly, of course, depending upon how the courts frame their own task in matrimonial proceedings, this orientation can result in varying approaches to practice, since in the perception of many welfare officers, courts are often as interested in having cases settled as they are in having them investigated:

> I think the courts are very pragmatic beasts really and the more agreements, the quicker they get through their lists. . . . I see that all the time. (Area C)

> There's this debate that goes on in ACOP and with High Court judges that seems so removed from the magistrates' and the county court. [...] the county court, for instance, don't seem concerned that one person conciliates and goes on to prepare a report. [...] the magistrates' courts hope that people will agree and give them every opportunity. (Area E)

However, in practice, these paradigms are often modified by the idea that an essential ingredient of professional practice is the provision of a service and the need to be responsive to the 'client', however defined. Many officers referred to the right of parents to have their needs and anxieties taken into account and the need to balance settlement-seeking with allowing couples their conflict. They were unhappy about bringing undue pressure to bear on parents, stressing the desirability of using a range of methods in responding to the needs presented. Many found the imposition of different practices in different areas, reflecting adherence to particular approaches to practice (such as the use of one-way screens as part of a systemic family-orientated approach to practice), a cause for concern.

The parties have an absolute right to have an adjudication on the dispute between them if they so wish. (Area A)

I'm always suspicious of social-work dogma. I never like it any more than any other dogma. I tend to believe that you learn various theoretical concepts as a social worker and you learn various social work techniques over the years. You then use those to fit the client's individual situation, but you don't start with a concept and fit the client in. That's what went wrong with Team X. [. . .] I don't believe you can say to people 'This is the way we work and if you don't like it, sod off.' [. . .] I don't like the thought of one area saying [. . .] everyone will be subjected to family therapy, or everyone will be investigated. It seems wrong that wherever you end up living, you'll have a different experience. (Area C)

Just because a family is divorcing doesn't necessarily mean it needs therapy. [. . .] people are already in a very vulnerable situation when they're getting divorced, so to expect them to come in and submit themselves under pressure is wrong. I don't think it is fair either on the adults or the children. To start sitting watching them behind a screen is atrocious. (Area C)

Such modifications allow the accommodation of competing paradigms. By acknowledging the sometimes uncomfortable reality that a service is being provided, both to courts and to families, and accepting the tensions and ambiguities which can result from this, both can be encompassed in the framing of the court welfare task.

In certain key respects, such issues revolve around the question of who welfare officers regard as their primary client. The large majority recognised that courts, families and children all have an element of client status. As officers from two somewhat different areas expressed it:

I have a dual function, to the child and the court . . . the court is where the work comes from . . . the court give me, or the agency, the authority to do this piece of work. The focus then is on what is the child's interest and welfare. (Area B)

Given that the court's primary client is the family, we and the court have families and children as our primary client [. . .] we and they are partners. (Area E)

Concluding comment

It is apparent that the way in which welfare officers frame their activities as report writers is much more complex than implied by the comparatively simple request from the court to 'investigate and report' on matters concerning the welfare of a child. Not only is there a range of complex and overlapping contextual factors relating to the process of divorce, the judicial framework and the organisational context of court welfare work, there are also competing paradigms of court welfare work rooted in differing professional orientations which have a profound influence over the way in which welfare reports are constructed.

This complex picture is compounded by the fact that there is still no consensus amongst either the social work or the legal profession about how best to discharge the shared responsibility for safeguarding the best interests of the child. Thus, there are no clear points of reference for the framing of welfare reports in terms of this centrally important objective. In a mirror image of the divorce process, although there is sometimes agreement and co-operation, sometimes there is strife and conflict about who is the most competent to decide such difficult issues.

What is apparent throughout this is that both welfare officers and parents have and use considerable amounts of power as fully self-conscious actors in a system which, perhaps more than any other, represents the power of the state and in which, at first sight, they appear as little more than minor functionaries and transient participants. Between them, however, they employ a range of strategies in negotiating some of the social realities of divorce and constructing the images of children and their welfare which are presented for the consumption of the courts in the discharge of their often largely symbolic duty in relation to divorcing families.

In the next chapter, we look at the ways in which other key actors frame the court welfare task, drawing particularly on the views of judges and senior probation service managers, and we consider in a little more detail the organisational context of court welfare practice.

6

Organisational issues

There are a number of widespread and complex problems that currently concern the organisation and management of family court welfare work. Many of these problems revolve around a set of broad social policy issues relating to the variety of 'structures', institutions and contexts within which court welfare officers have to operate and which permeate all aspects of their work. For example, the probation service, like other public-sector organisations, has been profoundly affected by the changes in social and economic policy resulting from the ideological commitments of four successive Conservative governments.

One result of this is that concern about some of the hallmarks by which we assess commercial organisations – most notably, economy, efficiency and effectiveness – are now as much in evidence within the probation service as they are within the business realm. Other preoccupations relate to the inherent tensions involved in determining and maintaining polices both nationally and locally. At one level, probation managers are having to work more than ever within the continually shifting frameworks of a national and bureaucratic probation administration with policies, priorities and resources being increasingly determined by the centre and filtered through area management. At another, they are having to contend with the special features, differential histories and exigencies of service delivery inherent in particular areas.

Behind these general concerns lie a range of more specific organisational issues, equally worthy of attention, which emerge primarily from the minutiae of everyday work. They need not be listed here in any detail, but they encompass *inter alia*: the movement of staff in and out of court welfare work; the amount of reports it is reasonable to expect an officer to prepare in any given period; attendance at case conferences; the amount of time that officers should devote to interviews, court duties and so on.

In this chapter we map out some of the forms that these organisational issues and dilemmas take, looking specifically at the way practice is formulated in the minds of middle and senior probation management and the judiciary. In so doing, we shall describe the ways managers and judges attempt to define the parameters within which court welfare officers have to work. These views, in turn, can be compared with the perspectives of welfare officers that we have described and commented upon in earlier chapters.

Summary of data

Our data in relation to organisational issues were gained primarily from asking welfare officers in each of the areas studied to complete a daily diary of their key activities for a calendar month (see James and Hay 1992: 95–107). These diaries reflected a number of variations in practice. There were wide discrepancies, for example, in the total number of hours that officers worked during the month in question. Excluding the area whose officers worked generically, this ranged from an average of 106 hours per welfare officer per month to 172 hours per officer per month. As one might expect for reasons of both geography and practice orientation, welfare officers in Areas A, B and C devoted a greater percentage of their time in activities related to home visits than did their counterparts in Areas D, E and F. Consequently, officers in Areas A, B and C inevitably spent more time travelling than those in Areas D, E and F.

Other differences included the amount of time that was devoted to pre-interview planning. For welfare officers in Areas D, E and F, who invariably worked in pairs, pre-interview planning in consultation with one's co-worker was considered to be an essential part of the process of preparing a welfare report. For other welfare officers, especially those who preferred to work on their own mainly by visiting parents and children in their homes, pre-interviewing planning may have consisted of reading affidavits, previous reports or the notes that they made of previous interviews. Thus, pre-interview planning may have meant different things to different welfare officers, particularly in relation to the degree of importance it may have been accorded.

Marked differences could also be discerned in the amount of time that was allocated to court duty/attendance both within and between areas. The percentage of total time that welfare officers spent on court duties in Area C, for example, ranged from 6 per cent to 19 per cent. Figures for other areas ranged from 9 per cent for one of the teams in Area E, to 28 per cent for Area D, the latter figure being largely explained by the fact that Area D was the only area to utilise a full-time court co-ordinator. Teams both within and between areas also differed widely in the amount of time devoted to team meetings, the range here being from 1 per cent of total monthly time in Area A to 13 per cent in one of the teams in Area E.

Thus these data also implicitly reflect some major divergencies of opinion about the nature of court welfare, the kind of roles that welfare officers adopt, and the kind of service they would like to provide. How these divergences are viewed by the judiciary and managed within the probation service will be discussed in more detail below. Before doing so, however, it is important to look briefly at perceptions of where court welfare work should be located, since these can be important determinants of organisational responses to key issues.

Which agency?

Whether court welfare work ought to remain in the probation service provides a useful starting point from which to examine some more general organisational concerns. Whereas the majority of main grade staff and senior probation officers felt that the probation service is an inappropriate home for a court welfare service, the reverse was frequently true for members of senior management. Meanwhile, as the following range of observations from circuit judges illustrates, judicial views ranged from complete indifference to strongly held beliefs that court welfare work should not be part of the probation service:

> I've never thought about it. It seems to me that this would concern the probation service more than us. I don't have a view.

I've never thought about it before. The beauty of the probation service is that it's so independent in children's matters. They're basically more qualified than social services' workers, aren't they? I don't know.

That is a matter for them. [. . .] They're very keen on it and have a sense of achievement, and they welcome the release from the criminal side. They regard themselves as being able to help and see the visible results of their work far more readily than they did working with criminals. In a way they find it more satisfying.

The two services are kept very separate, but I've never really thought of it, frankly. [. . .] As far as I am concerned a court welfare officer is a probation officer. I've never thought of segregating probation officers from the role of the court welfare officer.

However, in expressing a view that accords with that held by many court welfare officers, this judge argued:

I think it does not fit at all. I think it should be a separate service. [. . .] It requires a different approach and different skills. [. . .] Obviously the same sort of person can no doubt have a stab at both jobs, but I don't think there is any real link at all other than historically the probation service provided the pool from which court welfare officers would come. If you're starting a service now, you wouldn't use probation officers.

The divergence of opinion amongst judges on this issue is paralleled, in many important respects, in the minds of many of the services' senior managers interviewed, although they frequently argued their case according to different criteria and concerns. One Assistant Chief Probation Officer (ACPO), for example, argued that he would like to see court welfare work remain in the probation service so long as the training of probation officers remained firmly within a social-work context. However, in view of the changing role of the probation service within the criminal justice system and the implications of this for training, he foresaw a time when this might no longer be tenable. Another senior manager argued that one of the important features of probation practice was its work with offenders' families. For a number of reasons he felt that the service's commitment to such work was gradually being eroded. Thus for him, one corollary of losing court welfare work would be the further marginalisation of family work:

If we lost lost civil work altogether, then we're in danger of pushing family work and the skills associated with family work more and more down the line. So I take the view that I wouldn't like to see it separated out. (Deputy Chief Probation Officer (DCPO))

Others argued on strategic and instrumental grounds that court welfare work ought to remain within the service:

It's an appropriate task because it's court-based. I have the strongest possible interest in maintaining links with courts and if that got split between ourselves and another service, I don't think it would be in our interests. That's a very selfish view, but we gain from our links with the judiciary and we do that task fairly well. Chief Probation Officer (CPO)

Yet what was particularly striking was the degree to which some managers tended to argue in favour of retaining court welfare work within the probation service for pragmatic reasons:

Way back, the only really rational justification was to do with the court base, and to some extent the absence of any other agency. Times have moved on and a question mark must be put by that. But I'm not sure that it puts a big enough question mark by it. Is there really a pressure for social services to take on civil work? Is there really the mixture of court experience that probation officers have in particular? I'm not sure [that the case for transferring court welfare work] is all that compelling. [. . .] The views expressed to me about probation officers by judges and registrars seem much the same to me in 1992 as they did in 1972 and 1982. [. . .] On that basis, whatever the strong theoretical arguments for change, they haven't really amounted to enough to undermine confidence in the present structure. If in doubt, why change it? (CPO)

I take a fairly pragmatic view of it. I would like probation to hang on to civil work partly because we've developed skills in it, partly because there is a long tradition and people know what we are about. [. . .] I think that what civil work has brought to the fore is skills in conflict resolution which should feed back into the criminal part of the work. [. . .] So long as the focus and rationale is that we are the service which services the courts, both civil and criminal, then I think an argument can be made for keeping it within the probation service. (CPO)

In contrast, another chief officer adopted a similar starting position but reached a different conclusion:

There is an ever-developing school of thought which is asking should we be doing it anyway. There are those who say 'if I had to choose, I would say that we should get out.' On the other hand, others are saying that 'I am expanding it right, left and centre.' [. . .] I now find myself with a wholly pragmatic view about the matter. If the government declared that the civil work function be transferred to another body, then I think that would be a good thing. The issue of transferability of skills from one specialism to another is true, but it is less of a benefit than it has been made out to be. (CPO)

Such lines of argument tend to confirm the existence of a policy vacuum, as suggested in Chapter 2. However, it is important to note that there are compelling reasons why responsibility for the court welfare service should be transferred to another agency. One such reason propounded by some observers is that court welfare work should not be isolated from other areas of child-care policy and practice. This ACPO supported this view:

I would be happy to see an independent court welfare service. That's the logical outcome of what has happened in probation and social services in relation to guardians *ad litem*. I have major concerns about the management of guardian *ad litem* panels which is, I think, a much more pressing structural problem than civil work. [. . .] The only way to resolve the guardian *ad litem* dilemma is to bring civil work into some form of relationship with it. I have doubts about the service's ability to do that alongside its other concerns. [. . .] It would make the probation service have a major minority interest in something that has got nothing to do with criminal work. I'm not sure that the service would want to manage two big separate things that do not have much to do with each other when it comes down to it. (ACPO)

Whilst not necessarily disagreeing with the sentiments expressed here, it is important to remember that underlying these general concerns are a number of other specific difficulties which may need to be resolved before a specialist court welfare agency could be created. These include the pressures inherent in maintaining economic viability, establishing an appropriate management structure, and coming to terms with the restricted career prospects for staff.

However, the retention of court welfare within the ambit of the probation service is problematic for a number of complex reasons. It is undeniable that the service benefits in a number of ways from the high regard that judges have for court welfare officers. However, it can be argued that because it is sometimes regarded as something of an anomaly or a cinderella, court welfare cannot develop its full potential unless its organisational links with mainstream probation practice are severed. Moreover, we unearthed a strong feeling amongst many senior managers that parents and children would receive a better service if the court welfare task was located in a different agency. In the words of this manager:

> Civil work does not receive a great deal of attention, and there will always be this problem while it remains part of the probation service. [. . .] So there is a paradox. Civil work, in terms of its clients, might get a better deal from a separate service, but the probation service in its other work would very clearly lose. (ACPO)

What is perhaps inescapable, however, is the conclusion that the justification for retaining court welfare work within the probation service lies as much in arguments about the positive spin-offs for its work with offenders (which, as we argued in Chapter 1, was part of the historical rationale for its development within the probation service) as it does in an argument that this is the rational organisational locus for court welfare work.

Staffing courts

There has long been widespread disagreement amongst all grades of probation staff about the utility of staffing courts. However, staffing courts may mean anything ranging from routine presence at Directions Hearings to attendance throughout the hearing of contested cases. Whereas some welfare officers and their managers argued that staffing courts was not only worthwhile but essential, others argued the contrary, with various standpoints being adopted between these extremes.

Within this general context, the specific case for maintaining a high profile in court was argued by some practitioners on some or all of the following grounds:

- That it provides welfare officers with the opportunity to meet disputing parents early in the process, thus affording a degree of

influence in the proceedings whilst at the same time conveying the 'right kind of messages' to parents.
- Staffing courts is strategically desirable. It produces a variety of rewards, the most notable being that the high regard which judges have for welfare officers may be transposed to colleagues who work with offenders.
- It provides an opportunity for welfare officers to influence the number of reports requested.
- It provides opportunities to encourage judges to restrict enquiries to specific issues.

Whilst conceding that these points might have some validity, some senior managers remained unhappy about a policy that undoubtedly swallows up so many resources whilst producing no clearly measurable benefits:

> I think that [court duty] is useful. But I've got my doubts about whether it is value for money. [. . .] If one looks at it purely in terms of the officer attending, then it is very 'iffy'. If you look at it in terms of how the judges view the service, and how they then help with other practice, then that takes it on the plus side. But not much. (ACPO)

Clearly, managers are engaged in a complex cost–benefit analysis requiring them to steer a course between these competing standpoints.

Judicial views

Judges were also ambivalent about amount of time that should be devoted to court duty. Some judges welcomed the presence of the welfare officer:

> I find it very helpful to be able to say to parties that there is someone with whom you can have a word. Eight times out of ten it works. I also like to have a welfare officer around when I'm doing a family case because a bit of intervention can solve things and stop the quarrel.

> I'm very much in favour of officers being around as much as possible. [. . .] It is tremendously helpful to be able to have a quick word with an officer, and I think that the speediness with which something can be arranged is a tremendous help.

> If it's a contested case, I think it's always helpful to have the welfare officer who has prepared the report present throughout [. . .] quite

often things pop up and emerge in the course of the case and it would be very helpful to have the welfare officer's view. [. . .] It gives an added dimension to the contribution the welfare officer makes.

However, other judges viewed court duty very differently:

> In one sense it's a great waste of time. What I tend to say when giving directions is that the welfare officer should attend unless the parties indicate that their presence is not necessary. On reflection it's probably better to do it the other way round . . . to say that it is not necessary for the welfare officer to attend unless the parties want him to. [. . .] Frankly, they haven't been able to contribute very much. But usually one or other of the parties want to ask the welfare officer a question, so they have to be there for cross-examination.

Thus policies towards staffing courts appear to represent a set of organisational compromises which contain these tensions but do not in any real or lasting sense resolve them.

Conflicts of interest

As noted in Chapter 2, a view voiced by many welfare officers is that senior managers have not practised for many years and thus know very little about current court welfare practice. Such a criticism is not, of course, unique to court welfare work. However, given the radical changes that have occurred in the last decade both within the organisational and practice contexts of court welfare (see Chapters 2 and 3), it can be argued that there is some substance to this criticism. Indeed, it is a criticism that is acknowledged, to varying degrees, by those responsible for managing court welfare work. However, it is possible to agree with this criticism whilst also arguing that a certain distance from practice is in fact desirable:

> Because I've never done civil work, it is *the* area of work where I feel I've got the appropriate amount of ignorance as a manager. There are an awful lot of areas of practice of which I know too much and can meddle too often. But because civil work is not within my personal range of skills, I feel suitably remote from it. [. . .] The management task is about policy-making, structures and processes. But detailed knowledge at this level? Not really. (CPO)

Alternatively, some senior managers felt that this particular criticism was overstated and resented being thought of as out of touch. They often recounted how main grade staff have a tendency to forget that they, too, were once practitioners. Moreover it was, they stressed, part of their duty as managers to keep up-to-date with current practice. For some managers, this may mean observing various aspects of practice or even, perhaps, writing the occasional report:

> They certainly know more than I do about how to interview families and how to make recommendations. Of course they do. I last did a report two years ago just to get the feel of what it was like. I don't need to be as good at report writing as they are. I know a bit about it though. (ACPO)

In addition, many welfare officers drew our attention to a range of other concerns revolving around the belief that management frequently demonstrated their lack of understanding about practice. They cited issues such as the allocation of resources, the amount of work that court welfare officers are expected to undertake at any one time, and the number of reports that they are expected to prepare in any given period. Many senior managers were, however, well versed in these arguments. Whilst a number said that they took such criticisms seriously, they also found them to be a source of frustration and annoyance:

> The constant quibble here is on the question of weightings and how many pieces of work they can be expected to complete in a year. It's been a constant problem since I arrived. [. . .] People have heard me say that for good motives and professional reasons you are spending 'x' number of hours on these reports, and my view is that you could spend less and produce a good piece of work which would be just as useful to the court. [. . .] If I was a probation officer I'm sure that I would be saying that they don't understand; that they've forgotten since they were probation officers that there are issues of quality as well as quantity, and that all they're concerned about are the figures. It's irritating that the discussion goes on. You feel like you're trying to pin a jelly to a wall! (CPO)

Meanwhile, the burden of responsibility resting on the ACPO may be of a different order. For example, it was argued that one of the tasks of the ACPO is to recognise the problems of main grade staff in relation to the multitude of practice issues, dilemmas and pressures and to represent these interests in the senior management group. Once again, this situation is not unique to family court welfare work. However, the low priority that is generally accorded to this area of work means that some ACPOs have to fight their corner more than colleagues responsible for other specialisms in order to get court welfare issues on the agenda. As this ACPO noted:

> The danger of being a detached specialist division is that the experience of having to bridge the gap between the rest of the service and the civil work teams is very restrictive. So there tends to be a lack of appreciation [by the management group] in what it sees as being important and the context in which [court welfare officers] are working. In some ways civil work is in direct competition with what the rest of the service wants. [. . .] Ideally to represent them well I'd like to have some common criteria that are as meaningful in the other areas as they are in this area and which would have some clout. I see my role as representing them and trying to get what I can for them, but also mediating back to them some of the reasons why we don't get resources. (ACPO)

The role of the senior court welfare officer

Within this general managerial framework what specific part does the senior court welfare officer (SCWO) as a middle-manager play? What dilemmas and tensions do they face? In broad terms:

> He or she is the key person who holds it all together. [. . .] A senior has to be close enough to the action to be able to identify [the professional issues] and pass them up and to make the views of the team very clear if the thing is to be managed properly. (CPO)

According to this view the senior's role is both central and pivotal. But how do SCWOs themselves see their role? Once thought of as the senior practitioner, the role of a senior in both civil and criminal work has increasingly become identified with the tasks of management, including allocating work, liaison with courts and other agencies, supervising staff and monitoring staff performance. As a consequence a number of seniors, although by no means all, did not involve themselves in face-to-face contact with parents and children:

> My own thoughts towards the senior role generally have changed. When I first became a senior it was much more the feeling that you were a senior practitioner. [. . .] I now take the view that I am a manager of this team, a supporter of this team and an enabler of this team. [. . .] When you become a manager you lose some of the contact with clients and this is to be regretted. (SCWO)

> I've found myself moving away from the casework bit much more towards being office manager and holding people more accountable for what they're doing and what the task is about. There's still the opportunity to talk with people about their involvement with their work. [. . .] We don't have to do the work to know what it feels like. (SCWO)

A common theme referred to by SCWOs was the difficulty of managing very experienced practitioners who may be more skilled and knowledgeable than they:

> I don't see how I can claim through training or anything to have greater insights than they have. I say that from someone who regards himself, to use an old-fashioned term, as a good caseworker. But when you're talking to people who are specialising all the time, it's more difficult to come up with something clever. Any supervision needs to bounce things around. [. . .] If you gave me a choice I'd prefer to be more of a practitioner. Some say why should we have seniors at all? (SCWO)

It is perhaps because of these reasons, coupled with the kind of practice orientations (see Chapter 5) that are in part the product of team dynamics, that lead some SCWOs to take a more active practice role. In this regard, the team 'culture' was a key factor in helping to shape the senior's role. It was noticeable, for example, that those SCWOs who were responsible for teams whose practice orientation was geared towards conflict resolution were more likely to be actively involved in face-to-face work with parents and children, whereas the reverse was true for those seniors who managed teams orientated more towards traditional ways of working. This is perhaps a reflection of the fact that such teams may have been more closely knit than those that were more orientated towards investigation. Thus, a number of SCWOs argued that they would not have any credibility with their colleagues if they abstained from face-to-face practice with parents and children. In the words of this senior:

> I don't see how you can come into this work and have any credibility if you don't have experience of it. There is also the sense of needing to keep your hand in. [. . .] There is also the way in which this team operates in that it would be very difficult to have a manager who wasn't also a player because of the whole nature of shared working. You would be an outsider if you were always in the office. [. . .] The team also manages as well as plays. That is an integral way of functioning. So there's no way that you could have that sort of manager without the team being different. I don't know whether the team would have it. (SCWO)

Meanwhile, her counterpart in another team argued that it was misguided to attempt to separate face-to-face work with parents and children from the duties and obligations inherent in the management role:

> I've never believed in the notion that you can separate the task of doing the job and the task of being accountable. At the end of the day, a senior is accountable for certain things – that supervision takes place, and that the work gets done to a certain standard. I actually find it difficult to see how I can be accountable for those things without, at the same time, knowing what my colleagues are doing. If I separated out those functions I don't think I would have the same credibility. (SCWO)

These viewpoints in particular raise a number of interesting and important questions about the role of the senior, different management styles and the impact of team dynamics on the potential for change.

A crisis of confidence?

It is against this backcloth that managerial and judicial expectations of court welfare officers should be considered. Before setting about this task in more detail, however, it is perhaps necessary to address the question of how far members of management and welfare officers agreed over the broad thrust of court welfare policies. We encountered divergent views on this subject both within and between areas. For example:

> I don't have a strong sense of a split between management and the rest of the service. I think that staff are content to follow the policy line that we are taking. (CPO)

I would hope that one of the results of last year is more coherence. It is not yet as I expect. But one of the intentions of the practice document was to ensure that both within and without the service people had a much more clear and coherent view about what the underlying principles and expectations were. [. . .] I'm not saying that everybody will go along one hundred per cent with it, but I would want people to have had an opportunity to have taken part in an informed discussion about whether it should change or what it actually ought to be. (ACPO)

In contrast, when asked if there was a chasm between court welfare staff and members of senior management with regard to policy and practice, this SCWO replied:

That's hard to answer. It seems to me that this ACPO has done a better job of understanding where we are at than previous ACPOs have done. It sounds from what one hears that there is less understanding elsewhere. But there is still a gap there. (SCWO)

A colleague, however, was less equivocal:

I don't think that senior management are in the least bit interested in civil work itself, except when it has an effect on the probation service as an organisation or individual senior managers. It doesn't make any noises until something goes wrong or it wants to cut back on resources. But in practice that hasn't happened to us. [. . .] Why should they be interested? (SCWO)

We have already identified the degree of dissatisfaction that many welfare officers felt about the resources that are devoted to family court welfare work and their feelings of being overworked and undervalued as a result. We have also drawn attention to the fact that many felt that policies were insufficiently well informed by a close knowledge of practice, but their criticisms of management did not end here. For example, many welfare officers perceived the increasing emphasis on economy, efficiency and effectiveness as working inexorably towards reducing complex practice issues to technical solutions. Hand in hand with this was a widespread perception amongst welfare officers that quantity and not quality was what mattered most to those in positions of authority in the service. As we highlighted earlier, this perhaps partially explains the fact that welfare officers frequently took the courts or the parents and children as their primary reference points. As this Chief Officer notes:

> It seems as though they develop a whole new identity as members of the probation service. It shows itself in references to their sense of isolation and of being neglected. In its worst excess it takes the form that management doesn't care, that they have been left without a sense of belonging. They have developed a special sense of identity. I can encapsulate this by reference to their draft of their team objectives and to whom they are accountable. [. . .] It came across strongly that it was the judge with whom they had become familiar who they were accountable to for the quality of their work [. . .] rather than the organisation. (CPO)

Whatever the strengths and weaknesses of these arguments, the indications are that those who are ultimately responsible for service delivery both nationally and locally are, of late, asserting that family court welfare work needs to be managed much more effectively. Part of this drive lies in the need to be *seen* to be managing resources efficiently and effectively and part lies in the trend towards management by objectives (for a description, critique and proposed alternative managerial model, see McWilliams 1990 and Shepherd 1990). Yet another facet lies in the perception that court welfare work has been undermanaged for too long:

> The kind of individualistic approach has been allowed to continue to an extent which is perhaps not acceptable. Some management hasn't taken enough interest of the principles upon which court welfare should be founded, and the organisation which you need to meet those principles, and to keep a firm hand on that in terms of policy development. (CPO)

In such a fraught and unsettled situation tensions and disputes, sometimes acrimonious, between senior managers and court welfare officers are perhaps inevitable.

Principles of practice

One question that emerges from this discussion is: What should be the principles of court welfare practice? We have examined the values and beliefs that inform court welfare officers' practice in relation to this question. We now wish to address similar issues that arise from managerial perspectives. For this Chief Officer:

> There are two clear issues. One is that you should try and deal with these matters through mediation, conciliation, negotiation or whatever word you want to use in terms of giving the parties as much responsibility as you can to continue being parents even though they have separated. But there is a preliminary phase in that this should be done in a privileged state in which what they say to a welfare officer is not used in any report. That is clearly laid down in Practice Directions and we have to abide by them. To go outside that is wrong. The other involves investigations for the court when there are concerns about the welfare of the children. The subject matter is not privileged and that needs to be made clear to the parties. It also needs to be made clear that the welfare officer is preparing a report for the court and giving his or her opinion in it based on evidence which can be challenged in open court. Management has to be clear about that distinction in relation to those principles. (CPO)

In other words, court welfare practice needs to abide by both the *letter* and the *spirit* of the law. However, it can be argued that such principles are easier to abide by when they are applied to issues relating to conciliation *before* a report is ordered. What is more difficult is the task of disentangling the conflicting threads of settlement-seeking or conflict resolution and investigation *after* the request for a report:

> The situation is that if a court asks for a welfare report, I expect them to get a welfare report. I don't mind how the officers interview people, but if a party says 'No, I'm not prepared to come to a joint meeting', then I don't allow my officers to over-rule that. They can be persuasive but they must let people know that they have a choice about participating. That's the big difference. [. . .] I don't allow probation officers to write what is in effect a response to conciliation when the application in the first place was for a welfare report. (ACPO)

There is a sense, therefore, in which the status of Practice Directions and High Court judgments remains ambiguous. Moreover, many senior managers, court welfare staff and (as we saw in Chapter 2) judges were ambivalent about the relevance of such judgments and Directions:

> I don't think we have been desperately influenced by Mr Justice Ewbank's judgment. I spent a day in one of the offices not so long ago and it seems to me that the rationale for activity is to do with conflict resolution. And as far as the county court is concerned, I don't have a serious doubt that they have the support of the judges and registrars. I have never had a judge or registrar come up to me and say that they are not very keen on the way officers go about this. Magistrates are a little more edgy. I don't know that they feel that strongly about conflict resolution. Cerebrally they can accept it, but they feel uneasy about anything that leads to a situation where their sense of responsibility might be put out for scrutiny. (CPO)

> It's incredibly difficult. What has complicated matters here is that judges have rejected Mr Justice Ewbank's view. They are inclined to say that up there in the High Court they don't understand the issues at the basic level. [. . .] The difficulty I've got is that I agree with Mr Justice Ewbank about not writing a report after conciliation. [. . .] I think our position was that we said that we would support the judgment and were confounded when the practitioners were able to work with the judges in not doing so. [. . .] So in a way, that judgment has got overlaid on the reality which is utterly different from that. (CPO)

Given this situation, it is perhaps hardly surprising that court welfare practice has developed piecemeal and owes as much to pragmatism as it does to rational planning, a finding which is, of course, in accord with much organisation theory (see, for example, Morgan 1990: 80).

Notwithstanding these difficulties, senior managers were content, in general, with the way that the court welfare practice had developed in their own areas. At the same time, managers were also mindful that there is always room for improvement:

> I don't have any particular practice issues which we need to address now. What I do want to set up is a procedure whereby practice is looked at by practitioners and management on a regular basis and checked against what the expectations are. I want to be able to ask 'is this practice happening, yes or no?' If not, what are the major reasons? (ACPO)

More specifically, other senior managers identified a need for their service to improve communication between court welfare staff and management and to increase the opportunities for training and staff development. These are, of course, familiar concerns to welfare officers and management alike. However, they are of significance for two main reasons. First, many welfare officers expressed the need for more training in court welfare work (see Chapter 2) at a time when, they informed us, training had been severely curtailed, ostensibly as part of the drive towards ensuring efficient use of resources. Second, a number of welfare officers asserted not only that they felt isolated from their colleagues who worked with offenders, but also unappreciated by senior management.

Many senior managers did not seek to prescribe practice in any great detail, preferring to leave the nuts and bolts of policy implementation and everyday practice issues to middle-managers. Rather, the most pressing point for many middle- and senior managers was the general need to establish the kind of culture in which court welfare work could flourish. In this regard the organisational concerns of many were essentially to enable and facilitate practice. Yet there is a potential dilemma for senior managers – on the one hand, delegating responsibility may be thought of in a positive light but on the other, some might regard it, perhaps legitimately, as management by default. This dilemma is exacerbated by the fact that court welfare work frequently attracts some of the more capable and experienced probation officers. Thus:

> Time and time again a judge will say 'They are superb people.' [. . .] The abdication of managerial responsibility by CPOs is in my experience explained and, I might say, justified by knowing that they are so highly regarded, much more so than other teams. So it's a bit too easy to say 'let them get on with it', and one takes the line of least resistance. (CPO)

When senior managers did proffer an opinion on the merits or otherwise of particular practice orientations, it was frequently to cast doubt on the appropriateness of prevailing practice in *other* areas. It is perhaps interesting to note that the most vehement criticisms emanated from those senior managers in areas adopting traditional approaches to practice. The most voiced criticism in this regard reflected the negative feelings of some senior managers about the use of one-way screens and other techniques borrowed from family therapy. Thus, put simply, this Chief Officer felt that such techniques lie outside of the remit granted court welfare officers by the court:

> Technically you can lay out the rules in such a way as to say that we are going to do this because we feel it will be helpful, and because I cannot take in all the information, and I need someone else to prompt me and so on. [. . .] But the issue is not that the workers may be doing it in good faith, but whether they understand the rules under which they are working. [. . .] The welfare officer must be clear about the remit under which he is working and that sets up certain rules. If you are doing investigation the rules are quite clear – any information can be used and reported to the court. It must go through a due process which can be challenged in open court. It seems to me to be questionable that if you use therapeutic techniques that that is always clear. [. . .] Now family therapists may say 'well, we are not using those techniques', but it seems to me that they get dangerously close to it and are neglecting what the remit is. (CPO)

According to this view, to justify practice solely in terms of whether it might be successful or morally justifiable is not sufficient because this fails to address the issue of its legitimacy.

Tensions and dilemmas

Numerous questions need explanation in the light of these reflections, such as how have such differential forms of court welfare practice emerged? Does it actually matter whether there are significant differences in court welfare practice both between and within different areas? Should there be a consistent service based on a firmly grounded set of principles and, if so, what should these be? As the following observations of Chief Probation Officers from different study areas illustrate, there is no consensus amongst senior managers on these issues:

> We have a structure in ACOP which is supposed to try and deal with issues like [. . .] consistency between areas. But I have to say that in this particular area of work, the relationship between local judges and registrars is the most important dimension. We have a positive relationship at that level and there is a fair amount of satisfaction between them and us which will accommodate everyone's interests. That has to come first. If other areas come to other agreements, then so be it.

> I'm probably totally confused. The issue of consistency is around a lot at the moment. I can't justify this. [. . .] There are too many ponderables in civil work and it can be much clearer in criminal matters. I am a strong believer in national standards. But I don't know about national standards for civil work. The lack of any agreed criteria as to what counts as a quality service in civil work terms is going to bedevil [the exercise].
>
> I hope that we don't think that we have the philosopher's stone here and we know how to do it best. If we need to examine the differences then we'll do it. [. . .] It's part of our wish in ACOP to get the Home Office to take civil work seriously. I'm quite convinced that the Home Office do need to lay down certain national standards as long as they do that as a framework within which one has to make judgements according to local circumstances. The important thing about national standards is that they are advised by a good professional basis for an activity. Some of that involves arid things like saying people will be seen within a certain timescale, or that certain things will be taken up. Certainly we are waiting on a set of aims and values and we would want to ensure that the values which underpin any national standards are ones which we can all subscribe to.
>
> The proof of the pudding is in the eating. I suppose I get less and less wedded to central direction and regulation. I suppose I wouldn't be that troubled unless there was clearly some evidence that people were worst served on whatever criteria were deemed sensible. Then, of course, you have got to do something about it. [. . .] No. I will probably carry on tinkering around, pushing this way and that. [. . .] I don't feel under pressure to do anything about it because others are doing it markedly different.

Before beginning to unravel many of the puzzles set here, we are led almost inexorably into the sets of questions that we identified in Chapter 2 such as who defines the goals and is it possible and/or desirable to have shared values? Clearly, reference to values, beliefs and principles draws us into the realm of normative theory. Essential though this area is to explore, however, it is necessary to bear in mind Blau's reminder that a study of value orientations cannot be taken in isolation:

> While structures of social relations are, of course, profoundly influenced by common values, these structures have a significance of their own,

which is ignored if concern is exclusively with the underlying values and norms. Exchange transactions and power relations, in particular, constitute social forces that must be investigated in their own right, not merely in terms of the norms that limit and the values that reinforce them, to arrive at an understanding of the dynamics of social structures. (1964: 13)

In this regard, court welfare work is merely one element of a much wider network of socio-legal organisational frameworks and the issues raised therefore extend far beyond its own internal terms of reference. We have argued that court welfare practice is characterised by a multiplicity of rationales, some of which converge whilst other diverge in a number of significant ways. A number of inter-connected questions might therefore usefully be posed: how *does* court welfare intersect with other socio-legal institutions? What are the characteristics which give shape to the different sets of power relations and exchange transactions within court welfare work? And how best might we establish the philosophies, values and norms that court welfare officers, their managers and judges bring to bear within this structural framework? Answers to these questions, which are so fundamental to an understanding of practice, call for a considered exposition and analysis of theoretical perspectives. It is thus to the insights that can be offered by social theory that we now turn.

PART III

☐

Social theory and court welfare work

> In my view, we should recognise what might be called the *relative autonomy* of theory and research. Theoretical thinking needs in substantial part to proceed in its own terms and cannot be expected to be linked at every point to empirical considerations. The more encompassing or generalised a set of theoretical notions is, the more this is the case. Empirical work, on the other hand, cannot proceed in the absence of abstract concepts or theoretical notions, but these are necessarily drawn upon selectively and cannot be ever present.
> (Anthony Giddens 1989: 294–5)

> Just as intuition and empirical observation are blind without concepts and a theoretical frame of reference, so too the concepts and theoretical frame of reference are empty without intuition and empirical observation.
> (Immanuel Kant, cited by Munch 1987: 131)

7

From practice to theory: some emerging issues and problems

Determining the precise relationship between theory and practice is a particularly vexed and complex problem for practitioners and researchers alike. Faced with the everyday realities of people's problems, the importance (or otherwise) of a particular analytical paradigm may be of marginal utility to many practitioners (see Howe 1987), although as we have seen in earlier chapters, the relevance of and degree of commitment to certain theoretical models means that this is only partially true in the case of many court welfare officers.

Similar misgivings, though of a different kind, can also be detected in the field of research. As Giddens and Turner (1987) point out:

> many of those whose prime commitment is to empirical research find in the array of squabbling schools and traditions confirmation of what they have believed all along: theoretical debates are of little interest or relevance to those conducting empirical work. (1987: 3)

This raises the question as to whether theory is something that practitioners and researchers arbitrarily adopt or discard as they think fit. Whatever the answer to this question, both research and practice are, in their different ways, much the poorer for any dichotomy between theory and practice. Moreover, it is not only that ideas matter. The absence of any guiding theoretical framework, to paraphrase Pinker (1979), reduces practice to little more than a motley collection of skills which are applied, on a largely *ad hoc* basis, to a series of problems. The issue, therefore, is not whether we have to choose one at the expense of the other before we can proceed, but rather to recognise their inseparability.

It is against this backcloth that we wish in this chapter to tease out what it means to think theoretically about court welfare work. Of necessity this will entail a degree of abstraction. We begin by looking at the ways other commentators on court welfare have approached this task, highlighting the strengths and limitations of their relative positions. We then extend their analyses by drawing upon some of the central insights contained in the body of knowledge loosely termed 'social theory'. In doing so, we are not seeking to supplant or transcend the various approaches we review, or to say that our own framework is superior in any way. Nor, for that matter, are we claiming to have the key with which to unlock and resolve the multitude of conceptual and practical problems that we have been addressing throughout this book. However, we shall allude to a number of specific theoretical strands which are, in our view, of some importance in helping to understand many of the processes underpinning court welfare work.

The search for theory: the story so far

Theoretical analysis in the social sciences has always been characterised by deep divisions and dichotomies on a number of inter-related dimensions, not only between but also within different disciplines. How, then, are we to make sense of the plethora of conflicting and competing paradigms? To what extent is the application of a particular theory to a specific area of social enquiry merely a matter of idiosyncratic and arbitrary choice? Are all theories of equal worth or are some more useful or superior in particular ways than others? These difficult questions are made all the more complex by the fact that court welfare work occupies a nebulous space somewhere between the legal and social-work domain. Given these dilemmas it is perhaps unsurprising that much variation exists in the way that court welfare work has hitherto been theorised.

At this juncture, it seems sensible to pause briefly and reflect upon the ways in which others have approached this problem. Firstly, however, we must add a *caveat*. What follows is a highly selective and inevitably distilled review of the work of certain observers whom we have singled out because of their contributions to the study and understanding of court welfare work and for the usefulness of their theoretical insights in developing our own theoretical approach. In so doing, we recognise that we leave ourselves open to a number of criticisms, not least of which is the fact that we have chosen to concentrate only on particular, and some would say narrow, aspects of theory whilst ignoring others. In addition to such omissions, we have also chosen to defer commenting on the immense contribution to the analysis of court welfare made by certain feminist writers until Chapter 8.

Two important commentators in the field in recent years have been Mervyn Murch (see, in particular, 1980) and Gywnn Davis (see, for example, 1988a and 1988b). Both have commented widely on the nature of the court welfare task. Both have also based much of their work on empirical studies of the consumer. However, neither refer explicitly to a particular body of theoretical knowledge. Rather, we have to infer any theoretical framework from their writings which, in general, tend to emphasise normative rather than explanatory theories, although not to the exclusion of the latter.

Murch argues, quite rightly, that the views of consumers on the 'receiving' end are likely to be significantly different from service providers and these have their own validity (1980: 5). He thus draws upon research evidence from two research projects, the first of which involves a survey of petitioners in undefended divorce cases, the second, divorcing couples who were the subject of court welfare reports, highlighting the importance of the principles of justice which inhere in the divorce process. Davis, like Murch, also emphasises the importance of consumer views, drawing upon evidence from empirical studies on the basis of which he eschews many of the strong claims that have been made about the efficacy and desirability of settlement-seeking approaches. Whilst acknowledging that mediation provides a valuable complement to the existing court process, he nevertheless maintains that the expectations of mediation should not be overstated:

> The process seems to be associated with few or no consistent improvements in long-term compliance, spousal co-operation, and re-litigation. An analysis of child adjustment to divorce finds that mediation appears to have few measurable effects and private- and public-sector cost savings appear to be detectable only in compulsory programmes in large jurisdictions, where litigants are diverted to the process in the early stages of dispute. (1988a: 87)

Furthermore, he has reservations about the knowledge base upon which much of the dispute resolution approach is based, arguing that this approach is bound to be ill-understood by parents, with the result that this confers too much power on the court welfare officer (1988b: 159–60). In addition, he argues that parents are frequently bemused with the process, failing to distinguish between, on the one hand, the welfare officer's role as a reporting officer for the court, and her or his role as a conciliator, on the other (1988b: 147). These criticisms lead Davis also to focus, *inter alia*, on the principles and processes of justice and therefore to reject the option of leaving decision-making within the court welfare arena to conciliators and informal methods of dispute resolution.

It is not our intention, here, to arbitrate between Davis and advocates of settlement-seeking approaches as to what 'method' works best and nor, for that matter, do we seek to make judgements about competing differences of value. Nor do we wish, at this juncture, to enter the debate as to whether court welfare work ought to be subsumed within a broader, family-court-orientated organisational structure. Rather, our aim is to illuminate the theoretical assumptions (or lack of them) that underpin the kind of empirical research that Davis and Murch have undertaken and to subject this data to a theoretical analysis. Informative though their studies are, most notably for the insights derived from recipients of the court welfare service, we feel that their analyses are somewhat incomplete. In sociological terms: 'empirical modelling and empirical propositional schemes are not theory, but regularities in the data that require a theory to explain them. They are an *explicandum* in search of an *explanans*' (Turner 1987: 165). Thus, whilst empirical generalisations such as those offered by Davis and Murch can be useful as a means of testing the plausibility of abstract theories, models and propositions, nevertheless we find ourselves in agreement with Turner, who writes that

> without the abstract laws and models these more empirical approaches will not help to build theory. For if uninformed by abstract laws and formal models, then middle-range theories, causal models and empirical generalizations are constructed *ad hoc*, without concern for whether or not they illustrate an underlying dynamic of the universe . . . when one starts with the particulars, one rarely rises above them. (1987: 167)

How, then, might we build on the frameworks provided by Murch and Davis? Put simply, the need is for a much wider conceptualisation, a standpoint adopted by Maidment (1984). Her view is very much that of a family lawyer interested in the relationship between the law and the body of knowledge that is located within social science and how this can be utilised in the decisions that courts have to make when adjudicating in family proceedings. Indeed, Maidment makes the strong assertion that:

> the nature of divorce and custody decision-making can only be understood when the legal structure is located in its social context. Why and how judges decide custody cases can only be properly appreciated within an understanding of the social process involved in marriage and divorce, of the changes in the social institution of the family and of the social expectations of parenting. And this social context itself must be seen in an historical perspective. (1984: 1)

Although we find ourselves in agreement with the thrust of Maidment's assertion, especially for the need to place court welfare work in a broader context, we feel that she has taken a particular theoretical view which is incomplete. The limitations of Maidment's view stem, in large part, from changes in the social and historical context, to the significance of which she refers, in so far as she was writing before the full weight of the importance of alternatives to the adversarial process had become recognised. She therefore systematically underplays the influence of conciliation on the socio-legal processes involved in court decision-making and court welfare work.

Two other writers in the socio-legal realm are King and Piper (1990) who have sought to apply the ideas of constructivist legal theorists such as Teubner and social theorists such as Luhmann and Habermas to an analysis of the relationship between law and child welfare. King and Piper's work is broad in scope and ambition. Of necessity, therefore, we refer here only to the central propositions of their overall argument as they might be applied to court welfare work (for a fuller discussion see James 1992c). In particular we shall address ourselves to two distinct but intertwined strands of King and Piper's central thesis.

King and Piper take as their starting point the claim that the law, in 'conceptualising the world into rights and duties on which it can adjudicate' (1990: 11), actually 'thinks'. What do they mean by this? Two related propositions can be identified, both of which draw heavily on the work of Teubner (1989). The 'persons' the law deals with, King and Piper assert (following Teubner), do not have bodily form but are merely constructs produced by the legal discourse. A second central tenet of King and Piper's theory (drawn once again from the work of Teubner but also incorporating the work of Luhmann) is that the law acts as an self-referential system. They remind us of the ideological battle that is perceived as existing between the competing and conflicting claims and concerns of 'justice' oriented frameworks (see for example, Morris and her colleagues 1980) and those frameworks more overtly concerned with the 'welfare' of children. One solution to this dilemma, King and Piper point out, is for the elimination of either justice or welfare through the imposition of legal rules and procedures which would, in turn, allow the operation of only one ideology (1990: 7). A second solution lies in attempting to integrate the two philosophies (see Harris 1985). The trick is thus to transcend the dichotomy by incorporating the values of both models. In other words, a fusing together of law and child welfare discourses based on the recognition of the need to reconcile two seemingly polarised approaches. King and Piper, in accord with Teubner, argue, however, that such a hybrid discourse is not possible. Rather: 'All that results are simultaneous communications about the child and its problems, which, like parallel lines, never meet but continue along their own path' (1990: 19).

This view owes much to Luhmann's theory of autopoiesis, a term borrowed from the natural sciences referring to closed, self-sustaining biological systems, which is transposed to refer to closed and self-referential social institutions. Thus King argues:

> a genuine partnership cannot exist, for any attempt to merge child-welfare science with law as part of the legal system will inevitably result in the domination of law and the 'enslavement' of child-welfare knowledge to serve institutional legal objectives. (1991: 319)

King and Piper are thus arguing not only that the law deals with people as 'mere constructs', a product of its 'thinking' which is quite independent of key actors such as court welfare officers and judges, but also that it 'enslaves' other discourses according to, and to further, its own normative and institutional purposes. Space precludes a careful and considered reflection on the robustness of these assertions (for which, see James 1992c) but we shall consider briefly some of their implications later.

Elster is a social theorist who is primarily concerned with rational-choice theory and who sets out to deal with the scope, limits and failures of rational decision-making processes (Elster 1989). What interests us here is that Elster brings his substantive theory to bear on the specific topic of child custody. He asserts that rational-choice theory is first and foremost a normative theory and only secondarily an explanatory approach – that is, it tells people how they ought to act in order to achieve particular aims in the best way possible. His contribution is thus of great potential utility to both theorists and practitioners alike. However, our guiding concern in this chapter is largely that of seeking to explain the various aspects of court welfare work and how they stand in relation to one another. Therefore, we do not propose to spend too much time in a general elaboration or critique of Elster's theory. Suffice it to say that, in a wide-ranging discussion, he offers some incisive comments on the difficulties involved in the kinds of decisions that need to be made regarding the best interests of children.

Of particular interest, however, is that Elster draws upon some of the key theories of distributive justice. This leads him into discussion of, *inter alia*, some of the moral dilemmas that ensue. In this regard, he addresses himself to two highly problematic issues: firstly, to the question of competing rights, needs and obligations and the basis on which each of these might best be determined; secondly, to the inherent problem in decision-making as to whether decisions ought to be based on act-utilitarianism (the search on *each* occasion for the *act* that maximises utility) or rule-utility (the search for a *rule* that, if followed on *all* occasions, will maximise utility). The variations in court welfare practice which we outlined in Part II might be taken to confirm the dominance of the former of these, although the high priority that the large majority of welfare officers apparently accord to both settlement-seeking and to facilitating children's contact with the other parent perhaps lends itself more to explanation by the latter.

Also of importance is that Elster focuses our attention on the indeterminacy of the best-interests principle. In consequence, the courts must contend with the contradictions and tensions posed by the existence of a principle for determining issues of child welfare which is laid down in the law, suggesting rule-utility as the basis of decision-making, which is indeterminate in its application, implying act-utilitarianism as the basis of decision-making. Given this indeterminacy, coupled with his assertion that there is frequently little to choose between parental abilities, Elster raises the question as to whether the decision should be randomised – for example, by tossing a coin. He speaks of coin tossing as 'coming to symbolize the equal worth of parents, as well as the child's right to a speedy decision' (1989: 171). Having given due weight to this possibility he rejects this method of settling such disputes, arguing that a decision with such far-reaching consequences must be made by appeal to reason and argument, not by an arbitrary choice.

Elster thus begins his concluding remarks by saying that: 'It remains to be seen whether any other principle is superior, on balance, to the best-interest standard' (1989: 155). His central premise is that

> In the bulk of divorce cases, there is no basis for saying that the child will be better off with one parent than with the other. Nevertheless, the legal regime can and should incorporate the interests of children in two ways. First, custody should not be given to a parent who is clearly unfit. Second, the pain and stress to the child created by the custody decision itself should be minimized. This second consideration points to the need for a more mechanical and automatic decision procedure than the very finely tuned best-interest standard. (1989: 173)

Elster posits three possible alternatives: firstly, a return to the maternal presumption rule; secondly, the presumption that custody should be granted to the parent who has devoted the most time to the child; thirdly, that there should be some kind of compromise between the parents. Of course, there is nothing new here. The merits and detractions of each of these alternatives are something which judges, magistrates and court welfare officers regularly confront in their everyday decision-making processes. What is of interest is that Elster's concerns are part of a much wider scrutiny and reappraisal of the best interests principle. We take up these themes again in Chapter 8.

Common threads

These observers have, of course, approached the subject of court welfare in their own way according to their own disciplinary predilections and personal standpoints. It is, however arguable that each has sought to address issues of the 'function' of court welfare in furthering the needs of law, sometimes at the expense of recognising such issues as the role of the state, the nature of power relationships and the presence of conflict in societal relations. A number of criticisms have been made of functionalism (see, for example, Lee and Newby 1989; Rex 1976). We need not therefore rehearse the full weight of these arguments, but rather restrict ourselves to the core criticisms of functionalism and its relevance for an analysis of court welfare work.

The functionalist model of law, as with other sociological strains of functionalism, has as a common denominator a perception of a special form of social control that exerts pressure upon individuals towards conformity and stability rather than disintegration and conflict. If the 'system' – made up of the sum of its parts (organisms in King and Piper's formulation) – gets out of kilter, then pressures need to be imposed to restore stability and order once more. There is thus great importance placed on normative features of social organisation and the need to provide a shared set of values, meanings and beliefs.

There is much here that is worthy of attention. Norms shape the rules by which people live their lives and to this extent, at least, there is some kind of a shared belief system which serves to order and maintain purposive social relations. When court welfare officers, judges and solicitors interact with one another, they need to know the rules – those sets of 'patterned adaptations', in Goffman's terms (1971: 14) – which give shape to the nature of that interaction. They need to know the routines and rituals, when to speak and in what kind of ways. Similarly, when court welfare officers come into contact with parents it does not seem necessary every time to legitimise their role or to formulate anew the ground rules by which they are in a position to assess parental obligations towards children.

Yet we are sceptical that to concentrate merely on the way in which particular aspects of the socio-legal system 'function' cannot deal adequately with the complex problems that need to be addressed. One major problem involves the sense of amorphousness that the law embodies. As Feeley reminds us:

> law does not perform a unique social function, nor is it a singular form of social control. Hence it need not be singled out for separate theoretical concern. Legal rules are only one of a number of systems of rules, often overlapping and entwined, which shape people's aspirations and actions, and by which they are judged and resolve their troubles. In different cultures and at different times, law performs different functions and is entwined in different ways with other forms of social control and methods of dispute settlement. What may be regulated by

law at one time or in one setting may very well be controlled by informal peer group pressure, self-help, or other authoritative institutions in another. Law, unlike kinship, language or power, does not seem to be a fundamental phenomenon. Unlike these other phenomena law is not ubiquitous, and its nature varies; hence it does not capture a constant, identifiable activity, process, or set of relationships around which basic social theory is likely to be formed. (1978: 16)

Firstly this casts considerable doubt on the degree to which the law can be conceptualised in the way that proponents such as King and Piper (1990) suggest. For example, by claiming that the law 'thinks', King and Piper come very close to falling into the trap of reification by personifying the law as a social system. There is also considerable doubt about the sustainability of an analysis which conceives of the law as a closed, self-contained system in the organic sense (James 1992c). As Giddens points out: 'Social systems should be regarded as widely variable in terms of the degree of "systemness" they display and rarely have the sort of internal unity which may be found in physical and biological systems' (1984: 377).

Secondly, we are cautious about the degree of determinism that is latent in such an analysis – that is, the extent to which society is seen as having properties that impose themselves on individual actors. The stress that King and Piper place on the 'enslavement' of child welfare work is an illustration of this. In adopting this position, King and Piper are effectively saying that agents are acted upon independent of the motives, conscious or otherwise, of the actors themselves. The lack of sufficient attention to agency and to the ability of the actor to help shape social processes that is implied by such approaches is something that we shall take up later.

Thirdly, we acknowledge, although to varying degrees, the need to address issues relating to the integrative, consensual and normative aspects of social order. For example, as we shall go on to demonstrate, although there are clearly tensions, it is also apparent that many magistrates, judges and court welfare officers may share specific values and premises about certain issues, including the desirability of parents taking responsibility for their own decision-making and using the court only as a last resort when they are unable or unwilling to do so. In this regard, all actors may have shared or complementary aims governed by specific internalised norms. In the context of court welfare, many of these norms hinge upon the belief that parental conflict is, in general, detrimental to the welfare of the child. However, this is only part of a complex picture. As Rex points out:

> even if it is admitted that social integration is in part dependent upon value systems, there is also a substructure to social order which is determined by the struggle for power and the balance of power. Any complete account of a social system must describe the nature of this power. (1976: 111)

It is criticism of the functionalist approach that has led Turk to look for a better theoretical formulation. He argues strongly, and we think persuasively, that

> The conception of law as a set of resources, as power, is methodologically superior to the conception of law as conflict regulator in that the relationship between law and conflict is not assumed, but left open for investigation, and the distinction between legal and non-legal phenomena is grounded in empirical observations rather than normative assumptions. Instead of asking *how* law regulates conflict, the investigator is encouraged to ask *whether* law regulates or generates conflict, or in what ways and in what degree the use of legal power does both. (1978: 220; italics in original)

These general theoretical reflections raise a number of important specific questions about court welfare work: how can one begin to explain the complex matrix of relationships between the legal and other related structures and the multiple sets of social processes involved? What are the dominant ideologies which permeate this area of work? What inter-personal dynamics are involved within individual teams of court welfare officers and what impact do these have on practice, policy and socio-legal issues? Furthermore, what disciplinary and theoretical orientation is most appropriate for considering the organisational complexity of the court welfare task, in terms of both principle and practice? And how might the theoretical frameworks discussed above be developed further?

The next step

We suspect that, given the level of complexity of these issues, any answers to these questions can only ever be partial and that as with all social enquiry of this kind, they will lead not only to new insights but also to more questions. We propose to set about this task by exploring some of the central insights of social theory, drawing in particular upon the work of Anthony Giddens (1984, 1987) and Erving Goffman (1959, 1971, 1974), who have, in our view, developed some of the most valuable and original perspectives and theoretical frameworks.

Giddens

As Giddens points out, structuration theory is, in essence, an elaboration of Marx's comment that humans make history, but not in circumstances of their own choosing (1984: xxi). From this starting point, Giddens offers us a rich and complex theoretical system containing a number of diverse strands. Broadly, the theory stresses that there is a need to move beyond those approaches which stress only grand structure and those which concern themselves largely with the minutiae of action. Of particular importance in this analysis is the distinction that Giddens makes between 'structure' and 'system'. Structure, for Giddens, should not be conceived of as a skeleton or a framework of girders. Rather, structure should be conceptualised as those sets of rules and resources which give 'shape' to social and organisational encounters and behaviours and which are routinised, reproduced and stabilised over time. Giddens does not specifically relate law to his analysis, though it is easy to see that the emphasis on rules in particular indicates the relevance of his theory to the judicial realm and thus to some key areas of family law in general, and court welfare work in particular.

Meanwhile, 'system' refers to the reproduced relations between actors (judges, court welfare officers, legal representatives) or collectivities (the bar, the probation service), organised as regular social practices spanning time and space. 'Structure' does not in any crude sense 'determine' action, nor is it 'external' to individuals in the way that King and Piper seem to suggest. On the contrary, actors are knowledgeable agents who are free and have the ability, within certain constraints, to act upon those rules and resources. Structure and action are therefore inextricably interwoven into the fabric of everyday life in a variety of subtle ways. Thus:

> Crucial to the idea of structuration is the theorem of the duality of structure. . . . The constitution of agents and structures are not two independently given sets of phenomena, a dualism, but represent a

duality. According to the notion of the duality of structure, the structural properties are both the medium and outcome of the practices they recursively organize. . . . Structure is not to be equated with constraint but is always both constraining and enabling. (1984: 25)

As we shall go on to argue, especially in relation to issues of power, the stress on the fact that structure simultaneously constrains and enables is of central significance to enhancing our understanding of the sets of processes involved in court welfare work. We contend that this ensemble of concepts offers a rich array of perspectives from which to analyse much of the court welfare practice and the sets of influences that we have described in earlier chapters. Most notably, the degree of integration between the legal system, the court welfare service and parents depends not so much, we argue, on the law enslaving the influence of court welfare or parental interests in King and Piper's terms, but rather on the outcomes of negotiations which Giddens calls the 'dialectic of control', in which: 'all forms of dependence offer some resources whereby those who are subordinate can influence the activities of their superiors' (1984: 16).

Thus the basic contention here is that participants in the system, such as court welfare officers, judges and parents, are not acted upon in any crude deterministic sense, but rather participate in exchanges which are purposeful and rendered mutually intelligible by them as knowledgeable agents.

Goffman

The need also to locate institutionalised practices within the context of everyday action led us to consider the work of Goffman. There are two main strands to Goffman's work: the first is concerned with his thesis that a variety of institutions share a number of common features; the second is more concerned with concepts such as self, role, social encounters and routines. It is Goffman's interest in the nature and form of day-to-day interaction which is of relevance here. In particular, we are interested in Goffman's concern with how encounters are formed and re-formed in the context of daily life.

According to Goffman, daily life consists by the opening and closing of encounters in a variety of social settings or locales. Life therefore consists of a seriality of separate encounters which are relatively self-contained, or bracketed out. These encounters happen in situated places – in court rooms, in court welfare offices, in people's homes –

and they become routinised over time. However, these routines do not just occur by themselves. Rather, encounters are organised in and through the medium of the 'practical consciousness' of actors (to return to Giddens) – what actors know intuitively about their social conditions and ways of going about interacting with others. They thus draw on the rules and resources that these systems provide but, within certain constraints, act upon them in specific but not necessarily the same ways. As we have seen, for certain court welfare officers this will mean adopting a formal and legalistic approach with an orientation towards the courts, due process and legal accountability. In contrast, others show very little interest in legal proceedings and what are perceived as being its attendant trappings.

In our view, these theoretical orientations offer considerable scope for the interpretation of empirical data concerning the socio-legal processes which constitute the context in which court welfare officers work. For example, we suggest that the developments in court welfare work that we have described in earlier chapters did not occur because of time-honoured structures which in some sense determine particular courses of action. Nor for that matter can they be put down to immutable ideologies or norms which transcend both time and space. Rather, as Rex reminds us, key actors may pursue random ends or may be in conflict with one another over ends. If we transpose this to the court welfare discourse, we find that the behaviour of court welfare staff, judges and parents towards one another 'may not be determined by shared norms but by the success which each has in compelling the other to act in accordance with his interests. Power then becomes a crucial variable in the study of social systems' (Rex 1976: 112).

The significance of power

Power is generally conceived of and referred to in everyday terms as the ability to influence. It conjures up thoughts of conflict and in this sense cannot easily be separated from the potential to repress. Any extended discussion of power perhaps inevitably means addressing some of the difficult terrain that has been mapped out for us in the writings of Michel Foucault. For Foucault (1977, 1980) power permeates all areas of social existence and is not just confined to the overtly political. He writes:

in thinking of the mechanisms of power, I am thinking rather of its capillary forms of existence, the point where power reaches into the very grain of individuals, touches their bodies, and inserts itself into their actions and attitudes, their discourses, learning processes and everyday lives. (Foucault 1980: 39, quoted in Garland 1990: 138)

Central to the main thrust of his argument is the view that power is intrinsically related to and dependent upon knowledge that can be brought to bear in social situations. The strength of Foucault's writings lies in their capacity to sensitise us to some general aspects of the way power can be utilised, its pervasiveness and its capacity to create conformity and obedience. In tandem with Cohen (1985), Foucault alerts us to the ways that in modern times surveillance and coercion have steadily increased across the whole vista of society. On the other hand, the level of abstraction that is inherent in Foucault's writings makes it difficult to translate generalities into concrete situations and to differentiate between the various power relations and differential motivations of those wielding power. In this regard, Garland argues that Foucault's work often:

appears as a kind of empty structure, stripped of any agents, interests, or grounding, reduced to a bare technological scaffolding. . . . In the end, power is a kind of total confinement which envelops the individual, moulding the body and soul into patterns of conformity. Power is at once socialization and social control. It constructs the individual as a subject, but it is always an individual who is 'subjected' or subjugated in the same process. (1990: 170–1)

These are telling comments which are important for three main reasons. Firstly, they chime well with the centrality of the indivisibility of structure and action encapsulated in the concept of the duality of structure discussed above. Secondly, Garland's comments underwrite and further illuminate the importance of the two-way character of the distributive aspect of power. Thus no individual or institution has total power but rather those people who are often in a subservient position can bring some kind of influence, sometimes quite substantial, to bear. Rejecting both mechanistic and pejorative conceptions and definitions of power, Giddens argues that:

Power is not necessarily linked with conflict in the sense of either division of interest or active struggle, and power is not inherently oppressive. . . . Power is the capacity to achieve outcomes; whether or not these are connected to purely sectional interests is not germane to its definition. Power is not, as such, an obstacle to freedom or emancipation but is their very medium – although it would be foolish, of course, to ignore its constraining properties. (1984: 257)

Thirdly, these observations serve to remind us that any analysis of the nature of power needs to be located within specific contexts and settings. Once we move away from amorphous concepts, the more interesting questions then become: what is the nature of the power being used in this specific case in these particular circumstances? What form does it take and how is it being exercised? And what are the values and philosophies underpinning particular forms of power relationships?

Frameworks for power

We contend that three analytical frames of reference or meaning are needed within which such an analysis needs to take place: the general process of divorce (legal, administrative and interpersonal); the framework of the judicial system within which they also work; and the organisational framework within which court welfare officers operate. These frameworks were used in our analysis of the process of preparing welfare reports in Chapter 5 and therefore we do not propose to deal with each of these in turn, but rather to explore the potential interplay between each of them.

Such an approach necessitates an understanding not only of the social meanings and symbolism that exists between key actors but also an appreciation of the importance of locale and the way that particular activities are organised. Goffman (1974) argues that activities will be perceived by participants in terms of the rules or premises of a primary framework, either natural or social, and that such frameworks are not merely a matter of perception but also correspond in some sense to the way in which that activity is organised. These organisational premises he terms 'the frame of activity', although, as Burns (1992: 248) points out, Goffman gives no very clear definition of what he means by the term 'frame'. What can be discerned, however, is that frames provide those contexts of meaning which allow people to know what is going on, what to expect and the depth of their involvement.

One such frame of activity is the courtroom. What are parents who appear before the court to make of it all? The language used is frequently arcane and esoteric. It is thus rendered meaningful only to the legal participants. Informal alliances abound between key actors suggest a finely tuned hierarchical power structure. Within this frame, however, it is clearly judges and magistrates who are in the strongest position to dictate various terms of reference relating not only to the kinds of information which they consider to be of importance, but also arguably even the processes and methods by which it is obtained. Only the judiciary and the magistracy are accorded the right to interrupt and channel discussions in particular directions. In this sense, they have institutionalised and stable social identities conferred on them, emanating from the nature of the power that they are able to exert and backed up by the sanctions and prerogatives that they are able to enforce.

Equally clearly, however, this power is not untramelled. It is intrinsically linked to the temporal and spatial elements associated with the court as a locale. Meanwhile the kind of interactions that will occur in other locales such as court welfare offices or parental homes will be of a different kind of order. As we have seen, the framing of the interaction between welfare officers and parents and children in terms of the locale, particularly in offices with one-way screens, might be argued to have as much to do with maintaining the balance of power as it does to do with any guiding principles of philosophy or meeting what are perceived to be clients' needs.

A number of these interactions can be said to occur subterraneously. Thus, for example, Goffman (1974) refers to the relevance of 'out-of frame' activities, such as the concealment of some communications from other actors, which relate to the framing of activities themselves. Of particular interest here is Goffman's notion of 'paternal construction', whereby activities which are felt to be in the others' best interests but which they might reject, at least initially, if they discovered what was really happening, are fabricated, constructed or presented in a way which is calculated to give comfort and render the other person tractable. Such concealment is an element in welfare investigations, the highest levels being evident in office-based systemic work where 'out-of-frame' activities and communications between co-workers such as pre-case consultations, 'time-out' during family meetings, the use of one-way screens with telephone interventions and post-meeting debriefings are many and manifest.

For all the talk of empowerment, then, parents know, to greater and lesser degrees, that part of the court welfare officer's role is as an agent of the court. There are thus expectations on both sides as to the nature of the interaction and the agenda that is to be discussed. Moreover, as Dingwall and Eekelaar assert in their discussion of mediation, power exists by virtue of the sorts of occasion that mediation produces. Better, they argue: 'to discuss its regulation than to engage in fruitless attempts to wish it away' (1988: 173).

Yet, perhaps paradoxically, the real power, in terms of being able to determine children's best interests (and acknowledged in practice if not in principle by both court welfare officers and the judiciary alike), clearly lies with the parents themselves. Encounters with the court, with legal representatives or court welfare officers are time-limited and, in Goffman's terms, fade away. Parents' relationships with their children have the potential to be long-lasting, however. Thus the degree of power which courts or court welfare officers possess with which to influence matters might be of marginal significance in the long term, and even in the short term in those cases where parents are conscious of their own power as actors.

Goffman's analytical framework serves to highlight the fact that when in role, court welfare officers, judges, lawyers and parents may well have different 'frames of activity' in relation to their understanding of the separation experience, drawing upon different rules, premises and resources in terms of organising these. The frames for judges and lawyers will be predominantly drawn from the system of legal rules, values, procedures and processes of which they are a part. For the court welfare officer, the frame of activity is determined by their social work and methodological orientation, their degree of identification with the judicial frame, and the organisational context in which their practice is located. For parents, it is likely to be drawn from their perceptions of the separation process, from the legal system of divorce and from the information given to them by others, such as their lawyers, in connection with this. It is also likely to be influenced by more broadly based socially constructed notions of good parenting and child welfare, as well as interpretations of what is implied by terms such as 'welfare officer' and 'welfare report'. 'Given', writes Goffman, 'their understanding of what it is that is going on, individuals fit their actions to this understanding and ordinarily find that the ongoing world supports this fitting' (1974: 247).

The question thus emerges as to what happens if the encounter with the welfare officer fails to support this fitting – if they are not provided with the confirmation of a framed situation – for example if they anticipate an investigation of family *facts* and experience an investigation of family *process*. Goffman writes:

> It is perfectly possible for individuals . . . to be in doubt about what it is that is going on . . . the special doubt that can arise over the definition of the situation. . . . And insofar as the individual is moved to engage in action of some kind – a very usual possibility – the ambiguity will be translated into felt uncertainty and hesitancy. (1974: 302)

Goffman also argues that framed activities are geared to the continuing world by the person–role formula: 'The nature of a particular frame will, of course, be linked to the nature of the person–role formula it sustains. One can never expect complete freedom between individual and role and never complete constraint' (1974: 269). These reflections are relevant in that they offer an analytic framework that goes beyond the empirical generalisations offered by Murch and Davis and overcomes the weaknesses inherent in King and Piper's work. In particular, we feel that they provide a framework within which to examine the differential behaviours and values of judges, lawyers and court welfare officers to which we have drawn attention in previous chapters. They also confirm, in our view, the importance of examining the specific conditions under which decision-making processes occur, and how these processes may be shaped by such phenomena as differential power relationships, occupational specialisation, knowledge, established procedures and values. In the next chapter we thus address these concerns in more depth, seeking answers to questions such as: how can variations of practice within the same task be accounted for? What factors are involved in forging policies? What are the dynamics of teams and what impact do these have on practice, policy and organisational issues? And how is change brought about?

8
Understanding practice

It is time to begin to draw a few threads together. In the first part of this book we delineated the history of divorce and the context in which court welfare practice has developed. In the second, we mapped out the key features of practice revealed by our research. In this section we have been concerned to look at some of the ways in which social theory can be used to illuminate the complex processes that give shape and meaning to the court welfare task. In this chapter and the next, therefore, we wish to develop some of these themes further by considering how we might best make intelligible the way these disparate issues affect practice. In particular, we shall consider the ways in which welfare officers have responded to other frames of reference. In this respect we shall argue that as a result of contextual pressures, approaches to practice are beginning to cohere in some key respects in spite of their different theoretical roots.

The court welfare task

Ostensibly the court welfare task can easily be described. Faced with a parental dispute over their children, the court asks a welfare officer to prepare a report on its behalf which will enable the judge or magistrates to reach a decision about how disputes may be settled and the best interests of the child met. Yet there is no universal formula or agreed set of definitions which welfare officers can apply to this task. Rather there is a series of implicit expectations that the welfare officer will undertake particular enquiries, make a professional assessment and report the results of these enquiries to the court. There is thus infinite scope for interpreting not only the kind of information upon which the decision can be based, but also the process by which this information is gathered. As we have demonstrated, practice varies on a number of dimensions both within and between areas depending upon favoured practice orientations and the kind of ideological lens through which key actors perceive the task. Some of these differences can be located in applying divergent philosophies towards the task based on differing views of what the aims and objectives should be, and how effective particular strategies are in relation to achieving those objectives.

Since the introduction of the Children Act 1989, a series of benchmarks in the form of 'the checklist' have been introduced as an aid to the process of preparing a welfare report. In theory this should bring a degree of consistency to the task. But whatever the merits of the checklist, ascertaining the best interests of children cannot be reduced to restrictive definitions, or be ascertained by prescribed interventions, no matter how technically refined and theoretically sound they may appear to be. Determining the best interests of children will thus remain essentially problematic, not least because the debate between whether legal or welfare norms ought to prevail in court welfare work remains largely unresolved.

Skills, theory and knowledge

Given the central emphasis that we have placed upon key actors as knowledgeable and rational agents, it seem sensible to examine the theories, areas of knowledge and skills that enable court welfare officers to work effectively. Values, skills, knowledge and theoretical frameworks are, of course, intrinsically bound up with one another. Perhaps unsurprisingly, welfare officers frequently combined, confused or conflated these concepts, using one synonomously with another.

Skills
Our data suggests that most welfare officers can agree about certain 'core' skills. These cluster around such issues as:

- Eliciting information in a neutral and non-threatening way.
- Gaining the confidence and trust of parents.
- Communicating with children.
- Writing succinct and cogently argued reports.
- Presenting oneself well in court.

There were, however, also a number of divergent points of view about the range of other skills needed. For example, welfare officers in our study were equally divided about whether the skills needed to be a good probation officer were those that were also needed to be a good court welfare officer. Many (including most senior managers) regarded the two sets of skills as complementary:

> I think they are the skills you need as a probation officer. [. . .] It comes back to what you think your task is. [. . .] If you see the job as purely gathering information, then that demands that you need to appear to be seen as a nice person, to listen and get people's trust and that you have a basic level of social work and interviewing skills. If you see it as helping people to see how their behaviour is contributing to the problems [. . .] then I guess you're into a different level of social-work skills. But I see that as applying in criminal work as well. (Area C)

For others, although for different reasons, the opposite was true:

> I think that there are skills which you develop in court welfare which have little to do with social work. [. . .] A large part of court welfare work is drawing a line; looking at now and the future, particularly in terms of conciliation. Those are skills more in keeping with a negotiator. (Area C)

Welfare officers also placed differing degrees of emphasis upon other skills depending upon specific facets of a welfare officer's own practice orientation. For example, those officers who were primarily interested in the gathering of information stressed the need for skills in assessing parents' ability to parent and in liaising with other agencies. On the other hand, those welfare officers who were more interested in conflict resolution tended to stress the need for welfare officers to be skilled in group work and their ability to work within the fraught situations that may arise during joint meetings. Other welfare officers laid stress on the ability to understand the nature of the dispute by paying close attention to the family dynamics. For this latter group the skill lay in communicating this understanding to the parents and the court in meaningful and strategic ways.

Theory and knowledge

Welfare officers also differed in terms of the areas of knowledge and range of theoretical frameworks that they considered to be important.

Some officers had difficulty in identifying with any precision the kind of knowledge that they thought welfare officers needed to possess. What was particularly striking was that only one officer made reference to legal knowledge and the need for a solid grounding in the legislative frameworks of court welfare work. A number of welfare officers likened the process of divorce to that experienced during and after bereavement (see Kübler-Ross 1970; Parkes 1972); others said that court welfare work is just a matter of using common sense. Yet others answered that they did not apply a specific theory.

> I don't have a set theory that I apply to family breakdown or matters relating to children. I think I use some family therapy, but I think there's really quite a lot of behaviourist in me. I think that a large part of what we do in civil work is about crisis intervention. (Area C)

> I am not a great theorist. [...] I find myself quoting things like bits of research that I've read about kids and divorce and stuff like that. A certain understanding of the divorce process, how it feels and what the outcomes might be. I'm not one of these who has a pet theory. (Area D)

Other officers stressed the need for eclecticism and the need for:

> A bag of theories and knowledge – psychology, family therapy, knowledge of child development, counselling, psychotherapy, probably a few old casework theories. There is no body of knowledge which defines what we've got to know. (Area C)

In contrast, what was particularly striking was the pervasive influence of family therapy. However, it should be noted that welfare officers repeatedly stressed that whereas they found many of the techniques of family therapy helpful to their practice, they also argued that the theory was frequently not applicable or appropriate for court welfare work. Moreover, welfare officers were often unsure of some of the finer points of the theory. In this regard, this officer spoke for many in saying that:

> I have found ideas from family therapy useful: about how you structure meetings, hypotheses, circular questioning, geneograms and all that kind of stuff. [...] It's not really theoretical, they're techniques. [...] I wouldn't claim to understand it properly. I've not sat down and mastered the theory. I've just picked out bits and applied them. (Area D)

Meanwhile for this black welfare officer the theoretical frameworks that inform and guide practice were intrinsically problematic:

> Theories have always been a problem for me because most of the theories that are around do not always fit in a multi-cultural society. Most of them are white theories based on white values and so they don't always fit what is in front of me. So I don't find it easy to say to you that I use this theory or that theory. We are using the Milan method of systemic work. That allows me to be flexible. Beyond that I can't say 'yes' or 'no'. I certainly draw upon my culture and experience and that is very wide. (Area E)

We did not ask judges directly about the kind of skills and areas of knowledge that welfare officers should possess and display. We did, however, ask them whether they considered court welfare officers to be 'experts' (see James *et al.* 1992). In general, judges regarded the source of court welfare officers' expertise as lying in their life experience, particularly in relation to their work with offenders and the potential to prevent future family breakdown and delinquency, rather than any intrinsic knowledge of child care and child development. Such views are stongly reminiscent of the rationale which informed the early development of court welfare work (see Chapter 1).

As we have highlighted in Chapter 6, senior managers saw their role in terms of providing the infrastructure to facilitate good practice rather than prescribing it. Therefore, we did not ask senior managers to address the issue of the kinds of knowledge and theroetical frameworks that main grade staff needed in any direct way. However this is not to say that senior managers do not reflect upon their central relevance for practice, policy and other organisational issues. As the following observation by an ACPO makes clear, having a coherent theoretical framework and cogent body of knowledge to draw upon is clearly in many ways desirable. At the same time, it can have its drawbacks:

> It is unusual in social work to have a group of workers who have the level of agreement and commitment to use theoretical models in practice that they have here. [. . .] I've seen whole teams committed to systems and community-based approaches, but those approaches by their nature are pragmatic. They don't have the theoretical consistency and exclusiveness that the family-therapy model has achieved in civil work. Part of

what staff come for is to acquire a technical expertise. There is an area in social work where people move into developing technical expertise in spite of political pressures. That is what worries me about it. It seems very apolitical; a refusal to accept the context in which all this is happening and the concerns of other people having an equal legitimacy. Having a technical expertise is a way of escaping some of the moral dilemmas of social work.

Practice, power and legitimacy

This critical appraisal raises a number of important issues. At one level, it draws attention to the need that welfare officers have for an enduring and cogent practice framework with which to order their world and to make it meaningful. At another level, reference to the moral obligations and duties that are incumbent upon court welfare officers also remind us that practitioners should be wary of adopting highly formalistic or technical ways of working which may run counter to other social-work values or ignore wider contextual concerns.

In this respect, reference to legitimacy requires us to think deeply about a number of issues. In its wider sense the concept of legitimacy connotes the quest for validation of a set of given aims and objectives by moral means. Bound up in the term is an understanding of the codification of rules or laws which are rational and which can be shared by others. The struggle for legitimation is closely linked with issues of power and authority. Those who are powerful seek to establish themselves in the eyes of those who are subordinate to them without undue coercion. One way of achieving this is by means intimating that they have the authority to behave in ways which might elicit co-operation. At the same time, it is worth noting that there are dangers in accepting uncritically the notion that parents accept unquestioningly the values and norms which might underpin a particular practice orientation. As Held points out:

> According to some political and social analysts . . . the very fact that citizens comply with rules or laws means that the polity or political institutions are accepted, i.e. legitimated. But the problem with this conception of legitimacy . . . is that it does not take into account the different possible bases for obeying a command, complying with a rule, or agreeing or consenting to something. (1987:238)

In this regard, one example of an area of practice that received much criticism was the use of one-way screens. Such criticism generally took two forms. First, many practitioners in areas other than Area E (and indeed many from other offices in Area E) argued that one-way screens contribute to a dehumanising form of practice. The second concern revolved around issues regarding the potentialities for misuse of power. Practitioners from the office in Area E who used one-way screens laid much stress on parents giving full and informed consent prior to its use. However, some welfare officers from within this office, and a number of welfare officers from the other areas expressed doubt that consent can be freely given in the circumstances in which parents find themselves (see Chapter 5). The reasons for this are not hard to understand. Not only have they been asked by the court to attend such an interview, but they also have to be seen to be creating a good impression. It can also be argued that parents have a number of preoccupations when they first arrive and are not thus in a position or the frame of mind to make an informed decision. On both counts, therefore, parents can be said to be in a vulnerable position.

Clearly, much of this is of general relevance for court welfare practice inasmuch as one can see the way in which these abstract ideas are played out in the various frames of reference that we have alluded to in the previous chapter. More specifically, however, focusing on legitimacy returns us to some of the questions about the remit under which court welfare officers operate. Where does the court welfare officer's allegiance lie? To whom is he or she ultimately accountable? To what extent should welfare officers be free to frame their own terms of reference? It also raises interesting questions about the connections between rights, values, obligations and goals – is it the case that the ends justify the means?

However, although the robust assertions of the ACPO quoted above are both insightful and persuasive, we feel that an element of qualification is needed. It must be remembered that court welfare practice in Area E, for example, has been able to lay claim to a well-established and unbroken ethos of practice that has not occurred in other counties and the same observation could not have been made in Areas A and C, for example. This reminds us of the central importance of time and how practice can evolve at different rates, depending upon various contingencies and contextual pressures. In addition, it brings us face-to-face with the transformative capacity for change that can be invoked when the power that judges and senior managers possess is exercised.

Aims and objectives

As we have demonstrated, many of the differences of practice that we encountered can be located in divergent views about the philosophical and theoretical issues that ought to underpin court welfare work, and the kind of knowledge and practical skills that welfare officers need to function effectively. However, these factors cannot be disembodied from the aims, objectives and values that should inform the provision of a court welfare service, and the means by which they can best be realised. What, then, are these aims and objectives and what are the values that underpin them?

As we have shown, welfare officers in our study areas differed in the way they went about their duties. Differences were found in whether the parents were seen separately or jointly, or a combination of both; the order in which parents and children were interviewed; the setting in which parents and children were seen; and whether the children were present or not. Other significant differences of opinion revolved around issues of when, where and how the children were seen and how officers obtained information from children.

What is apparent is that some of the court welfare officers we interviewed and observed in their contacts with parents and children believed that their remit was very clearly defined by the court. In this sense, aims and objectives cannot be separated from how the court welfare task is defined in relation to legal processes and the role that is ascribed to and adopted by the welfare officer in this context. Some welfare officers clearly gave priority to establishing the 'facts' that could be deduced from their enquiries, supported by evidence from other agencies and welfare professionals:

> To investigate thoroughly the situation that exists and to look at what each party has to offer the child or children. To look at all the surrounding bits – the child's health, whether there are any allegations of any description which need following up. To get a fairly clear picture of what is going on now and what has been going on in the past which has led to the present situation. (Area A)

> The ultimate aim is to provide information for the court to enable them to resolve the difficulty. Everything that is done is geared to that end. It is a matter of interviewing all the people who seem to be significant in the life of the children... and trying to draw some picture as to how they influence or affect the environment in which the child lives or is going to live. (Area C)

Conversely, other officers saw their primary aim as the resolution of conflict by facilitating agreement.

> A starting point for every report is sitting down with the parents and saying to them 'if we can find a solution [. . .] that will be reported to the court. If we can't do that, then [. . .] I will have to do an investigative report.' [. . .] I will contact the school, doctor, and determine how and when I'm going to see the children. (Area B)

Meanwhile, other officers had equivocal views about the objective of reaching agreements. For them, the issue was not so much about the awkwardness inherent in attempting to reconcile competing paradigms, but rather about working with families and children in ways which will enable parents and children to have greater understanding of the underlying reasons for the dispute:

> We can either be called report writers where our brief is just to write a report. I do not see my role as that. I see myself as someone who is also helping and nurturing parents through the process to help them look at their children's needs. (Area B)

Such a view, in part, hinges on the belief that welfare officers should be realistic about what they can achieve. Whereas the ideal may be to resolve the conflict, some welfare officers argued that in practice very often little can be done about the kind of deeply entrenched situations which characterise court welfare work. Their hope was that parents could learn from their involvement with the court welfare service and that eventually they would be able to make informed decisions about their children without reference to the legal system. This orientation, with its emphasis on self-determination, thus adds an *aspirational* dimension to the task as it has customarily been defined and developed.

> My first aim is to see whether there is scope for agreement. If that is not possible then to prepare a report which gives the best information to those people who will make the decision and to do it in such a way that it can be a constructive experience for everyone involved, hoping that even if they don't get to an agreement that they will have been encouraged to think about the way ahead. (Area E)

My primary aim is to get the parents, or the families, to come to see what is, in the long term, the best thing for the children. Often that is not what either of them want. It is often getting them to hear and see what their children hear. (Area E)

These orientations cannot thus be separated from some of the broader issues relating to social-work values. Timms refers to the evolution of two general approaches to social work. They are:

> that which concerns any imperative governing social work as concern with results, and that which sees the substantive effort of social work revolving around ideas of the morally 'good' social worker and of 'good' social work judged according to moral criteria. Social work, in the first perspective, is good only if it effects some externally validated result; in the second perspective, the results of social work are seen as a moral good achieved within the relationship of social worker and client.
> (1983: 7)

We contend that Timms's distinction is not as sharp in practice as it is in theory. Nevertheless, we feel that his observations are of import to understanding court welfare practice. As we have pointed out in Chapter 2, concern with 'results' is increasingly a feature of practice. Success or otherwise is frequently measured in terms of the number of agreements that are made either during the process of preparing a report, or at the court door once the report has been submitted. But restricting measurements of effectiveness to this narrow criterion is problematic for a variety of reasons (Hay et al. 1992). However, issues relating to the *moral* worth of social work revolve in part around the central social-work values of respect for persons, the ideal of promoting self-determination and the aim of helping people to cope with distressing personal problems by offering insight, succour and support. It is clear that such concerns occupy a central place in welfare officers' thinking. At the same time, many stressed that maintaining a neutral stance and striving to empower parents cannot be tenable in any absolute form. In this regard, welfare officers frequently added the *caveat* that they must relinquish impartiality whenever there is an allegation or question of child abuse. Thus, issues relating to parental responsibility, the welfare officer's values, beliefs and authority and state power interact in an infinitely complex way.

Clearly, then, court welfare as it is presently constituted cannot be firmly located in any coherent and enduring framework. Yet, perhaps paradoxically, despite the various ambiguities and antimonies, there is a wealth of evidence to suggest that practice is becoming more homogeneous in a number of key respects. With few exceptions, welfare officers in all of the areas we studied routinely combined the information-gathering task traditionally associated with the preparation of a welfare report with a focus on the nature of the dispute and any potential for its resolution. Thus:

> The primary task is the investigation because that is what the court expects me to do, and orders me to do. To investigate and provide a report – they sometimes word it almost like that, and that's what I'm about. [At the same time, this does not preclude the option that] in the process of investigating we can reduce the conflict by bringing the parties together then as far as I am concerned that's right and proper. (Area C)

> I have got two rather different aims of conciliation and enquiry in mind. Can you get them together with a little bit of help and effort to come to an agreement, or do you see, in fact, that they are not going to do that? [. . .] Therefore it's more an enquiry mode, a digging under stones which may make them farther apart because you've got to get this stuff out and explore it. [. . .] There are two possible modes. Can you get them to agree? But at the same time you never take your welfare hat off all-together. (Area E)

It is important to note, however, that some welfare officers felt that any attempt to reconcile the two aims was untenable:

> I don't think you can say to people that they are *your* children and *you've* got to be responsible and then go off and investigate all sorts of things and put in totally unrelated information to a court. And then to say that they should be responsible, and this information suggests this should happen, is, I think a contradiction in terms. Although it is very understandable why we do it. (Area D)

The point that we wish to make is that contrary to conventional wisdom, an increasing number of welfare officers do not see information-gathering and settlement-seeking as necessarily being mutually exclusive or contradictory tasks. Nor for that matter are they necessarily considered as being a sufficient end in themselves. On the contrary, a *modus vivendi* has emerged whereby the two features of practice coexist and intermingle in a variety of ways. The questions raised are thus not which side of the same coin should be prioritised, or whether the twin strategies are compatible but whether joint meetings are an appropriate way of gaining information?; or can practice which focuses upon seeing parents individually best facilitate agreements? or what kind of information is deemed appropriate and/or required and who defines this?

Practice is thus shaped by a number of influences, constraints and processes. As we sought to portray in Chapter 7, such processes do not happen by accident or occur randomly. Nor are they determined in any crude sense by structural pressures. Rather, they emerge and are shaped by the complex interaction between the motivation of welfare officers and other key actors and the contextual circumstances and structures within which such motivations are played out. Court welfare practice may thus best be understood as a purposeful activity in which welfare officers and judges are autonomous within certain constraints to give priority to particular aspects of the work, but not to the exclusion of all others. Given the continual reflexivity that this engenders, practice can never remain static. Court welfare officers and judges have continuously to attempt to resolve the dilemmas that arise out of the tensions inherent in straddling the legal and social frameworks that permeate court welfare work.

Some emerging themes

This fluidity is fully illustrated by this officer, albeit from a particular theoretical standpoint:

> I suppose the systemic stuff has been enormously influential. But I think we are in a slightly post-systemic phase in the sense that we are no longer in the first flush, wholesale application. We are now having to hold on to the good parts, but it is a modified system. We are seeing that we have got to integrate it more with an enquiry mode and with the emphasis upon seeing children and giving them a fair hearing. In some ways the systemic mode has given us a rather false idea that the real

macho way was to have everybody together all the time, and that you work best that way. [. . .] Now we no longer think that this is so. It has taken us a while to see that. (Area E)

But this is only part of a much larger picture. As noted in earlier chapters, much of the court welfare discourse has revolved around issues of joint meetings and the extent that these are used to fulfil therapeutic purposes. However, this debate has frequently been conducted without an adequate knowledge of practice in the areas criticised for offering therapy. As a result, much knowledge of practice in other areas is ill informed. Our data suggest, for example, that in many respects the virulent critique of therapy-oriented approaches is overstated. Welfare officers in all areas frequently referred to family therapy as being a cogent theoretical framework which gave both shape and meaning to their work. Furthermore, they argued that many family therapy techniques (though by no means all) were well-suited to court welfare work. Notwithstanding this, many stressed that their primary aim was aiding the parents and the court to resolve the dispute rather than counselling parents and children. Therapeutic spin-offs were thus something to be *hoped* for rather than *striven* for. Moreover, because of the many tensions, ambiguities and ambivalences regarding the statutory responsibilities of court welfare officers highlighted throughout this book, we doubt whether any fully fledged 'therapeutic model' ever existed for very long even in those areas that pioneered some of the original thinking about therapeutic potentialities.

Such criticisms also need to be viewed in the context of welfare officers being first and foremost social workers who are involved in an area of acute personal distress. Given, therefore, the traumatic situations with which welfare officers have to engage, it is perhaps surprising, if not ironic, to find welfare officers being critical of colleagues for offering, in passing, some therapeutic assistance to parents with their problems. However, it should also be remembered that offering support for people undergoing the trauma of divorce is not the sole preserve of those welfare officers who are more overtly interested in family therapy.

Prominent though these issues remain, in many ways this debate is already beginning to give way to more pressing concerns. To the forefront of these are issues of gender and, to varying degrees, race, reflecting changes in the probation discourse more generally:

> The area in which [practice] has changed is that there is much less intensity about therapeutic goals. So that from my point of view as a worker, I have much less expectation about the degree of change that can be achieved with families. The other significant change in practice has been that initially issues were about the theoretical model of working. Over the years, it has been much more about issues of race and gender. As a result changes of practice have taken place. In relation to gender, various gender-monitoring exercises have been done regarding content of reports and in relation to family interviews. Male members of the team no longer work together unless there is an absolute need to. In relation to race, the whole development of cultural consultants and having a working relationship with cultural consultants rather than a worker-interpreter relationship has been an outcome of those particular areas of practice. (SCWO, Area E)

In addition, close attention has also been paid to the way that issues of gender and race intersect with issues of differential power relations. Of course, such concerns are part of a much wider inter-disciplinary discourse. However, within court welfare practice they frequently find expression in an acute form. Smart and Sevenhuijsen argue that:

> the question of custody and child welfare in the 1970s and the 1980s has developed largely outside a feminist informed framework and has become the terrain of the social work profession, the conciliators, and legal and social policy makers. It is not that the women's movement has had nothing to say on these vital issues, nor that the movement is unconcerned with the welfare of children; rather it is that recent political debates on child custody have been successful in disregarding areas which seem to give voice to women's concerns. (1989: xvi)

Notwithstanding this, a number of socio-legal theorists and practitioners are currently seeking to to redress this imbalance. This is not to say that this discourse is proceeding in unitary fashion. Views on how the various ambiguities, dilemmas and tensions within this discourse may be best resolved thus vary greatly. Sandberg (1989) argues that a primary caretaker preference that we referred to earlier in relation to Elster's work should replace the present best-interest principle and that such a shift enables the past to be taken into consideration while at the same time taking account of parents' needs. Thèry (1989) also attacks the best-interests principle but makes the point that any opposition to the principle leads into the double-bind situation of appearing not to have the best interests of the child in mind. Brophy's (1989) concern is not so much with competing rights but with the fact that no amount of emphasis on joint parenting will alter the multitudinous aspects of inequality that exist between men and women in the way they care for children on a day-to-day basis. Similarly, Holtrust and her colleagues assert that the movement to enshrine fathers' rights that the Netherlands is experiencing (which has, of course, its parallels in England and Wales) systematically works against women's interests. 'The rhetoric of the human rights argument becomes so powerful that other considerations on desirable arrangements in the sphere of child-rearing and parenthood are becoming illegitimate and a "real" public debate becomes impossible' (1989:75).

They argue that child-custody issues should be informed by the 'power approach' that the women's movement has brought to political debates. By this they mean that child-custody issues should not be limited to the best-interests principle or a narrow discussion of rights but viewed from a wider perspective which takes into account the broader power relations between men and women. As they put it:

> A power approach questions the role of law in enforcing day-to-day relations and contacts, and debates the meaning of 'rights' in this context. It asks for a discussion of the reasons and motives for a strong state intervention in this field, and looks for problems that are solved or created by the proposed reforms, especially the effects for women. (1989: 52)

What is of importance in considering these reflections is that many of these conceptual disagreements about how to proceed also find their parallel in court welfare practice:

> What really worries me [about the joint meeting approach] is the issue of power and the risks to women and the number of cases where men have been violent. (Area C)

> We wrote to a couple where there had been allegations of violence – address not to be disclosed and so on. She was nervous about coming in and I reassured her, as we always do, that there would be separate waiting rooms, that they wouldn't be alone together and that she would be able to leave the office separately. She agreed to come. On the day of the interview [. . .] her husband tried to strangle her. [. . .] She said he

was dangerous. I'd heard that one before and you tend to discount it. [. . .] When you realise that she could have been killed outside the office, you begin to wonder at the power that you have got to insist that these two people come to the office together. (Area B)

How then do welfare officers attempt to reconcile these tensions? Once again opinions varied depending upon the philosophical and ideological lens through which the problem was viewed. Clearly, the welfare officers we interviewed and saw practise struggled to mediate between competing rights, obligations, interests and needs. For those welfare officers working in Area A who interpreted Mr Justice Ewbank's judgment in a literal sense and acted upon it, the problem was perhaps not quite so vexed:

> I think it is difficult for people [to meet jointly]. But in a sense that is one of the arguments for separating out conciliation from welfare reports. (Area A)

Some welfare officers in the other areas argued that there is no easy resolution to this problem. Because it is endemic to the work, it is something that welfare officers have to live with continually. However, it is interesting to note that practice has been reshaped as a result. In the words of this welfare officer:

> Both feminist critiques and ideas about race have made people less sure of themselves, less sure that they have an approach and that they can apply it. It is hard to believe that and hold on to ideas of racism and sexism. [. . .] So we are much gentler now about whether we push people to come to joint meetings. There is much more reluctance to force women [to come to joint meetings]. [. . .] Although we never did force women to come, we used to 'stonewall' a lot more effectively to get what we wanted. (Area E)

Others argued that this particular set of tensions cannot be reconciled. It is precisely because this particular circle cannot be squared, they argued, that welfare officers have a moral imperative to see parents individually in order to ascertain their wishes and feelings prior to arranging a joint meeting.

Consensus, concerns and consequences

Despite these new areas of fragmentation, it is nevertheless possible to identify from this convergence of practice several objectives which will satisfy the requirements of both court welfare officers and judges. Most notably these are to establish the following:

- The background to the dispute.
- Parental points of view.
- Parental anxieties.
- What they are proposing.
- What objections they have to the other person's proposals.
- Where applicable, the child(ren)'s views and wishes.

However regardless of an officer's practice orientation, there is almost universal agreement that the court process is inherently an unnecessarily intrusive and destructive experience which parents should avoid. As one officer put it, if she has a single aim it is

> simply to see if there is any way that parents can agree something which takes them out of the torture of having to go through this horrific court process. (Area C)

At another level, and perhaps more importantly, some officers stressed that parents have a right to their dispute and their 'day in court' if that is their wish. It is neither morally right, nor fruitful, they argued, to coerce or rush parents into making compromises or settlements which they might later regret. However, given the emphasis on results as the prime measure of effectiveness, there is clearly much pressure to get parents to agree.

It is perhaps important also to draw attention to some of the unintended consequences that might stem from seeking to 'divert' parents away from the formal court process. There is a great danger that such antipathy to the court process (well founded in certain respects though this may be) might, intentionally or otherwise, stigmatise parents who choose to opt for the formality of a court adjudication, rather than other means. In its strong form, welfare officers might admonish parents for actively choosing to engage in such a 'destructive' process. In its weaker (but insidious form), parents can be made to feel inadequate for being unwilling or unable to take responsibility for their own decisions about their child(ren). An additional, and some might argue more important, unintended consequence may be the denial of due process. The potential for a range of misunderstandings is illustrated in the following comments made by a welfare officer during an interview with both parents:

> We really have been struggling to find a way out for you. Like a lot of people when a welfare report is ordered we come along with the hope that we can help resolve the problems. We haven't been able to do that with you. [. . .] So at the end of the day it is going to be the court who will decide who is right and wrong and they will weigh evidence as in a criminal case. [. . .] So I will write the welfare report on the information that I have and you will go through it with your solicitors and decide what evidence to present. You are having your power as parents taken away from you and given to the court. You run the risk of it not working out in the way you might have hoped. Courts also compromise and it might not suit either of you. (Area D)

Concluding remarks

In this chapter we have sought to reveal the range of factors which together constitute practice including such elements as the values, beliefs and theories which court welfare officers hold and utilise, and the skills that they need to undertake the work. In so doing we have sought to illustrate further the way in which court welfare officers construct and order their views in specific and meaningful ways according to the context and sets of power relations in which they find themselves. In addition we have demonstrated that court welfare work stands on shifting sands. Issues which once dominated the discourse of court welfare revolving around debates about the relative standing of therapy in court welfare have given way to other pressures and influences as the discourse has broadened out with the introduction of new epistemes. Of particular importance in this regard is the influence of the feminist movement. However, a clear pattern for the way forward cannot yet be discerned. There are some obvious points of agreement within the movement about the way that law acts primarily in the interests of men whilst, it is argued, it remains impervious to women's needs and aspirations. Law, it is argued, is gendered in that continually enshrines patriarchal family values.

However, beyond these general points of unity lies the potential for much confusion and division. For some, Smart (1989, 1992) points out, the issues revolve around the dilemma of whether the law should be geared more around legislating on the basis of equal rights and responsibilities or upon a framework which recognises such things as biological and other differences. For others, the possibility of a feminist jurisprudence is a chimera which cannot be redeemed. The way forward therefore can only lie in a complete reconceptualisation of justice.

An example of the way these competing issues manifest themselves in court welfare practice is perhaps exemplified in the ever-increasing emphasis on equal parenting which, according to some commentators, slots more easily into a judicial discourse of 'rights' than it does that of welfare. This returns us to the question of whether law enslaves welfare. In keeping with King and Piper, Smart certainly believes, if we read her rightly, that this is largely true:

> We should also be alert to the way in which law can transform appeals couched in the discourse of welfare into issues of rights – hence reasserting law's traditional dominion over the matter. One example of this is the question of access to children by fathers after divorce. In this case the idea of parental rights has diminished as a valid appeal to make to law, but the claim for access has been substantiated by the 'psy' discourses which maintain that it is in the child's best interests to see his/her father. The courts have accepted this, but have reconceptualised the issue into one of rights. Hence the law argues that access is the inalienable *right* of the child . . . *This transformation of power conflicts into the language of rights enables law to exercise power rather than abdicating control to the 'psy' professions and the mechanisms of discipline.* (1989:19–20; italics in original)

As we have argued, we do not see the issues raised by Smart in quite the same way, particularly as it leaves out many of the realities of parental power from the equation. Moreover, we do not feel that such a simple division between rights and welfare is helpful or, indeed, necessary. Rights, needs, interests, responsibilities and obligations are inextricably bound together and cannot be disembodied from each another any more easily than can the judicial and social frameworks which surround parental separation and divorce. Furthermore it is never easy to determine courses of action when rights clash. In this regard, there may not be a 'correct' solution. But this is not all. Court welfare officers regularly have to face the complexities of having to meet simultaneously the demands of justice and welfare and many we interviewed would find themselves in conflict with such a simple separation.

It is against this backdrop that many of the present dilemmas within court welfare need to be addressed. It is not that we seek to 'disqualify knowledge' (Smart 1989: 13), but rather to make the point that there is a need to be clear about those areas of practice which require conceptual clarification and those which can be determined empirically. Our data suggest that in practice (perhaps contrary to some of the theoretical writings that we have considered in this chapter), much weight is given to the reality that it is mothers who in many cases continue to be the prime carer for the children. Whether this is by design or default is difficult to say. What is clear, however, is that welfare officers place a great deal of emphasis on where children reside. Because this is more likely to be with their mothers, it follows that women are much more likely to have the support of court welfare officers, if only on the grounds that the best interests of children will be met by not disrupting the *status quo*.

What is also clear is that a number of practitioners who have been influenced by feminist perspectives in general, and their impact on court welfare practice in particular, are unsure about how these various tensions can be resolved. Practitioners cannot stand outside or above these conceptual divides. They are frequently caught in the trap of wishing to decentre the importance of law without knowing how to ensure that people's 'rights' are protected without it, and in the full knowledge that, in any case, the law is reluctant (if not powerless) to enforce its decisions.

To echo Smart's phrase, court welfare thus represents 'a site of struggle'. The parameters of this struggle continue, however, to be in a permanent state of flux. For Cantwell (1992: 158), one of the ways forward is to accept that parental disputes take time to resolve themselves, possibly with the help of the court welfare service. The court should not therefore 'force parents to stop fighting'. Better, he argues, to acknowledge 'raw feelings' and perhaps to think a little more about using 'therapy by consent' that can be offered by the Family Assistance Order. A number of other commentators, including King and Trowell (1992) are calling for less court intervention. Meanwhile,

Davis, aligning himself with the 'legal partisans' says: 'I don't think we have enough trials. I think that the nature of the trial process needs to be transformed, so that trials are made less alienating, less expensive – and we can have more of them' (1988b: 204–5). This argument may find a degree of support among some observers. It may also draw our attention to important deficiencies in the nature of the trial process and reflect important concerns about due process. However, viewed in the light of the many and major changes in the last decade, for many others – including a number of judges and probably all court welfare officers – this call is at best anachronistic and at worst, borders on the absurd.

9
Synthesis and synergy

One of the major issues to emerge from all aspects of this study is the existence of substantial variations in the practice of court welfare work – variations between areas, teams and individual officers – but as a result of the gradual synthesis, described in the previous chapter, of differing approaches to court welfare work as it has evolved, there is perhaps a greater uniformity of practice than is suggested by the court welfare discourse described in Chapter 3. However, although this process seems likely to continue in the short term, since we have argued throughout that such changes are profoundly affected by the behaviour of knowledgeable actors forging policies within changing structural and legal constraints, it is impossible to divine the direction of developments in the longer term.

However, it is quite clear that there remain considerable variations in a number of important dimensions of practice which result in significant, and some might argue unacceptable, variations in the kind of service offered both to courts and to divorcing families. As we showed in Chapter 5, some welfare officers are highly critical of such variations, arguing that where divorcing parents happen to live should not determine the kind of service which they receive from court welfare officers. Others, believing that, as professionals, they are best placed to determine how the needs of divorcing families can most appropriately be met, are less concerned about such distributional anomalies.

Similarly, our data suggest that there is no consensus amongst senior managers in the probation service about whether greater uniformity is desirable and if so, along what lines this might be established. Views on this are determined according to widely varying criteria: for some, it is a matter of pragmatism, defined in terms of providing a service which is acceptable to local courts; for others, it is a matter of principle, reflecting concerns about issues of justice; and for yet others, the situation is so confused that they have no clear view on the issue.

However, it is clear that the Home Office do not regard variations in the services available to courts as acceptable. Having taken steps to minimise these in relation to the work of the probation service for the criminal courts, both directly and indirectly, through the introduction of national standards and the reform of the structure and function of probation committees, they are initiating similar steps in relation to the family court welfare work of the probation service (Home Office 1993). In so far as services will need to be relevant to the needs of local areas, however, it is inevitable that any such measures will need to be couched in fairly broad terms and that variations will still exist. Moreover, although it is clear from the analysis we have offered that there are some substantial areas of agreement, particularly amongst practitioners, there is little evidence of any overall clarity about the aims and objectives of court welfare work, either nationally or locally. Two related questions must therefore be considered: to what extent is it *desirable* and to what extent is it *possible* to achieve uniformity?

In terms of the prevailing rhetoric and ideology of empowerment, consumer choice and the citizen's charter, as well as in terms of traditional social-work values such as respect for persons and client self-determination, important questions are raised about the desirability of more uniform provision. For example, should parents and children be pressurised into participating in processes which they find uncomfortable if these cannot be proven to be essential in order to achieve the agreed outcome, solely because no other form of service is being made available? Should parents and children, during the highly emotional and deeply unsettling experience of divorce, have the right of access to services which are appropriate both to their needs and to the needs of the court?

Such questions might suggest that each probation area should be responsible for either making available or, under the umbrella of local strategies for partnership with other agencies, ensuring the availability of a range of services addressing the many and varied needs of divorcing families, a prospect hinted at by the Home Office (1993). Such a role would also be valuable in ensuring the co-ordinated provision of services for couples considering divorce envisaged by the Law Commission, which are discussed in more detail below. However, this case rests on the belief, which is not shared by a number of court welfare officers, that there is more than one way in which court welfare officers can offer an effective service which is of value to families and courts and that welfare officers cannot and should not be the sole arbiters of the nature of the service which is offered in any given area. Arguably, therefore, the single most important issue in determining the extent to which such variations in service provision might be regarded as justifiable, in a context where greater uniformity is seen as desirable by policy makers in particular, is the extent to which these will be determined by variations in local needs as opposed to variations in the views, commitments and practice orientations of local courts and court welfare officers.

The extent to which it is *possible* to achieve greater uniformity is more problematic, however, because of the many and varied factors which lead to variations in the availability of services and the practice of welfare officers. It might certainly be argued that practice along more 'traditional' lines might be more amenable to the clear prescription of practice in order to achieve such uniformity, although the effectiveness of such an approach would depend in large part on associated arrangements for monitoring. However, the greater variety and complexity of approaches involving joint working and family meetings seem likely to limit the impact of such an approach.

In addition to such issues, uniformity is difficult to achieve for a number of other reasons. We have drawn attention in previous chapters to the importance of local accommodations between welfare officers and the judiciary and these seem likely to continue to be a pervasive influence. Indeed, such arrangements may even be more likely in the wake of the Children Act 1989 and the developing Home Office strategy encouraging closer formal liaison arrangements (1993: para. 15). As one senior member of the judiciary commented:

> with the limitation on the number of Circuit Judges involved in family work there will grow up a system in which a particular welfare officer becomes used to preparing reports for particular Circuit Judges. Each will come to know the particular needs and strengths of the other. In this sense it is perhaps less important that welfare officers should have a uniform approach across the country than that they should produce what is useful for their particular Judges and that *their working practices*

should be effective to that end. Uniformity is desirable but usefulness is the priority.

(personal correspondence, 2 October 1992; emphasis added)

Policies which fail to take account of such views and the pressures which they create, the need to manage these effectively, and the absence of any effective means for so doing (see Chapter 2) therefore seem doomed to fail in this respect.

Also of considerable significance are geographical factors, variations in which tend to favour particular approaches to practice, although by no means to determine them. Thus, the teams studied in Area E were able to operate a predominantly office-based approach to practice, with less emphasis on home visits than other areas by virtue of being based in the city centre of a largely urban area. This enabled them to complete their reports in a shorter time, based on fewer interviews overall. Even had they favoured such an approach, this would have been much more difficult for Areas A and F, for example, both large rural counties, in which it would have been extremely difficult to expect the majority of parents to travel many miles for office-based family meetings. Such considerations may also lead to different emphases being placed upon contact with non-custodial fathers and with new partners, given the cost of home visits in terms of both time and money.

This raises the interesting question of the extent to which the different locales in which court welfare practice takes place and the weight given to these, both in the methods used and the way in which reports are constructed, is determined by such issues of geography and space. Such issues may also, in turn, exercise a powerful influence in the construction of ideologies of practice. In other words, to what extent are the practice ideologies of individuals, teams and areas constructed around issues of practicality? Not surprisingly, we cannot provide an unequivocal answer to this question. However, it seems clear that such issues are one important element in determining variations in practice.

Other elements reflect the different values and theoretical orientations of welfare officers; others reflect different team ideologies; yet others reflect situational accommodations to factors such as the views of local courts. These in turn may be based upon pragmatic considerations such as the need to process an ever-growing number of cases as efficiently and expeditiously as possible, or a commitment to a new and different approach to resolving the issues raised by marital breakdown, or a combination of these.

Yet other variations are a reflection of the need for the legal process and decisions concerning the welfare of children to be transacted according to the needs and constraints of individual cases, as opposed to being determined solely by overarching legal rules and precedents. This is a factor which not only inheres in the very nature of such decisions but which is also determined by the attitudes and behaviours of the key actors involved, such as judges, lawyers, welfare officers and, in particular, parents. Although the latter might appear to be relatively powerless once they enter the legal process, we have shown they can and do exercise a substantial degree of control over how the 'story' of their marriage and its breakdown is constructed and how the solutions to the subsequent problems are shaped.

The significance of this is that it reflects the *social* context and processes of divorce *within which* the legal process and court welfare work are situated and, as we have argued, these are constantly changing with the passage of time. Certainly, the framework provided by the law is important for the full-time cast of players in the legal system, in which parents and children are but transitory 'bit-players'. However, this framework is but one component, itself transitory, in the social and emotional contexts of divorce as experienced by parents and their children.

One of the key questions for court welfare work therefore is whether its focus should be dictated solely by the legal framework of divorce, or whether it should be determined by the social framework. The answer to this question, which is not accessible through the application of any particular set of principles, may help to determine what the aims and objectives of court welfare work should be. It will also therefore provide some of the answers to a wide range of subsidiary questions about the nature and extent of court welfare work and will help to provide answers to some of the additional questions raised.

If the view is taken that court welfare work should be located solely within the legal framework, this may provide important clues about the nature of the service to be provided, its place within the system, its orientation and its accountability. It will also highlight questions about how the broader issues raised by viewing the divorce process in its social context are to be addressed and by whom. If the position is taken that court welfare work should be located within the broader social framework, this might also provide important clues about the nature of the service and its orientation. However, the question of whether such a service can also discharge a set of legally constructed responsibilities within the framework of the legal system and, if so, what these should be or, if not, who should bear this responsibility, will also need to be addressed.

The view might also, of course, be taken that the court welfare service can do both, for, as we have argued, this is a pivotal feature of the development of court welfare work. However, as we have also argued, this particular feature is equally pivotal to an understanding of much of the confusion and conflict which has been so much a feature of the court welfare discourse. This has occurred largely because of a failure to address a number of key questions of policy and practice which have arisen from the very nature of its development. Central to these key questions are those which revolve around the issue of whether such a view takes sufficient account of the organising frameworks which give shape to the phenomenon of divorce and to court welfare work and the extent of the many changes in these.

In previous chapters, we have outlined and analysed court welfare practice in terms of these frameworks. The issues arising now need to be considered in the context of the major changes in family law embodied in the Children Act 1989 and those related to the need for further reform of the law relating to divorce.

The Children Act 1989

The Children Act signifies, as we argued in Chapter 1, a major shift in law from an emphasis on the rights of parents in relation to their children towards their responsibilities. In the relatively short time since our research was conducted, court welfare work has already undergone further changes as a result of the Act. However, whilst such a shift is of undoubted significance in legal terms and for those operating in the legal framework, its relevance to the construction of child welfare issues by *parents* in terms of the social context of divorce is more doubtful. A major factor where there is conflict over children in divorce is a common-sense notion of justice, of *moral* rights, which may often bear too little resemblance to legal definitions. As Eekelaar argues:

> it is perhaps inevitable that the law on the allocation of parental responsibility and child care after divorce should become enmeshed in

arguments over ideology and practice relating to the roles of men and women ... the substitution of fathers' rights by the welfare 'test' has, according to some, merely masked the preservation of socially ascribed roles to the sexes. The welfare test clearly fails to diffuse these conflicts. (1991: 136)

Smart, on the basis of a small empirical study of how divorced and divorcing parents 'negotiated' the question of child custody, reached the conclusion that there are important moral issues which are 'being silenced by the dominant discourse of contemporary family law' (1991: 486–7). These issues revolve around an important distinction between 'caring for' children, which is morally (and economically) undervalued work done predominantly by mothers, and 'caring about' children, which underpins many fathers' arguments for custody and which 'seems increasingly to occupy a sentimental and sacred place in the dominant moral and legal order ... [which] is part of the discursive reconstruction of fatherhood' (Smart 1991: 494). The stress placed by the new law on joint parental responsibility is undoubtedly an important element in this reconstruction which presents a new challenge to these common-sense, moral perceptions of justice, leading Smart to argue for

> a different conceptual framework in which to interpret or hear what is said. In other words, we should cease to treat statements of 'caring for' as synonymous with 'caring about'. . . . The moral discourse of care is such a framework and while it does not promise a solution to the difficulties of divorce and child custody, at least it allows all the parties a legitimate voice. (1991: 499)

This clearly raises important issues for the practice of court welfare work, as we saw in Chapter 8, in which issues of gender and related ideologies are closely related to practice in the structuring of accounts of and reports on child welfare issues. Our findings concerning the lower levels of contact with fathers and investigation of their home circumstances and their new partners suggest that although fatherhood may be in the process of being reconstructed, welfare officers tend to focus their enquiries more on mothers who do the 'caring for'. This may be justifiable on all sorts of pragmatic grounds, but it raises questions concerning the nature of Smart's proposed discourse of care and the extent to which fathers still struggle to find a 'legitimate voice' with which to articulate *their* common-sense notions of justice.

As we argued in Chapter 1, when legal definitions begin to become too far removed from such common-sense notions of justice, history has shown that the pressures for change in the law begin to build and eventually become irresistible. It is conceivable that this shift of emphasis in the Children Act in relation to parents may mark the start of another such episode of separation between legal and common-sense definitions. However, the moral discourse of care outlined by Smart remains an essentially adult-focused discourse. This raises again the basic question which permeates the entire court welfare discourse – *why are court welfare officers involved in divorce proceedings?*

The central legal and social purpose of divorce is to end a marital relationship and it is therefore quintessentially a provision for adults. Where there are children of the family, the law traditionally regarded them as but one element of the property of parents requiring distributive decisions in the event of the breakdown of a marriage, reinforcing the adult-centred nature of divorce. Thus, divorce is not for children in most cases. On the contrary, it happens, often *against* their wishes (see, for example, Mitchell 1985; Walczak with Burns 1984; Wallerstein and Kelly 1980), because their parents decide that they can no longer live together. Therefore, although increasingly the law has implicitly recognised that divorce may not necessarily be the best solution to marital problems in terms of children's welfare, it remains a provision for adults, which is precisely why, paradoxically, children's interests must be paramount and the state, through the legal system, must both regulate divorce and protect children's interests.

This fact is central to some of the ambiguities which surround the involvement of welfare officers in divorce, the competition between the legally and socially orientated components of their work and their associated statutory and discretionary responses. It is also central to understanding the court welfare discourse, since it tempts many commentators, both academics and practitioners, to fragment the issues by focusing on adults rather than on children and on particular aspects of court welfare work at the expense of others, rather than on the complex inter-relationships that bind them inextricably together.

Therefore, a key issue is how welfare officers respond to these competing imperatives and the ambiguities which they create for them in framing their role in divorce proceedings. The Children Act places a major emphasis on the wishes and feelings of children in determining their best interests. The fact that the literal application of the provisions of s.1(3) of the Act is quite limited does not detract from their impact on the discourse about children's rights which is much more substantial and far-reaching (James 1990b). All aspects of our research have confirmed the suggestion that, although many welfare officers regard children as their clients and see the protection of their welfare as one of the major responsibilities of court welfare work, comparatively little emphasis is given to ascertaining their wishes and feelings and reporting these directly to the courts.

In addition, although the Act provided some direct enhancement of the rights of children, as Eekelaar and Dingwall argue, this was much more limited in reality than the debate surrounding the introduction of the Act suggested, and 'it seems that the decision-maker's views will normally take priority over those of the child if there is a disagreement' (1990: 23). Therefore, if the court welfare function is to be framed in terms of its contribution to the legal process, the welfare officer will continue to occupy a crucial position in relation to children in divorce proceedings since, in the vast majority of cases, it will be only the court welfare officer who will be in a position to provide independent information to the decision makers, the judges. However, it is arguable in the light of our findings that this will need to be on the basis of more thorough investigation and assessment of children's wishes and feelings than is currently the practice of many welfare officers.

Eekelaar argues that child welfare issues might best be resolved by taking these developments a stage further and creating a framework constructed around the legal concept of children's *rights*, which would be capable of clearer specification than the welfare-orientated 'best-interests' criterion. He argues that a child has the following:

- Basic rights: to be protected against emotional, physical and intellectual harm – which should hardly ever (if at all) be put at risk.
- 'Developmental rights': to expect parents to develop its capabilities so as to put it in the most favourable position they can reasonably achieve to achieve its life chances when it enters the adult world. This views the child as a potential adult and implies/requires a broader perspective than that provided by childhood alone. The child should be *entitled* to the disposition which offers the most advantageous prospect for its development.
- 'Autonomy rights': the *right*, with increasing age, to fashion its own life-style free of adult domination (at least where this does not threaten the first two interests).

Such an approach would not pre-determine a particular outcome in marginal cases, but it does, he argues, provide: 'the basis for principled reasoning which would need to articulate how the decision related to the rights of the child in a particular case' (1991: 137).

Eekelaar's approach represents an attempt to address the problems raised by divorce by locating it in its legal context and finding a legally appropriate solution in terms of articulating rules to guide decisions – rule-utility in Elster's terms (see Chapter 7) – while Smart's approach locates divorce within its social context and seeks to identify a moral discourse of care within which to locate these difficult decisions – a process based on act-utilitarianism. Thus, the struggle between competing discourses continues. However, it is clear from our analysis that divorce and divorce court welfare officers presently straddle the legal and the social frameworks, as they must because of the very nature of divorce as both a legal and a social phenomenon. In the process, they struggle in their daily work to reconcile the fundamentally different perspectives produced by these frameworks, adopting different forms of practice in the process. Might it be desirable, therefore, to consider ways of achieving a degree of synthesis of these presently competing perspectives, creating the potential for synergy and the exploration of new responses based upon co-ordination, co-operation and complementarity?

The reform of the law relating to divorce

The proposals of the Law Commission, made following consideration of responses to an earlier discussion paper (1988), reflect many of these issues and represent the possibility of a further step in bridging the apparent gap between the legal and social frameworks. Of particular significance in view of the arguments outlined in Chapter 1 about the social processes underpinning legal change is the fact that, in addition to responses from a range of professional and other groups to the discussion paper, these proposals were informed by a specially commissioned survey of public opinion about the law relating to divorce. It was designed to 'identify what people see as its good and bad features, to assess the acceptability of a variety of bases for divorce and to probe two possible reforms in more depth' (para. 1.3). This process of consultation revealed widespread criticisms of the current law and the practice which it contained, widespread concern to encourage amicable resolution of problems arising from divorce whilst minimising the harm caused to children, and support for the retention of the irretrievable breakdown of marriage as the fundamental basis of the ground for divorce. This led to 'the firm conclusion that there is one particular model for reform which is to be preferred' (para. 1.8). This model is that of divorce after a period of consideration and reflection. The key elements are that after the process has been initiated by one or both parties making a statement indicating that they believe their marital relationship has broken down, a 'cooling-off' period lasting a minimum of twelve months ensues. This is intended both to demonstrate that the marital relationship has broken down irretrievably and to give the couple a realistic time to resolve the practical consequences of any ensuing divorce. At the start of this period, both parties are to be supplied with a comprehensive information pack, explaining the process and, *inter alia*, 'the nature and purposes of counselling, reconciliation, conciliation and mediation and the services which are available in the area' (para. 7.15(iv)). Such services, recourse to which is to be on a voluntary basis, are described as 'an important element in developing a new and more constructive approach to the problems of marital breakdown and divorce' (para. 7.24). After a minimum of eleven months from the filing of the statement, the parties may apply for a divorce or separation order.

This very brief summary of the proposed model reflects a number of important issues. Firstly, it clearly reflects a move towards a more administrative system of divorce, moving many of the issues and processes away from the formal dispute-resolution machinery of the legal system towards informal processes. Secondly, it also clearly reflects many of the principles embodied in the Children Act 1989: the principles of parental responsibility and parental involvement; the principle of minimum intervention and positive intervention – courts will still be able to make orders where appropriate during the 'cooling-off' period. The welfare principle is reflected in the implicit assumption that encouraging parental responsibility and decision-making, thereby reducing conflict, is the best way of ensuring that the child's welfare is met. Thirdly, it represents an endorsement of thinking behind many of the developments which have been at the heart of the revolution in court welfare work and clarifies some of the key issues central to the discourse, such as the privilege to be attached to conciliation or mediation procedures. And fourthly, it acknowledges explicitly the need for a range of services for families contemplating divorce and implicitly, the need for greater co-ordination and co-operation between the legal and the social, the statutory and the independent. It is in this context that the family court welfare strategies of local probation services (Home Office 1993) might have a major impact in terms of providing both a link between these elements and a framework for co-operation with and between independent sector agencies such as RELATE and mediation services.

The proposals also reflect some of the concerns which have been central to the history of divorce and court welfare work, described in Chapter 1. It is clear that one effect of such proposals would be to reduce the increasing burden on the legal process represented by divorce proceedings, whilst at the same time potentially increasing the burden on statutory and voluntary services. Such an increase also, of course, represents a considerable and formally sanctioned expansion of the sphere of influence of such services. In contemplating such a prospect, we should be mindful of the warning offered by Dingwall and Eekelaar that 'Welfare can be a more insidious form of social control than law, although it is always a fine judgment as to whether its enticements to conformity may not be preferable to outright coercion' (1988: 179).

It is also clear that concerns about the prevalence of divorce, and the possible impact of proposals which might be seen to be making divorce easier to obtain, have led to a number of provisions designed to facilitate reconciliation where possible, to which the notion of a 'cooling-off' period is central. Such concerns have been evident in comments made by the Lord Chancellor in response to the proposals (Family Policy Studies Centre 1991), stressing the need to strengthen the institution of marriage and expressing concern about current divorce rates and trends.

What cannot be clear at this stage is what unintended consequences might result from the introduction of such a model in terms of deliberately introducing an unavoidable delay into the process of divorce (in essence, reflecting predominantly *adult*-orientated and *marriage*-saving concerns – Law Commission 1990, para. 5.66), in the context of the provisions and principles of the Children Act 1989 relating to minimising delays in family proceedings (in essence, reflecting predominantly child-orientated and *child*-saving concerns). This is of particular significance in the light of the experience of the 1969 reforms of the law relating to divorce and the subsequent widespread use/abuse of the unreasonable-behaviour ground by many couples, aided by their lawyers, in order to secure more speedy divorces.

It is possible, for example, that parents might, perhaps encouraged by their lawyers, seek an order under section 8 of the Children Act 1989 to deal with any number of issues that might arise during the cooling-off period, or that courts might consider making use of their power to make orders of their own motion under section 10. This might also lead to a section 16 family assistance order being considered when exercising the powers proposed by the Law Commission (1990, para. 5.39) to adjourn hearing an issue for the purpose of enabling parents to participate in conciliation or mediation. Indeed, the Law Commission explicitly envisages the use by the courts of their powers to make orders (e.g. paras. 5.13 and 5.53–5), particularly in the context of their recommendation for a preliminary assessment. This should be held by the court not later than twelve weeks from the date of the statement of marital breakdown being made, in order to monitor progress on the making of the necessary arrangements and so that parents might 'be encouraged to get on with making those arrangements and not to defer decisions which need to and can be made' (Law Commission 1990, para. 5.50).

Such provisions could well result in more orders being sought and made than was intended in the framing of the Act, thereby undermining some of the important principles which the Act and the Law Commission's proposals have in common. Whether these eventualities occur remains to be seen, but the lessons of history suggest that some unintended consequences are almost inevitable because those who bring their disputes to law will seek to use it to achieve their own ends rather than necessarily those of legislators or the law.

Practice and theory

In embarking on a study of the civil work of the probation service, our purpose was to generate some much needed empirical data about the work of court welfare officers and their approaches to practice. However, perhaps predictably, this alone has proved to be insufficient to provide a full understanding of court welfare work. It has become clear that in order to begin to do this more fully, it is also necessary to consider the history of court welfare work, the values and political agendas which have underpinned its development, as well as the values of welfare officers themselves and how these have changed in response to a changing social, economic and political climate. In addition, it is necessary to understand the relevance, if not the detail, of the theoretical perspectives drawn from social work and other disciplines, such as law, which constitute the 'epistemological bundle' (King 1991) used by social workers and used in part by court welfare officers to conceptualise their practice.

In seeking to understand much of our data about the practice of court welfare officers, these theoretical perspectives alone have proved inadequate in terms of explaining important aspects of practice and in particular the nature of the dynamic relationship between welfare officers, courts and families. Such perspectives, although valuable in their own right, fail to address pivotal issues concerning the way in which such encounters and relationships are structured and how these are not only perpetuated over time but also enabled and, indeed, required to respond to the widely varying parameters presented by individual cases and by continually changing circumstances.

We have therefore argued that in order to understand key aspects of the world of court welfare work revealed by our study, it is necessary also to consider aspects of social theory in order to make better sense of our empirical data. In so doing, we have, of necessity, been highly selective and emphasised certain of the theories of certain authors. The work of Giddens and Goffman has been given particular attention because of its relevance to the analysis and understanding of court welfare work. In the process, we have been able to bring closer together, if not completely to reconcile, some of the apparent paradoxes revealed by our study – the relative powerlessness of the courts to resolve the bitter emotional conflicts which often surround divorce, in spite of their position of apparent omnipotence; the comparative power of welfare officers in relation to some parents and some courts, but their relative impotence in relation to others; the relative power of some parents, when they are able or choose to recognise and exercise this, and the apparent loss of power experienced by others as soon as they enter the legal process; and the way in which issues of time and space, of process and locale, are fundamental to the transaction of such dynamic issues.

In taking this particular approach to our analysis, our purpose was to illustrate the major contribution which social theory can make to understanding a complex empirical world such as that in which court welfare officers exist, rather than to attempt a comprehensive discussion of the many different areas of social theory which might illuminate this particular empirical world. The purpose of our enterprise has therefore been to try to identify a further theoretical and explanatory dimension which will inform the crucial considerations currently being given to the future development and management of court welfare work.

The future organisation of court welfare work

Our analysis has identified not only the complex history of court welfare work, the complicated policy context in which it exists and the far-reaching impact of changes in practice in the last decade, but also the many and varied factors which have shaped its development and which determine the minutiae of practice. Faced with these complexities and the need to identify a more coherent way forward, Hooper and Murch (1990) have argued that the current array of child-welfare services currently supporting the courts (excluding social services departments) – that is, court welfare services, guardians *ad litem* and conciliation services – should be merged under the responsibility of the Department of Health to provide an integrated welfare service in family proceedings. This is a superficially persuasive argument in the post-Children Act era, with the creation of a combined jurisdiction and much greater emphasis on inter-professional co-operation, and there may indeed be an argument for closer co-ordination for a variety of economic and pragmatic reasons.

However, there is an important distinction to be drawn between integration of *management* and integration of *function*. Certain advantages may indeed accrue from the former, particularly in terms of making an improved service – in terms of training, resourcing, management, uniformity of provision and quality control – available to the courts, parents and children. This may have particular significance in the context of the Law Commission's proposals for the reform of the divorce law which would require a range of services to be made available to the courts and divorcing couples. Our analysis of court welfare work would suggest, however, that the nature of such services is determined by a wide range of complex and inter-related factors and that integration of management would not necessarily yield such benefits.

In contrast, an argument for the integration of function would seem to be predicated upon the view that such services rest on a common set of child-saving/child-protection assumptions and values and, as we have argued, this underpins a significant part of the current confusion surrounding court welfare work (and, arguably, conciliation!). The role of the guardian *ad litem* revolves principally around the assessment, protection and representation of children. Court welfare work, particularly if located in the legal framework, is essentially about investigating on behalf of the court of issues relevant to determining what is in the best interests of a child, including ascertaining their wishes and feelings, with a view to communicating information about these to the court. It is not directly concerned with child protection or representation and to confuse these ingredients with those already in the melting pot would provide a recipe for continued confusion and conflict about both policy and practice.

It is tempting, at the conclusion of such a detailed study of court welfare work and in responding to proposals such as these, to begin to think in terms of making recommendations. However, we have resisted this temptation. Although this might cause disappointment to some and leave us open to the criticism of not having the courage to nail our colours to our mast, or of having ducked important issues about the future of court welfare work, we hope that it will prove to be more helpful to have taken the alternative course of identifying a number of important issues which will need to be borne in mind, whichever of the various options are chosen by those responsible for the framing of policy.

Indeed, we do not believe that any particular organisational structure or context for court welfare work is necessarily inherently superior to any of the alternatives, or that the existing structure is so fundamentally flawed that it cannot be made to work satisfactorily. This is because we have concluded in the light of our research that the processes we have described and the issues that emerge as a result of these, which we have identified throughout this book and summarised briefly at the start of this chapter, are intrinsic to the very nature of court welfare work. In consequence, we believe that they will exist in the context of *any* organisational framework which might be designed for court welfare work.

Should court welfare work remain the responsibility of the probation service, there is no doubt that the tension between the criminal and civil responsibilities of the service in terms of organisational objectives and ethos, knowledge and skills, resources and manpower will need careful management. In addition, although probation officers have a tradition of providing services to the courts and are well regarded by many judges and magistrates, it is clear that this is no longer sufficient justification for the continuation of this arrangement and that important and difficult issues about the development and management of practice will have to be faced as the legal and social context of divorce changes.

It is equally clear that many of the issues which we have identified are inherent in the problem of determining and providing for the best interests of children, in the process of divorce and in the dynamics of dispute resolution, by whatever means, in a judicial context. They are a product of the interaction of a range of complex social, structural and human factors and it would be naïve to believe that they would or could be eradicated by the simple device of transposing court welfare work to a different organisational context.

It is also clear that major issues lie in the management of court welfare officers and the development of their practice, particularly at the level of middle-management, whatever the organisational context in which they are located. It is at this level that issues of practice, standards, policy implementation and the monitoring of these can and should be most effectively dealt with. What is less clear is how the nature and purpose of the court welfare task and its contribution to the legal and social processes of divorce are to be determined. Although the process of attempting to achieve this major task is at long last under way, effective decisions about how to structure services accordingly, and to select, train and supervise both managers and practitioners and the practice of each, cannot be made until this process is well advanced, if not actually complete.

Concluding comments

Arguably, the proposals of the Law Commission for the reform of the law relating to divorce will be of crucial importance in influencing the next stages in the development of the legal and social phenomenon of divorce. These proposals, like the provisions of the Children Act, reflect the continuing struggle not only to shift the balance but also to bridge the gap between the social and the legal frameworks which structure marital breakdown and divorce. This struggle is evident in the picture revealed by this study. And yet divorce, as currently constructed and until (if ever) it becomes a totally administrative process, is both a legal and a social phenomenon, involving and belonging to both the legal and social worlds and existing in the context of both legal and social processes.

The confusions which this generates are clear, but they are confusing because they are constructed as and assumed to be competing frameworks, whereas in reality, they overlap and complement each other. Law is a social as well as a legal construct. Legal institutions and processes are also social institutions and processes, designed to deal with issues defined as legal for certain specific purposes, for instance breaking legally binding arrangements such as marriage contracts, or resolving disputes, or making symbolic and/or normative statements.

In order to overcome the confusion resulting from these supposedly competing paradigms, it must be acknowledged that they are indivisible and complementary and services must accordingly be constructed which reflect the entire range of issues raised, in such a way as to acknowledge the different frameworks and processes implicit in them. Might such a synthesis be brought that much nearer by returning to the question of who divorce is for? It is the parents who, although only transitory players, cross and recross the boundaries between the legal and the social in the course of divorce and its aftermath; it is they who bring together the different institutions, professions, frameworks, structures and value systems which comprise the divorce system; it is they who have been given the responsibility for determining their children's welfare; and it is arguably they who have the ultimate power. If they become the starting point for any analysis of the divorce process and the services needed to assist them in going through this particularly painful transition, rather than the competing discourses, paradigms and professions, perhaps some of the many issues we have raised might become clearer.

In the light of this analysis of practice and theory, therefore, should the divorce system, bolstered by the prevailing ethos of empowerment, consumer rights and the citizens' charter, become much more responsive to parents' needs and wishes in the difficult circumstances surrounding divorce, as well as those of children? What would be the implications of such a change? It would certainly suggest the need for greater flexibility, for much closer co-ordination between the different parts of the legal system, and for greater sensitivity to the needs of those seeking divorce, which would signify the need for substantial changes in the perspectives, attitudes and practices of those many professionals involved in providing services to divorcing families. Such a perspective, which acknowledges and responds to the power which parents already possess and will continue to exercise, presents a major challenge in terms of defining the context and content of court welfare practice. However, it is also a perspective which might, in the process of rising to the challenge, create the opportunity to build upon the firm foundations of current practice and provide a service which better meets the needs and interests of all concerned.

References

A Group of Devon Probation Officers (1972) 'Children and divorce', *Probation Journal*, 18 (2).
Association of Chief Officers of Probation (1987) *Civil Work Handbook.* Wakefield: ACOP.
Association of Chief Officers of Probation (1989a) *Position Statement on the Preparation of Welfare Officers' Reports*, 8 December. Wakefield: ACOP.
Association of Chief Officers of Probation (1989b) *Position Statement on the Probation Service Contribution to Support Services for the Family Jurisdiction*, 10 August. Wakefield: ACOP.
Association of Chief Officers of Probation and the National Association of Probation Officers (1991) *The Probation Service and Civil Work*, February. Wakefield/London: ACOP/NAPO.
Association of Chief Officers of Probation, Central Council of Probation Committees and the National Association of Probation Officers (1987) *Probation – the Next Five Years: A joint statement.* London: ACOP, CCPC and NAPO.
Audit Commission (1989) *The Probation Service: Promoting value for money.* London: HMSO.
Audit Commission (1991) *Going Straight: Developing good practice in the probation service* (Occasional Paper No. 16). London: HMSO.
Beldam Committee (1991) *Report of the Committee on Alternative Dispute Resolution*, General Council of the Bar, October.
Blau, P. (1964) *Exchange and Power in Social Life.* New York: John Wiley.
Bochel, D. (1976) *Probation and After-Care: Its development in England and Wales.* Edinburgh: Scottish Academic.
Booth Committee (1985) *Report of the Matrimonial Causes Procedure Committee.* London: HMSO.
Bottomley, A., James, A., Bochel, C. and Robinson, D. (1993) 'A study of the

probation service response to the "tackling offending" initiative', *Research Bulletin*, HORPU, 33.
Bottoms, A. (1977) 'Reflections on the renaissance of dangerousness', *Howard Journal of Penology and Crime Prevention*, 16 (2).
Bretherton, H. (1979) 'Court welfare work: Practice and theory', *Probation Journal*, 26 (3).
Brophy, J. (1989) 'Custody law, child care and inequality in Britain', in C. Smart and S. Sevenhuijsen (eds) *Child Custody and the Politics of Gender*. London: Routledge.
Burgoyne, J., Ormrod R. and Richards, M. (1988) *Divorce Matters*. Harmondsworth: Penguin.
Burns, T. (1992) *Erving Goffman*. London: Routledge.
Burrett, J. and Gibbons, F. (1981) 'Catching the fall-out from exploding nuclear families', *Social Work Today*, 28 April.
Cantwell, B. (1992) 'Welfare reports after the children act: Setting a new agenda', *Probation Journal*, 39 (3).
Cantwell, B. and Smith, N. (1990) 'A systemic approach to Divorce Court welfare work', *Journal of Family Therapy*, 12.
Central Council of Probation Committees (1991) *Policy Statement on Civil Work*. London: CCPC.
Chapman, J. (1979) 'Should "probation" be involved in marital work?', *Probation Journal*, 26 (2).
Chester, R. (1971) 'Contemporary trends in the stability of English marriage', *Journal of Biosocial Science*, 3.
Clulow, C. and Vincent, C. (1987) *In the child's best interests? Divorce court welfare and the search for a settlement*. London: Tavistock.
Cohen, S. (1985) *Visions of Social Control*. Cambridge: Polity Press.
Conciliation Project Unit (1989) *Report to the Lord Chancellor on the Costs and Effectiveness of Conciliation in England and Wales*. University of Newcastle Upon Tyne.
Craib, I. (1992) *Anthony Giddens*. London: Routledge.
Davis, G. (1982) 'Conciliation: A dilemma for the Divorce Court Welfare Service', *Probation Journal*, 29 (4).
Davis, G. (1983) 'Mediation in Divorce: A theoretical perspective', *Journal of Social Welfare Law*, 131–40.
Davis, G. (1985) 'The theft of conciliation', *Probation Journal*, 32 (1).
Davis, G. (1988a) 'The halls of justice and justice in the halls', in R. Dingwall and J. Eekelaar (eds) *Divorce Mediation and the Legal Process*. Oxford: Clarendon Press.
Davis, G. (1988b) *Partisans and Mediators*. Oxford: Clarendon Press.
Davis, G. and Bader, K. (1985) 'In-court mediation: The consumer view – I and II', *Family Law*, 15.
Davis, G. and Murch, M. (1988) *Grounds for Divorce*. Oxford: Oxford University Press.

Davis, G. and Roberts, M. (1988) *Access to Agreement*. Milton Keynes: Open University Press.
Denning Committee (1947) *Final Report of the Committee on Procedure in Matrimonial Causes*, Cmnd 7024. London: HMSO.
Dewar, J. (1989) *Law and the Family*. London: Butterworths.
Dingwall, R. (1986) 'Some observations on divorce mediation in Britain and the United States', *Mediation Quarterly*, 11 (March).
Dingwall, R. (1988) 'Empowerment or Enforcement? Some questions about power and control in divorce mediation', in R. Dingwall and J. Eekelaar (eds.) *Divorce Mediation and the Legal Process*. Oxford: Clarendon Press.
Dingwall, R. and Eekelaar J. (1988) 'A Wider Vision', in R. Dingwall and J. Eekelaar (eds) *Divorce Mediation and the Legal Process*. Oxford: Clarendon Press.
Dingwall, R. and James, A. (1988) 'Family law and the psycho-social professions: Welfare officers in the English county courts', *Law in Context*, 6 (1).
Dominian, J. (1982) 'Families in divorce', in R.N. Rapoport, M.P. Fogarty and R. Rapoport (eds) *Families in Britain*. London: Routledge.
Dormor, D. (1992) *The Relationship Revolution: Cohabitation, marriage and divorce in contemporary Europe*. London: One plus One.
Edwards, H. (1986) 'Alternative dispute resolution: Panacea or anathema?', *Harvard Law Review*, 99.
Eekelaar, J. (1991) *Regulating Divorce*. Oxford: Clarendon Press.
Eekelaar, J. and Clive, E. (1977) *Custody after Divorce*. Oxford: SSRC Centre for Socio-Legal Studies, Wolfson College.
Eekelaar, J. and Dingwall, R. (1988) 'The development of conciliation in England', in R. Dingwall and J. Eekelaar (eds) *Divorce Mediation and the Legal Process*. Oxford: Clarendon Press.
Eekelaar, J. and Dingwall, R. (1990) *The Reform of Child Care Law: A practical guide to the Children Act 1989*. London: Routledge.
Elliott F. (1986) *The Family: Change or continuity?* London: Macmillan.
Elster, J. (1989) *Solomonic Judgements*. Cambridge: Cambridge University Press.
Family Policy Studies Centre (1991) *Family Policy Bulletin*, December.
Feeley, M. (1978) 'The concept of laws in social science: A critique and notes on an expanded view', in C. Reasons and R. Rich (eds) The Sociology of Law: A Conflict Perspective. Toronto: Butterworths.
Finch J. (1989) *Family Obligations and Social Change*. Cambridge: Polity Press.
Fineman, M. (1988) 'Dominant discourse, professional language, and legal change in child custody decisionmaking', *Harvard Law Review*, 101.
Finer Committee (1974) *Report of the Committee on One-parent Families*, Cmnd 5629. London: HMSO.
Fisher, T. (ed.) (1990) *Family Conciliation within the UK: Policy and practice*. Bristol: Family Law.

Forster, J. (1982) *Divorce Conciliation: A study of services in England and abroad with implications for Scotland.* Edinburgh: Scottish Council for Single Parents.
Foucault, M. (1977) *Discipline and Punish.* Harmondsworth: Penguin.
Foucault, M (1980) *Power/Knowledge:* Selected interviews and other writings 1972–1977, ed. C. Gordon. Hemel Hempstead: Harvester Wheatsheaf.
Fraser, D. (1980) 'Divorce Avon style – the work of a specialist welfare team', *Social Work Today,* 2 (13).
Freeman, M. (1982) 'Questioning the delegalization movement in family law: Do we really want a family court?', In J. Eekelaar and S. Katz (eds) *The Resoultion of Family Conflict: Comparative legal perspectives.* Toronto: Butterworths.
Frisby, C. and Wilson, V. (1946) Report of investigation by the National Institute of Industrial Psychology for the Probation Training Board of the Home Office on the work of the probation officer (unpublished), 14 November.
Garland, D. (1990) *Punishment and Modern Society: A study in social theory.* Oxford: Clarendon Press.
Gathorne-Hardy, J. (1981) *Love, Sex, Marriage and Divorce.* London: Cape.
Giddens, A. (1984) *The Constitution of Society.* Cambridge: Polity Press
Giddens, A. (1987) *Social Theory and Modern Sociology.* Cambridge: Polity Press.
Giddens, A. (1989) 'A reply to my critics', in D. Held and J. Thompson (eds) *Social Theory of Modern Societies: Anthony Giddens and his critics.* Cambridge: Cambridge University Press.
Goffman, E. (1959) *The Presentation of Self in Everyday Life.* Harmondsworth: Penguin.
Goffman, E. (1971) *Relations in Public.* Harmondsworth: Penguin.
Goffman, E. (1974) *Frame Analysis: An essay on the organization of experience.* New York: Harper and Row (Northeastern University Press Edition).
Goldstein, J., Freud, A. and Solnit, A. (1973) *Beyond the Best Intersets of the Child.* New York: Free Press.
Goldthorpe, J. (1987) *Family Life in Western Society.* Cambridge: Cambridge University Press.
Greatbatch, D. and Dingwall, R. (1989) 'Selective facilitation: Some preliminary observations on a strategy used by divorce mediators', *Law and Society Review,* 23.
Griffiths, A. (1988) 'Mediation, conflict and social inequality: Family dispute processing amongst the Bakwena'; in R. Dingwall and J. Eekelaar (eds) *Divorce Mediation and the Legal Process.* Oxford: Clarendon Press.
Guise, J. (1983) 'Conciliation: Current practice and future implications for the probation service', *Probation Journal,* 30 (2).
Gulliver, P. (1979) *Disputes and Negotiations: A cross-cultural perspective.* New York: Academic Press.

REFERENCES

Guymer, A. and Bywaters, P. (1984) 'Conciliation and reconciliation in magistrates' domestic courts', in T. Marshall (ed.) *Magistrates' Domestic Courts* (Research and Planning Unit Paper 28). London: Home Office.

Hammersley, M. and Atkinson, P. (1983) *Ethnography: Principles in practice*. London: Tavistock.

Harris, R. (1985) 'Towards just welfare', *British Journal of Criminology*, 25 (1).

Haxby, D. (1978) *Probation: A changing service*. London: Constable.

Hay, E., Hay, W. and James, A. (1992) 'Measuring the effectiveness of court welfare work: I', *Probation Journal*, 39 (3).

Held, D. (1987) *Models of Democracy*. Cambridge: Polity Press.

HM Inspectorate of Probation (1991) *The Work of the Probation Service in Serving the Needs of Children Involved in Separation and Divorce*. London: Home Office.

Holdaway, S. and Mantle, G. (1991) 'Probation committees: A perspective on policy-making', paper presented at the British Criminology Conference, York, 24–6 July.

Holdaway, S. and Mantle, G. (1992) 'Governing the probation service: Probation committees and policy-making', *Howard Journal of Criminal Justice*, 31 (2).

Holtrust, N., Sevenhuijsen, S. and Verbraken, A. (1989) 'Rights for fathers and the state: Recent developments in custody politics in the Netherlands', in C. Smart and S. Sevenhuijsen (eds) *Child Custody and the Politics of Gender*. London: Routledge.

Home Office (1966) *Report on the Work of the Probation and After-Care Department, 1962 to 1965*, Cmnd 3107. London: HMSO.

Home Office (1976) *Report on the Work of the Probation and After-Care Department, 1972 to 1975*, Cmnd 6590. London: HMSO.

Home Office (1979) *Marriage Matters: A working party report*. London: HMSO.

Home Office (1984) *The Probation Rules, 1984*, SI 1984 No. 647. London: HMSO.

Home Office (1991a) *Organizing Supervision and Punishment in the Community: A decision document*. London: HMSO.

Home Office (1991b) *Cash Limits for Probation Services CPO, 23/1991*, 22 July, Probation Service Division, Home Office.

Home Office (1992a) *Summary of Probation Service Performance Indicators and Background Information: 1990*. HM Inspectorate of Probation, Home Office.

Home Office (1992b) *Probation Statistics: England and Wales, 1990*. London: Home Office.

Home Office (1992c) *The Probation Service: Three year plan for the probation service, 1993–1996*. London: Home Office.

Home Office (1993) *Helping the Court to Serve the Needs of Children Involved in Separation or Divorce: A strategy document for probation service family court welfare work* (Draft: January). C6 Division, Home Office.

Hooper, D. and Murch, M. (1990) *The Family Justice System and its Support Services*, Concluding Report to the Nuffield Foundation. Bristol: Socio-Legal Centre for Family Studies, University of Bristol.

House of Commons Expenditure Committee (1972) *First Report of the Expenditure Committee of the House of Commons, session 1971-72: Probation and after-care, 1971*. London: HMSO.

Howard, J. and Shepherd, G. (1982) 'Conciliation – new beginnings?', *Probation Journal*, 29 (3).

Howard, J. and Shepherd, G. (1987) *Conciliation, Children and Divorce: A family systems approach*. London: Batsford/BAAF.

Howe, D. (1987) *An Introduction to Social Work Theory Making Sense in Practice*. Aldershot: Wildwood House.

Humphrey, C. (1991) 'Calling on the experts: The Financial Management Initiative (FMI), private sector management consultants and the probation service', *Howard Journal of Criminal Justice*, 30 (1).

Hurst, P. (1986) 'Civil work practice: A non-conciliation approach', *Probation Journal*, 33 (3).

Jackson, C. (1992) 'Re H (conciliation: welfare reports) – revisited', *Family Law*, November.

James, A. (1988) ' "Civil Work" in the probation service', in R. Dingwall and J. Eekelaar (eds) *Divorce Mediation and the Legal Process*. Oxford: Clarendon Press.

James, A. (1990a) 'Conciliation and social change', in T. Fisher (ed.) *Family Conciliation within the UK: Policy and practice*. Bristol: Family Law.

James, A. (1990b) 'Conciliation, welfare reports and the Children Act 1989', *Journal of Social Welfare Law*, 4.

James, A. (1992a) 'Continuity, change and contradiction: The Children Act 1989 and the stepfamily', in B. Dimmock (ed.) *A Step in Both Directions? The Impact of the Children Act 1989 on Stepfamilies*. London: The National Stepfamily Association.

James, A. (1992b) 'Family mediation', paper presented at the Lord Chancellor's Department Legal Aid Advisory Committee conference on Alternative Dispute Resolution, 4 June.

James, A. (1992c) 'An open or shut case? Law as an autopoietic system', *Journal of Law and Society*, 19 (2).

James, A. and Dingwall, R. (1989) 'Social work ideologies in the probation service: The case of civil work', *Journal of Social Welfare Law*, 6.

James, A. and Hay, W. with Greatbatch, D. and Walker, C. (1992) *Court Welfare Work: Research, practice and development*. Hull: Centre for Criminology and Criminal Justice, University of Hull.

James, A. and Wilson, K. (1983) 'Divorce court welfare work – present and future?', *Probation Journal*, 30 (2).

James, A. and Wilson, K. (1984a) 'Reports for the court: The work of the divorce court welfare officer', *Journal of Social Welfare Law*, March.

James, A. and Wilson, K. (1984b) 'The trouble with access: A study of divorcing families', *British Journal of Social Work*, 14 (5).

James, A. and Wilson, K. (1986) *Couples, Conflict and Change*. London: Tavistock.

James, A., Hay, W., Greatbatch, D. and Walker, C. (1992) 'The welfare officer as expert? Reporting for the Courts', *Journal of Social Welfare and Family Law*, 5

Jones, M. (1986) 'Conciliation: A family affair', *Marriage Guidance*, 22 (2).

King, M. (1991) 'Child welfare within law: The emergence of a hybrid discourse', *Journal of Law and Society*, 18 (3).

King, M. and Piper, C. (1990) *How the Law Thinks About Children*. Aldershot: Gower.

King, M. and Trowell, J. (1992) *Children's Welfare and the Law: The limits of legal intervention*. London: Sage.

Kingsley, J. (1990) 'The court welfare officer: Aims, procedures and practice – a research project', *Family Law*, 183.

Kübler-Ross, E. (1970) *On Death and Dying*. London: Tavistock.

Law Commission (1966) *Reform of the Grounds of Divorce: The field of choice*, Cmnd 3123. London: HMSO.

Law Commission (1988) *Facing the Future: A discussion paper on the ground for divorce*, Law Com. No. 170. London: HMSO.

Law Commission (1990) *Family Law: Ground for divorce*, Law Com. No. 192. London: HMSO.

Lee, D. and Newby, H. (1989) *The Problem of Sociology*. London: Unwin Hyman.

Lloyd, C. (1986) *Response to SNOP: An analysis of the Home Office document, 'Probation Service in England and Wales: Statement of National Objectives and Priorities' and of the subsequent local responses*. Cambridge: Institute of Criminology, University of Cambridge.

Mace, D. (1947) 'A marriage welfare service', *Probation*, 5 (8).

McGregor, O., Blom-Cooper, L and Gibson, C. (1970) *Separated Spouses: A study of the matrimonial jurisdiction of magistrates' courts*. London: Duckworth.

McWilliams, W. (1990) 'Probation Practice and the management ideal', *Probation Journal*, 37 (2).

Maidment, S. (1984) *Child Custody and Divorce: The law in social context*. London: Croom Helm.

Mair, G. (1989) 'Some developments in probation in the 1980s', *Research Bulletin*, HORPU, 27.

Matthews, R. (ed.) (1988) *Informal Justice?* London: Sage.

Minamikata, S. (1988) *'Kaji Chotei*: Mediation in the Japanese family court', in R. Dingwall and J. Eekelaar (eds) *Divorce Mediation and the Legal Process*. Oxford: Clarendon Press.

Mitchell, A. (1985) *Children in the Middle: Living through divorce*. London: Tavistock.

Mnookin, R. and Kornhauser, L. (1979) 'Bargaining in the shadow of the law: The case of divorce', *Yale Law Journal*, vol. 88.
Morgan, G. (1990) *Organisations in Society*. London: Macmillan.
Morison Committee (1962) *Report of the Departmental Committee on the Probation Service*, Cmnd 1650. London: HMSO.
Morris, A., Giller, H., Szwed, E., and Geach, H. (1980) *Justice for Children*. London: Macmillan.
Morton Commission (1956) *Report of the Royal Commission on Marriage and Divorce*, Cmnd 9678. London: HMSO.
Mount, F. (1982) *The Subversive Family: An alternative history of love and marriage*. London: Cape.
Mullins, C. (1938) 'The matrimonial work of the courts', *Probation*, 3 (1).
Mullins, C. (1943) 'Probation officers and post-war problems', *Probation*, 4 (5).
Munch, R. (1987) 'Parsonian theory today: In search of a new synthesis', in A. Giddens and J. Turner (eds) *Social Theory Today*. Cambridge: Polity Press.
Murch, M. (1980) *Justice and Welfare in Divorce*. London: Sweet and Maxwell.
National Association of Probation Officers (1984) *Discussion Paper on Conciliation*, PP.7/84, Probation Practice Committee, February.
National Association of Probation Officers (1988*) The Role of the Court Welfare Officer*, Draft Policy Document PP.66/88, Probation Practice Committee, September.
North West Regional Divorce Court Welfare Officers (1976) *Welfare of Children in Divorce and Domestic Dispute: A practical guide for all those who provide the service to the magistrates' court (domestic) county court and family division through the probation service and its divorce court welfare officers*, August.
Office of Population Censuses and Surveys (1980) *Marriage and Divorce Statistics: Review of the Registrar General on marriages and divorces in England and Wales, 1979*, Series FM2 no. 6. London: HMSO.
Parkes, C. (1972) *Bereavement: Studies of grief in adult life*. London: Tavistock.
Parkinson, L. (1983) 'Conciliation: Pros and cons (I) and (II)', *Family Law*, 13.
Parkinson, L. (1986) *Conciliation in Separation and Divorce: Finding common ground*. London: Croom Helm.
Parkinson, L. (1989) 'Co-mediation with a lawyer mediator', *Family Law*, 135.
Philips, R. (1988) *Putting Asunder: A history of divorce in western society*. Cambridge: Cambridge University Press.
Pinker, R. (1979) *Social Theory and Social Policy*. London: Heinemann.
Piper, C. (1988) 'Divorce conciliation in the UK: How responsible are parents?', *International Journal of the Sociology of Law*, 16.
Preston-Shoot, M. and Agass, D. (1990) *Making Sense of Social Work*. London: Macmillan.
Pugsley, J. (1986) 'The court welfare role: Finding the balances', *Probation Journal*, 33 (2).

REFERENCES

Pugsley, J. and Wilkinson, M. (1984) 'The court welfare officer's role: Taking it seriously?', *Probation Journal*, 31 (3).
Rees, J. (1939) 'The social and psychological aspects of marriage', *Probation*, 3 (6).
Report of the Departmental Committee on Grants for the Development of Marriage Guidance (1948), Cmd 7566. London: HMSO.
Report of the Departmental Committee on the Social Services in Courts of Summary Jurisdiction (1936), Cmd 5122. London: HMSO.
Rex, J. (1976) *Key Problems of Sociological Theory*. London: Routledge and Kegan Paul.
Richards, M. and Dyson, M. (1982) *Separation, Divorce and the Development of Children: A review*. Cambridge: Child Care and Development Group, University of Cambridge.
Rimmer, L. (1981) *Families in Focus: Marriage, divorce and family patterns* (Occasional Paper No. 6). London: Study Commission on the Family.
Roberts, S. (1983) 'Mediation in family disputes', *Modern Law Review*, 46 (5).
Roberts, S. (1992) 'Mediation in the lawyers' embrace', *Modern Law Review*, 55 (2).
Robinson Committee (1983) *Report of the Inter-departmental Committee on Conciliation*. London: HMSO.
Rutter, M. (1975) *Helping Troubled Children*. Harmondsworth: Penguin.
Sandberg, K. (1989) 'Best interests and justice', in C. Smart and S. Sevenhuijsen (eds) *Child Custody and the Politics of Gender*. London: Routledge.
Scarr, D. (1978) 'The divorce experience', *Probation Journal*, 25 (1).
Shepherd, G. (1990) 'Mangement: Short of ideals?', *Probation Journal*, 37 (4).
Shepherd, G. and Howard, J. (1985) 'The theft of conciliation? The thieves reply', *Probation Journal*, 32 (2).
Shepherd, G., Howard, J. and Tonkinson, J. (1984) 'Conciliation: Taking it seriously?', *Probation Journal*, 31 (1).
Silbey, S. (1981) 'Making sense of the lower courts', *The Justice System Journal*, 6.
Simpson, B., Corlyon, J., McCarthy, P. and Walker, J. (1990) 'Client responses to family conciliation: Achieving clarity in the midst of confusion', *British Journal of Social Work*, 20 (6).
Smart, C. (1989) 'Feminism and the power of law', in C. Smart and S. Sevenhuijsen (eds) (1989) *Child Custody and the Politics of Gender*. London: Routledge.
Smart, C (1989) *Feminism and the Power of Law*. London: Routledge.
Smart, C. (1991) 'The legal and moral ordering of child custody', *Journal of Law and Society*, 18 (4).
Smart, C. (1992) 'The women of legal discourse', *Social and Legal Studies*, 1 (1).

Smart, C. and Sevenhuijsen, S. (1989) *Child Custody and the Politics of Gender*. London: Routledge.

SPCK (1966) *Putting Asunder: A divorce law for contemporary society*, report of a group appointed by the Archbishop of Canterbury. London: SPCK.

Stone, L. (1990) *The Road to Divorce: England 1530–1987*. Oxford: Oxford University Press.

Straker, D. (1979) 'In the throes of divorce', *Probation Journal*, 26 (3).

Teubner, G. (1989) 'How the law thinks: Towards a constructivist epistemology of law', *Law and Society Review*, 23 (5).

Thèry, I. (1989) ' "The interests of the child' and the regulation of the postdivorce family', in C. Smart and S. Sevenhuijsen (eds) *Child Custody and the Politics of Gender*. London: Routledge.

Timms, N. (1983) *Social Work Values: An enquiry*. London: Routledge.

Turk, A. (1978) 'Law as a weapon', in C. Reasons and R. Rich (eds) *The Sociology of Law: A conflict perspective*. Toronto: Butterworths.

Turner, J. (1987) 'Analytic theorizing', in A. Giddens and J. Turner (eds) *Social Theory Today*. Cambridge: Polity Press.

Walczak, Y. with Burns, S. (1984) *Divorce: The child's point of view*. London: Harper and Row.

Wallerstein, J. and Kelly, J. (1980) *Surviving the Breakup: How children cope with divorce*. London: Grant McIntyre.

Wells, T. (1990) 'Conciliation and the probation service', in T. Fisher (ed.) *Family Conciliation within the UK: Policy and practice*. Bristol: Family Law.

Wilkinson, M. (1981) *Children and Divorce*. Oxford: Blackwell.

Name Index

Agass, D., 96
Association of Chief Officers of Probation (ACOP), 3, 6, 26, 36, 38, 42–3, 45, 53, 56, 122, 143, 144
Atkinson, P., 4
Audit Commission, 51

Bader, K., 32, 59
Beldam Committee, 59
Blau, P., 144
Bochel, D., 20, 21, 22, 25
Booth Committee, 26, 44, 77
Bottomley, A., 37, 42
Bottoms, A., 23
Bretherton, H., 60, 61
Brophy, J., 34, 182
Burgoyne, J., 14
Burns, S., 25, 196
Burns, T., 164
Burrett, J., 63
Bywaters, P., 42

Cantwell, B., 75, 187
Central Council of Probation Committees, 25, 44, 45, 56
Chapman, J., 60, 61
Chester, R., 14
Clive, E., 33
Cohen, S., 163
Conciliation Project Unit, 28, 59
Craib, I., 35
Davis, G., 26, 32, 33, 59, 63, 64, 65, 70, 71, 76, 151, 152, 167, 188
Denning Committee, 20, 22

Dewar, J., 22, 23
Dingwall, R., 1, 19, 20, 21, 24, 26, 31, 32, 40, 59, 71, 91, 115, 166, 197, 200
Dominian, J., 14
Dormor, D., 14
Dyson, M., 25

Edwards, H., 58
Eekelaar, J., 19, 21, 24, 25, 26, 29, 30, 31, 32, 33, 34, 166, 194, 197, 198, 200
Elliott F., 81
Elster, J., 154, 155, 156, 181, 198

Family Policy Studies Centre, 14, 200
Feeley, M., 157
Finch J., 81
Fineman, M., 76
Finer Committee, 24, 25, 59, 62
Fisher, T., 25, 52, 71
Forster, J., 52, 71
Foucault, M., 162, 163
Fraser, D., 63
Freeman, M., 59
Frisby, C., 18

Garland, D., 163
Gathorne-Hardy, J., 14
Gibbons, F., 63
Giddens, A., 149, 158, 160, 161, 162, 163, 202
Goffman, E., 103, 157, 160, 161, 164, 165, 166, 167, 202
Goldstein, J., 61, 62, 71

219

Goldthorpe, J., 14
Greatbatch, D., 6, 59
Griffiths, A., 58
Guise, J., 66
Gulliver, P., 58
Guymer, A., 42

Hammersley, M., 4
Harris, R., 154
Haxby, D., 24
Hay, E., 177
Hay, W., 5, 82, 103, 108, 126
Held, D., 173
Holdaway, S., 45
Holtrust, N., 182
Home Office, 5, 13, 18, 23, 24, 27, 36, 37–8, 39, 40, 42, 45, 50, 51, 52, 55, 56, 77, 144, 190, 191, 200
Hooper, D., 203
House of Commons Expenditure Committee, 24
Howard, J., 63, 64, 65, 70, 71
Howe, D., 149
Humphrey, C., 51
Hurst, P., 74

Jackson, C., 76
James, A., 1, 5, 14, 22, 23, 24, 25, 26, 29, 40, 52, 57, 59, 60, 66, 76, 82, 91, 103, 108, 115, 126, 153, 154, 158, 172, 197
Jones, M., 71, 72

Kelly, J., 25, 62, 71, 196
King, M., 35, 60, 74, 153, 154, 157, 158, 160, 167, 186, 187, 202
Kingsley, J., 59
Kornhauser, L., 16
Kübler-Ross, E., 171

Law Commission, 7, 22, 30, 33, 47, 48, 53, 191, 198, 200, 201, 203, 205
Lee, D., 157
Lloyd, C., 38, 40, 42, 52
Lord Chancellor's Department (LCD), 6, 39–40, 44, 50, 56, 58, 200

Mace, D., 21
Maidment, S., 28, 152, 153
Mair, G., 37
Mantle, G., 45
Matthews, R., 58

McGregor, O., 16
McWilliams, W., 139
Minamikata, S., 58
Mitchell, A., 196
Mnookin, R., 16
Morgan, G., 141
Morison Committee, 25
Morris, A., 154
Morton Commission, 21
Mullins, C., 17, 19, 21
Murch, M., 1, 25, 26, 33, 61, 151, 152, 167, 203

National Association of Probation Officers (NAPO), 26, 43, 45, 56, 60, 61
Newby, H., 157
North West Regional Divorce Court Welfare Officers, 43

Office of Population Censuses and Surveys, 23

Parkes, C., 171
Parkinson, L., 24, 25, 59, 71, 72, 77
Philips, R., 14
Pinker, R., 149
Piper, C., 32, 35, 59, 153, 154, 157, 158, 160, 167
Preston-Shoot, M., 96
Pugsley, J., 68, 69, 77

Rees, J., 18
Report of the Departmental Committee on Grants for the Development of Marriage Guidance, 20
Report of the Departmental Committee on the Social Services in the Courts of Summary Jurisdiction, 17
Rex, J., 157, 159, 162
Richards, M., 25
Rimmer, L., 14
Roberts, M., 59, 76
Roberts, S., 57, 58, 59
Robinson Committee, 27, 28, 44
Rutter, M., 25

Sandberg, K., 181
Scarr, D., 60
Sevenhuijsen, S., 84, 181
Shepherd, G., 63, 64, 65, 67, 68, 69, 70, 71
Silbey, S., 40

INDEX

Simpson, B., 59
Smart, C., 34, 84, 181, 186, 187, 195, 198
Smith, N., 74
SPCK, 22
Stone, L., 14, 15, 23, 32
Straker, D., 60, 61

Teubner, G., 35, 153, 154
Thèry, I., 181

Timms, N., 177
Trowell, J., 187
Turk, A., 159
Turner, J., 149, 152

Walczak, Y., 25, 196
Wallerstein, J., 25, 62, 71, 196
Wells, T., 52, 53
Wilkinson, M., 61, 62, 63, 68, 69, 70
Wilson, K., 14, 25, 66

Subject Index

adversarial system, 1, 61, 69, 153
  synthesis with settlement-seeking, 74–8
  traditional approach, 58, 62, 65, 66
agreements (*see also* settlement-seeking and conflict-resolution), 24, 63–6, 71, 77, 111, 121

best interests of the child, 47–8, 64, 68, 81, 92, 111, 119–20, 124, 156, 168–9, 182, 196, 204

children
  ascertaining wishes and feelings, 96, 100, 197, 204
  child-saving, 25, 28, 70–1, 75, 200, 204
  parental competence, 69
  working with children, 8, 100–2
Children Act 1989, 7, 9, 29, 30, 34, 36, 38–9, 42, 47, 49, 54, 56, 92, 100, 106, 109, 169, 191, 194–8, 199, 200, 201, 203
conciliation (*see also* mediation), 1, 4, 7, 16–17, 18, 19, 22, 24–8, 38, 39, 41, 53, 58, 59, 61–72, 76, 90–1, 140, 153, 199, 204
  costs, 37
  in-court, 26
  inter-agency initiatives, 52, 190
  out-of-court, 25
  religious enthusiasm, 17
conflict-resolution (*see also* agreements and settlement-seeking), 94, 96, 111, 140

court welfare reports
  contextual factors, 108–19
  data collection, 3–4
  increasing demand, 60
  minimising delays, 2, 48
  purpose, 63
  recommendations, 107–8, 120, 121
  summary of main findings, 103–8
courts
  High Court, 16, 18, 21, 105
  magistrates' courts, 105
  staffing of, 131–3
co-working, 8, 94–6
criminal justice, 2, 17, 23, 25–6, 31, 36–7, 50, 53, 77, 135, 204
divorce
  ancillary matters, 23
  and the Church, 13
  grounds for, 22, 30
  rates, 14
  reform, 14–24, 198–201
  regulation of, 30
  significance of, 14–15
  statistics, 23
  trends, 14–15

empowerment, 99, 111, 166, 178, 190, 206

Family Assistance Order, 188, 201
family meetings, 8, 96–100
family therapy, 58, 64–72, 94–6, 122, 180–1

INDEX

feminism, 15, 151, 182, 186

gender, 33–4, 81, 84, 181, 195
guardian *ad litem*, 130, 203–4

health visitors, 175
High Court Judgments, 40–1, 55, 72–4, 89, 91, 140, 183
home visits, 8, 85–9, 104, 119, 120, 121, 192

ideology, 29, 108, 195
   of empowerment, 192
investigation, 24, 63, 65–6, 68, 81, 89, 94, 121, 124, 140, 197

joint meetings, 89–94, 175, 191
judiciary, 8, 40–1, 46, 72–4, 76, 89, 115, 127–8, 157, 165, 179, 191–2, 197, 205
justice, 1, 39, 151, 154, 155, 190, 195

knowledge base, 54, 114, 171–3

legislation
   Criminal Justice Act 1991, 53
   Divorce Reform Act 1969, 22, 33
   Guardian of Infants Act 1925, 28
   Guardian of Minors Act 1971, 28–9
   Matrimonial Causes Act
      1857, 13, 16
      1878, 16
      1923, 13
      1963, 21
      1967, 22
      1973, 23, 27
   Matrimonial and Family Proceedings Act 1984, 22
   Summary Jurisdiction (Domestic Procedure) Bill 1934, 16
   Summary Procedure (Domestic Proceedings) Act 1937, 17–18, 64
legitimacy, 34, 77, 91, 143, 157, 173–5

magistracy, 16, 42, 45, 105–6, 156, 165, 205
   number of reports for, 22
management, 3, 7, 35–6, 39, 44, 46–7, 49–55, 118, 127, 133–5, 142, 203, 205
   divergent views with court welfare officers, 137–9
   resources, 139

senior court welfare officer, 8, 135–7
Marriage Guidance Council, 19, 21
measuring effectiveness, 51–2, 125, 138, 177, 184, 191
mediation (*see also* conciliation), 61, 76, 151, 199
National Association of Probation Officers (NAPO), 43, 45, 56, 60–1
national standards, 40, 144, 190
neutrality, 61–2, 74, 177

office contact, 82–4, 104, 119–20
one-way screens, 122, 142, 165, 174

paradigms of practice
   as free-floating professional, 119–21
   as officer of the court, 121–3
paramount principle, 28–9, 31, 47, 67, 196, 199
performance indicators, 2, 108
power, 124, 156, 162–7, 173–5, 202
   frameworks of, 164–7
   of judges, 111–14
   of parents, 110–11, 124, 206–7
   of welfare officers, 75, 111–15, 120, 124
Practice Directions, 24, 39, 41, 140
President of the Family Division, 24, 39, 42
principles of practice, 139–43
probation committees, 36, 44–6
Probation Rules, 22

race, 77, 172, 180, 181, 183
reconciliation, 18, 21, 24–8, 30, 38, 62
RELATE, 200
reports (*see* court welfare reports)
research, the
   study areas, 4–5
   methods, 3–6
   data base, 5–6
rights, 17, 34, 48, 77, 122, 155, 156, 174, 182, 184, 186–7, 194–5, 197–8
   custody and visiting, 16
   obligations, 29, 187
   parental responsibility, 29–30, 47, 98, 113, 157, 177, 195, 199
settlement-seeking (*see also* conflict-resolution and agreements), 31, 41, 59–66, 87, 93, 121, 140, 151–2, 156, 179

alternative dispute resolution, 58–9
  synthesis with adversarial, model 74–8
skills, 54, 67, 169–71
social theory
  dialectic of control, 161
  functionalism, 156–7
  legal constructivist theory, 35, 153
  normative theory, 144, 154, 157
  rational choice theory, 154–6
  relationship to practice, 149–50
  social control, 31–2, 200
  structure and action, 160–2
solicitors, 110

Statement of National Objectives and Priorities (SNOP), 37–8
statutory responsibility, 55, 108–9
stigma, 43, 20, 185

training, 54–5

utilitarianism, 155, 198

values, 81, 102, 174, 177–8, 202, 204

welfare reports (*see* court welfare reports)
welfare test (check list), 29, 34, 169